Born in 1959 in Hemel Hempstead, Dougie Brimson left school with 11 'O' levels and went directly into the RAF where he trained as a mechanical engineer. After serving for over eighteen years – including the Falklands and Gulf conflicts – and attaining the rank of sergeant, he left to become a freelance writer and actor. He is married with three children.

Eddy Brimson was born in 1964, also in Hemel Hempstead. After leaving school, he trained as a graphic designer.

They are the authors of one previous book, the bestselling *Everywhere We Go*, published by Headline in March 1996.

Also by Dougie and Eddy Brimson

Everywhere We Go

England,
My England

The Trouble with the National Football Team

Dougie and Eddy Brimson

HEADLINE

First published in 1996
by HEADLINE BOOK PUBLISHING

10 9 8 7 6 5 4 3 2 1

ISBN 0 7472 5508 3

Typeset by Avon Dataset Ltd, Bidford-on-Avon, Warks

Printed and bound in Great Britain by
Cox & Wyman Ltd, Reading, Berks

HEADLINE BOOK PUBLISHING
A division of Hodder Headline PLC
338 Euston Road
London NW1 3BH

Contents

With special thanks to Tina, Harriet
and the whole family.
Thanks also to Ian, Mark,
and football fans everywhere
(except L*t*n),
particularly those that took the
time to contact us.
Thanks for your support and remember:

Don't follow us, follow the 'ornets.

You know it makes sense!

Preface
Borehamwood

On 30 March 1996, the two of us and a friend attended a match between Borehamwood and Yeovil Town. This ICIS Premier League fixture held great importance for the supporters of both clubs, as victory would keep their slender hopes of the championship alive and bring with it automatic promotion to the GM Conference.

Our attendance at the match was admittedly fuelled by curiosity, as we had been informed that the supporters of both clubs had been known to include an element of fans willing to indulge in violence. Many years ago I had personally witnessed Yeovil fans playing up at a midweek cup fixture with Wycombe Wanderers at the old Loakes Park ground before they attained League status. Our friend, a keen follower of non-League football, had visited Yeovil many times and had witnessed aggression involving their fans on more than one occasion, including hot tea being thrown over old men, fighting inside and outside their ground, and trouble when they visited the ground of his own team. To say he was not a lover of Yeovil Town and their supporters would be something of an understatement. We had also been told that the supporters of Borehamwood had been playing up throughout the season, but nothing prepared us for what we were about to witness.

Borehamwood's Meadow Park ground is a compact, well-maintained stadium with an average gate, according to the programme, of around 300. The importance of the fixture and the additional 150 to 300 Yeovil fans present (not bad for a Tuesday night trip from Somerset to Hertfordshire) brought the crowd to close on 600. Those who regularly attend non-League football will know that usually you are able to move around the ground at will, and that the movement of the supporters is usually dictated by the direction in which their team is kicking, as fans like to stand behind the goal their team is attacking. Borehamwood's little mob – around twenty blokes – took up their position, while the Yeovil fans took up theirs at the other end of the ground. We, however, stood along the side of the pitch, a position enabling us to keep a discreet eye on both ends and the game.

The first half went off quietly. The football was appalling and Yeovil were soon 1–0 up, but a particularly good rendition of 'Who Ate All The Pies' aimed at Graham Roberts (yes, the ex-Spurs player), and an interesting variation on the famous 'You're shit! aaaaargh!' chant accompanying a goalkick from a bunch of schoolboys ('You wankaaaaaargh!') made the whole thing worthwhile. However, as we stood at the end of the half, we overheard a comment made by a man to his son, who had asked to move behind the goal to join in the singing. His reply was: 'No son, let's stay here because they [the Borehamwood fans] won't let them [the Yeovil fans] stand down there, and there could be a bit of trouble!'

By half time, all the Borehamwood lot had disappeared to the bar and, as expected, the Yeovil supporters made their way around the ground and took up their position behind the opposite goal. Interestingly enough for us, though, the two police constables on duty, along with the stewards, kept the area occupied by the home fans clear. Obviously, that father's fears were justified. As the second half got underway, the Borehamwood mob returned and took up their position and the verbal aimed at the Yeovil fans took on a very different edge. The 'Sheep-shagger', 'Where are your carrots?' taunts of the first half became 'We don't run from no one', 'Where's your famous 2000?', 'No surrender to the IRA', and the obligatory 'You're gonna get your fucking heads kicked in'. Things were turning very nasty. The whole thing was led by four particularly mouthy twats who by now were pushing past the stewards into the Yeovil fans and starting to shove people around. All the stewards did was to follow them and drag them back while the police did nothing.

Midway through the second half, due almost certainly to the lack of police intervention, the four twats had grown in number to nine or ten when, as luck would have it, Yeovil scored. The Yeovil fans, pissed off at all this grief, started to go mental, celebrating wildly. Unfortunately for them, the goal was disallowed, much to the amusement of our friend and the Borehamwood mob, who then started to move towards the Yeovil fans. The police, finally realising that they had to gain control of the situation, took the subtle approach. They drew their truncheons and seemed to hit out at anyone within reach. Unfortunately, though, this did not include the ringleaders who had, by now, got past the stewards and were slapping those Yeovil fans who were too old or slow to move out of their way. The stewards managed to regain order and dragged the Borehamwood supporters back to where they had come from, while the police became busy calling for assistance on their radios. Within minutes, four more coppers arrived and took up a position between the two groups, truncheons drawn.

Clearly it would not have been difficult for the

stewards, who see these blokes at every home game, to point them out to the police so that they could have been arrested. Even we could have done it from where we were, far from the action. But they didn't, and if that was because they didn't want trouble with people they knew, then they have no right to be stewards. Similarly, the police could have taken the decision to move the Yeovil fans round to the other end to avoid further confrontation, but, again, they didn't. With the two sides separated by a line of six policemen and the Borehamwood mob getting more and more lary, Yeovil found the net again, only this time it was given. That was it. The locals steamed in and the Yeovil fans did a runner into the corner of the ground. More people got hit and, once again, it seemed to us that the police reacted by moving in on those left behind, rather than those doing the fighting. By this time, a few fans had got onto the pitch, a steward had been lumped and all the Yeovil fans simply wanted to do was to get on their coach and go home. The father, still standing by us, watched all this in amazement while his son, thankfully, remained focused on the game. Crazy.

As the last few minutes ticked away, more police entered the ground in no great hurry, and joined their mates behind the goal. Only, by now, the locals had left the ground and that end resembled a Met Police FC supporters' mob instead. It was a somewhat subdued cheer that greeted the final whistle, but of more interest to us was that, despite the aggressive and foul language and the fighting, there had been no arrests or ejections. The stewards directed the Yeovil fans to leave at the other end of the ground from where they were positioned and we followed. As we exited the ground and walked through the turnstiles towards the car park housing, among other things, the Yeovil coaches, I offered my congratulations to a policeman on the gate over the way they handled the trouble. Obviously, sarcasm hadn't

4

reached that part of Hertfordshire yet, and he seemed genuinely grateful. Bizarre. The very next face we saw was that of one of the Borehamwood ringleaders, who shouted: 'Where's your famous slashing-up crew then, you fucking shitters?' Very nice! Behind him stood the rest of the mob, completely unsupervised, and we were suddenly faced with the very real possibility of getting a slap ourselves because they thought we were Yeovil supporters. We had to walk straight through them and up the road to our car, expecting the thunder of feet as they came up the road after us, and it was only when we were in the car and moving that we were able to relax. The silence was only broken by our companion, who came out with the gem, 'Serves those bastards right, I fucking hate those wankers.'

We have opened this book in this way because if ever there was an indication that football-related violence is alive and kicking in this country, then this was it. We went to this game, a fixture that meant nothing to the two of us, and witnessed a horrible incident which illustrated perfectly how pathetic, futile and ugly the whole thing has become. The fact that we almost became embroiled in it, despite having seen enough trouble over the years to know the danger signs and avoid it, was, quite frankly, scary. However, of greater relevance is the fact that this wasn't at The Den, Stamford Bridge or Elland Road; it was at a tiny non-League ground on a warm Tuesday night in the middle of Hertfordshire. The morons involved would never have got away with playing up like that at a League game, but that is not the issue here.

The simple reality is that, from the FA Cup final to the Sunday hackers league, violence is always possible at football matches and that is tragic. However, before you say that this incident is irrelevant to what goes on among England fans, think about this. The next time England play, look at the flags on the terracing. The names of small towns and villages you've never heard of which adorn many of those Union Jacks may well have been put there by supporters from non-League clubs. They may well be up for it and may even have been active for some time. It is almost certain that they will not be on any police computer, nor will their photographs be on file, but they will still turn out for the big games and fill the pubs on big occasions. They may not support Chelsea or Leeds, but that doesn't make them any less violent or dangerous and if you think they don't 'practise' just as much as the largest mobs, then you are sadly mistaken.

Having reflected on the Borehamwood incident, we became disgusted at ourselves. We had gone along to this game expecting and, in truth, hoping to see trouble, and we'd been ashamed when we had seen it. The realisation that in the past we had behaved like that was quite alarming. It was pathetic to witness. Those who suffered at the hands of the Borehamwood fans will remember how frightened they were for many seasons – while, next season, Yeovil will bring a serious mob to extract revenge, because that is how these rivalries start. In any case, as is the way of these things, the following week the Yeovil fans crossed their home pitch on two separate occasions to launch violent attacks on Enfield fans, possibly by way of retribution for the attack at Borehamwood.

We know that what we saw is the responsibility of people like us, because we caused trouble in the past. But we are big enough to admit we were wrong, and we have grown up. However, football shouldn't be like that; we shouldn't have to be scared to take our kids, or have to watch our backs simply because some idiots want to cause trouble. We, as supporters, have to win the game back for the good of all who want to watch and play it. The game isn't about players, the FA, the latest shirt supplier or the television company with the deepest pockets. It's about us, the people who pay at the gates and who play it on Sunday mornings. The fact that there is an acute shortage of referees for amateur football is due in no small part to the violence and intimidation they regularly suffer. From the school yards to the Premier League, players and officials have to sort out this issue and end the abusive language and the foul play, backed by both the football authorities and the supporters. Similarly, the hooligan elements have to realise that they are still causing irreparable damage to the game because they are stopping people from watching it and, if people do not push through those turnstiles, eventually the game will die.

In our first book, we were condemned by many who reviewed it for any number of reasons. In truth, and as we said at the start of *Everywhere We Go*, we expected it. But, without exception, all the letters we received from fans of clubs all over the country as a result of the book were supportive. So too were all the people who sought us out at Watford games and during Euro 96. It was for those people that we wrote – not for the reviewers.

However, we have to answer those critics because they got it wrong, primarily because they do not understand what we are about. We have to stress again that we are not writers by profession – Dougie wrote occasionally for a small motorsport magazine and sat through much of a ten-week creative writing course, while Eddy could hardly type when we started. We are just two blokes who became fed up with reading the same old stereotypes about us, and people like us. Furthermore, we saw violence creeping back into the game, and wanted to try to help stop it. We were driven by a desire to get that first book in print. Also, we never set out to glorify football violence in any way because, since we stopped, we have become very anti-violence and will continue to maintain that stance.

We will do whatever we can to help the game rid itself of violence, but the sad fact is that the game does not want our help. We wrote to the FA warning them of the growth of violence while we were researching *Everywhere We Go*, and received a reply stating that it wasn't a problem any more – on the morning of the Millwall–Chelsea riot. Just before the publication of *Everywhere We Go*, we contacted the FA again to warn of the potential for trouble at Euro 96 and, despite meeting with members of the organising committee at

Lancaster Gate and repeated discussions by telephone and letter, they refused our help. We offered our advice as former hooligans to work with supporters so that they could police themselves and be involved in the security for the tournament. Again, the FA didn't want to know. On the day they turned down our assistance, *Everywhere We Go* sat at the top of the sports book listings and at number seven in the paperback bestseller charts, which suggested to us that we were able to reach our target audience.

On top of the FA ignoring us, we were accused of moral fuzziness, which was another way of attacking our beliefs, yet we would argue that when you walk through the turnstiles, all rational theory and common sense are left behind so what you do and what you say bear little relation to what you would say or do at home or at work. Secondly, and most importantly, we received a great deal of backing and not one single word of condemnation from those who matter most, the supporters. Others seemed to believe that all the accounts in the book were based on our own experiences, but neither of us has ever run with another mob, nor will we ever run with a mob again (it is unlikely Dougie could ever even run again in any case!). The accounts were not about us and what we had got up to: as in this book, they were obtained from real people.

Finally, we have to say that what we say and write is what we truly believe: no more, no less. The overwhelming majority of people we speak to, and who contact us, think exactly as we do on many issues which, if nothing else, proves that we are just average fans. In fact, we wrote this second book because there was so much that we didn't say in *Everywhere We Go* and so much more that needs to be said. So far, there is no one else to say it.

We were driven into writing because, as fans, we have no real voice. There is no place where we, or others, can have our say and people will listen, and there should be. By writing these books, the two of us have created a voice for ourselves and hopefully we can put across the feelings of many others. But we can only hope that we continue to speak for those

8

other supporters and that someone will eventually listen to us. As fans, we deserve that.

Introduction

This book is about England. Not the team: whatever you think, enough has been written about them already. No, this book is about the much-maligned England supporters and, in particular, the travelling fans. In the post-Euro 96 euphoria it will be clear to many that the corner has been turned and, as the fans largely behaved, that all is well. The pre-tournament hype surrounding the threat of hooliganism was just that – hype. Euro 96 was proof at last that the game has been cleansed of thugs and all is now wonderful.

If only it were true. This image is one to which a great many people, including the two of us, aspire; but it is sadly wide of the mark because, in the battle to defeat the hooligans, Euro 96 was very much a false dawn. We shall attempt to explain why in the pages that follow.

We will try to delve into the background of the hooligan problem which has, over the years, been irrevocably linked to the national team. Similarly, we will look at the history of those forays of England supporters to foreign shores, and at Euro 96 and the lessons that the game can hopefully teach us (although that's a bit of a long shot!) and what else can be done to take the game even further forward than it has come in the last twelve months.

What we haven't done is to dig too deeply into the problems

surrounding club sides, and their excursions into Europe and beyond. This is because there are similarities between the reasons club sides play up abroad and at home.

The situation with the England team, and its supporters, is different, as there are so many additional factors involved: historical oppression, the Empire, nationalism, patriotism, jingoism, xenophobia and so on. We will hopefully shed a little light on all of these. That isn't to make light of the problem at club level because it is clearly a major one as any Chelsea, Manchester United or Arsenal fan will be only too happy to tell you after their recent trips abroad. But one of the unique things about the problem as it affects England is that while at club level, everyone is united under their club colours, at national level they are brought together under the flag and that can have extra resonances. Club rivalries occasionally surface during England trips, but in the main they are buried, as we will see. An examination of the nationalism issue is an integral part of this book, because whereas Euro 96 saw an explosion of mostly healthy patriotic fervour, the defence of the Cross of St George has long been an excuse and a reason for violence abroad. As well as looking at the various influences on supporters, such as the media, the FA and the police, we will also look in detail at some of the nations whose own hooligan elements have provided conflict for the travelling England faithful.

As with our first book, we have included within these pages anecdotes from all sides of the hooliganism equation and, also as before, they are based both on our own experiences and on interviews with, and letters from, genuine football fans who have become involved in this issue in one way or another. While we will have inevitably missed things, we may well bring to your attention things you either didn't know or had not thought about. It is a simple fact that one of the strange features of the hooligan issue is that everyone involved in an incident sees it differently from the next person. Certainly those who get run see it as a tactical withdrawal, while those who do the chasing see only that the other mob bottled it.

Similarly, the police will say that they took action to defuse a given situation, while the fans will say that the situation never existed in the first place and the police provoked them into a response. In one particular instance, we received three separate letters about the same incident – two from one side and one from the other – and they were all so different from one another that it was only when we wrote back to the correspondents that we realised what had actually happened. It is also important to stress that wherever possible we have copied interviews and accounts verbatim, but, as always, we have changed or omitted certain details, such as names, to protect both the provider and ourselves from any incrimination or recrimination from the boys in blue. As for the rest, well, all we can do is to tell things as we see them or they are told to us, but we are certain that we have done the best we can in the only way we know how.

PART ONE
They Think It's All Over

———————————

Chapter 1

Why Club, Why Country?

Every Saturday afternoon from August through to the following May, hundreds of thousands of people will be attending football matches, listening to radios, waiting for the teleprinter or, if they're really sad, watching teletext. They do it all in the vain hope that their team will finally unleash their obvious potential, and let the rest of the nation know what they already know – that this team is indeed the best ever to grace these shores. The belief, pride, passion and dedication shown every Saturday by the masses that follow football in this country astound those who view the game from a distance.

But come 4.45pm, when most of us will be trudging home from yet another mind-numbing display of ineptitude, or sitting at home moaning into our tea, the predominant feeling will be of loss, disappointment and shame, fading into frustration that they have let us down yet again. While we ask ourselves, 'Why do we do it?', we know that come the next fixture, we will do it again because the belief always resurfaces. The hope that the next game will be *the* game, where the lads finally turn the corner and come of age, always returns. That is the attraction of football, and why it becomes addictive.

For many, the choice of which club to support is made for

17

them. They are born into families who follow a certain side (and perhaps this information should be included, together with name, date of birth, sex, and the details of both parents, on birth certificates). Others will find their own way, by rebelling against parents who stick to family alliances, and the influence of school friends, or even by choosing a team which wins all the time (it does happen, strangely enough!). But once that decision has been made, there really is no turning back. When the individual attends their first live game, usually with one or both parents, that match will become an initiation ceremony into the faith that is the football club.

What follows is Eddy's account of how he fell in love with the Hornets. From what we have learned over the years, his story represents a fairly typical chain of events.

THE LONGEST AFFAIR

Personally, I fell in love with my club, Watford, after seeing them on *The Big Match* one Sunday afternoon. Surprisingly enough, on my tenth birthday my dad, a Tottenham Hotspur fan and obviously somewhat confused, took me to see my first ever live match, L*t*n T*wn vs Millwall. I already knew that I was supposed to hate L*t*n despite the fact that I had never seen *my* club play, and I cheered Millwall as loudly as any ten-year-old can from the safety of the main stand. The thing I remember most about that match was watching the L*t*n end being overrun by the Millwall fans, and my dad being worried about the trouble and telling me that there had been three stabbings. I don't know what effect that had on me personally but I continue to hate L*t*n with a passion, orange is still the colour I hate most and I am not over-impressed with Millwall either because they lost 3–0.

Over the next few years, I attended more and more matches and was proud to identify myself as a supporter of what was, and still is, an unfashionable club. I would

18

go with the same people, stand in the same place, recognise the same faces and cheer my heroes on, week in and week out. It didn't matter to me that no one else at my school knew who Ross Jenkins was – I had something to identify with and so did those who shared my love for Watford FC. I would wear the black and gold wherever I went and to this day, when anyone asks who I follow, I am proud to tell them, 'Watford, of course' as if there could possibly be any other club on the planet.

Watford belong to me, they are mine and they carry my hopes and dreams. The love affair I have with that club is like no other love. No matter how badly it treats me or rubs my face in the dirt, I could never leave or turn my back on it because when it's good, it's fantastic, beautiful, awe-inspiring, and it's mine. It isn't like being married or living with someone, you can always give them the elbow. There are, after all, plenty more fish in the sea, to coin a phrase, but could you ever honestly imagine changing the football club you support? There is only one Watford or Darlington or Southampton, so to jump ship . . . well, there are names for people like that.

The love affair with our own clubs is total and all-consuming, and while most supporters (all right, real supporters) would never dream of switching allegiance to another club, most of us only grudgingly follow the national side. That is not to say that it is not important, but if Watford were playing on the same night as England we know where we would be whatever the circumstances. The fact is, following the national side is different because they do not belong to us in the way that our clubs do.

At club level, we have an identity. We sit, shout, sing, and some even fight, to protect that identity, and we are proud to do so and proud of what we have. That isn't just true of any hooligan element, it is true of all fans. The England team are rapidly losing that identity simply because we can't be seen to be proud of it, and that is one of the main reasons why people do not seem to care. As the merchandisers and sponsors take over, the England team's identity is eroded more and more, and we, as fans, stand by and do nothing. The brief for the team kits now seems to be slanted more towards what it will look like when worn with jeans, than towards anything to do with tradition or the national flag, while the sponsor's name looms large on the chest. That is a disgrace and yet, because the marketing departments promote the kit as a 'trendy must-have', people are stupid enough to buy it.

Another of the problems with the national side is that the players out on the pitch are usually the same players that the majority of us enjoy abusing week in, week out. For example, it must be very difficult for any Arsenal fan attending an international to find himself cheering a Teddy Sheringham goal! Similarly, in these days of high-profile foreign imports, it must be hard to be critical of your club's own players when they are busy doing their utmost to put one over on you at international level. The demise in the identity of the national side means that we, as fans, travel to watch how our own players, rather than the side as a whole, perform. When Watford were in their prime (many moons ago, sadly), we had the opportunity, on odd occasions, to watch our players pull on an England shirt, but it was as if they were representing us rather than the whole country.

This is obviously a feeling that is widely shared by supporters of other clubs. When Matt Le Tissier finally got the chance to shine at international level, the number of Southampton shirts and flags seen at the match rose tenfold, and this has happened with many clubs, even those with only the odd international in their squad. It gives the fan someone to identify with, something that the team as a whole cannot give. It may well be that the same is true for Rangers and Celtic fans, but the Scots have the advantage of being able to revel in their Scottishness without being branded racist, and that helps to bring them together in a way that is impossible for the English.

There are, of course, other problems that foster this apathy. With the introduction of satellite television into almost every pub in the country, the most entertaining way to watch an England game now seems to be while propped up against the bar with a pint in your hand, or catching up with the good bits when it's not your turn at the pool table. Watching, along with 15,000 schoolkids, England play Bulgaria in some meaningless friendly in a stadium that is half closed, and has little or no atmosphere, is hardly conducive to the big-game experience which should be provided if you are having to shell out between fourteen and seventy-five pounds to get in.

Indeed, the pricing policy is an important factor because as crowds at League games increase, crowds for internationals are falling. Surely any international match should be a showpiece event, but even a half-full Wembley is a bonus these days and one of the main reasons is that it is just too expensive. The FA must take the blame for this because it is they who set the prices, without considering what people can afford. This was never more clearly illustrated than at the FA Cup semi-finals, played in March 1996. Manchester United can sell out Old Trafford over and over again, and yet they were unable to take up their full allocation of tickets, because of the prices imposed by the FA for the game with Chelsea at Villa Park. Chelsea also returned tickets, as did Aston Villa and even Liverpool for their semi-final tie at Old Trafford. This was a clear indication, if any were needed, that supporters had simply had enough. English football, we are often told, is the best in the world, and yet two of the biggest games in the English footballing calendar, featuring some of the best-supported teams in the country, could not sell out.

The embarrassment of seeing empty seats at these two games should serve as a warning to those who continually ignore paying customers and sell the game to the sponsors and television companies with the deepest pockets. Supporters have allowed themselves to be bled dry by the game for far too long. At club level there is no choice because, as compulsives, we simply have to go; but at least at club level we can complain or demonstrate against the board. For England games, we just stay at home or go down the local.

If the manager or chairman of our own club turn out to be a complete waste of space, then we can come together, get organised and do something about it. It may take a long time (ask any Norwich fan) but we, as fans, can have an effect on what happens. If a player is crap, we can let him know in no uncertain terms on any match day, and there are thousands of incidents of crowds influencing managers' decisions during games. But with the national side, what can we do? We simply have to rely on the press to do the work for us in order to see any progress. Yet as we saw during the build-up to Euro 96, even the media are fickle. While we accept that the England team manager is there to be shot at because he is an easy target, can you imagine Messrs Kelly or Millichip lasting as long as they have at a League club? Just how these two have escaped criticism from fans for so long is mystifying. Indeed, as these gentlemen are at the forefront of our game, any long-term resentment – not just about the England team, but about the game in general – should be directed at them. They are the equivalents of a club's board and, as with club football, the fans know whether it is the tactics (and so the manager) or the set-up (the board's responsibility) that has caused the team's failings. With England there have been occasions where both parts have let people down, yet it is nearly always the manager alone who takes the blame.

Obviously we would all love to watch our side perform as well as, if not better than, the Brazilian side of the seventies; but in reality, they don't, and we're lumbered with whatever runs out onto the pitch on match days. It's not our fault we follow Coventry, Exeter or, yes, Watford, just unfortunate: but that's life. We live with that and accept it, but it is a sad fact that the only people who really care about *our* clubs are us, the supporters. There are obviously people who work at the club who love it as we do, but they are supporters too. But those within the game who do not care about our clubs should, because they supposedly run our game. It is a disgrace that those in control can watch clubs go to the wall for the price of a second-rate midfield carthorse while players, managers, agents and God knows who else meet – allegedly – in motorway service stations and take backhanders of amounts that probably would have saved Newport County, Aldershot and Maidstone.

Now, we are not saying that the game should bale out every club that has been badly managed, but when the 'haves' (such as Tottenham) and the 'have-nots' (such as Swindon) of this world are treated so differently, supporters become very angry. What the FA must realise is that when a club such as Aldershot go to the wall, the supporters of that club don't just give up and go home. Nor do they start supporting Arsenal or Everton. It may well be the hope of those at Lancaster Gate that the Premier League cash register rings just a little louder, but in reality, those supporters fight back. They regroup, and launch a mission to prove to the fat cats that they can't just kill off a club for the price of a team holiday to Barbados. They keep that identity because it is too important to them to allow it to be lost but they will resent forever the fact that they came so close to losing something so dear.

Once again, it has to be said that football is not about players or managers, it is about supporters. And the game owes everything to those of us who pay at the turnstiles. With the advent of that latest money machine, pay-per-view television, the possibility that every League club will be able to beam their fixtures into the living room of any home willing to pay for the privilege could well spell the end of the game as we know it. We have seen, over recent seasons, that clubs such as Manchester United have banned away fans because their grounds are being redeveloped, but the downside of this is that the atmosphere within those grounds has suffered, sometimes dramatically. Football support has, of course, an element of tribalism to it – that sense of belonging to a group, the chanting, the display of loyalty and sometimes aggression. When there are no opposing fans, just who can you display your vocal support to? When the scummers up the road banned away fans following the Millwall riot, the little atmosphere that their sad and deluded supporters were able to generate all but vanished. Every home game must have been as exciting as a visit to the local library – with almost certainly about as much movement off the ball!

Indeed, the implementation of all-seater stadia has dampened the atmosphere at many grounds. Arsenal have actually displayed posters introducing a scheme to concentrate the vocal element into a specific area of the ground, while both Tottenham and even Manchester United have been forced to appeal to supporters to generate more noise. At most games, the visiting supporters seem, in any case, to make much more noise than the home fans. This may be because they represent the hardcore travelling support of their own club, or because they are concentrated in a specific part of the ground, but the vocal element is a vital part of the stadium atmosphere. If pay-per-view were to become the norm, the possibility of clubs such as Newcastle and Liverpool banning away fans to satisfy the demand from both their own supporters and clamouring advertisers would become a reality. The problems would then start when other clubs started banning their fans. For example, Newcastle could hardly complain if they were not given tickets for their match at Elland Road if they made none available for Leeds fans to visit St James Park. Once on this spiral, there is no going back. Many will lose the right to watch their team play live football, and the game will run the risk of losing those fans forever.

With the price of watching football these days so expensive that even the most ardent supporter is being forced to pick and choose which games they attend, the habitual act of going out to a game is in danger of being broken. Once that habit is lost, it is hard to convince people that football provides value-for-money entertainment (and over recent years the England team usually have not, in any case). For many families, attending a game is already out of the question as an option for an afternoon out, so the main make-up of the support base remains that of the bloke out for an afternoon with his mates, away from his family. Every bloke wants his kids to follow the same team he does. It makes life so much easier. You don't have to explain to your mates what went wrong, or fund some other club's money machine by paying for an overpriced replica shirt every six months. It's much easier to convince a kid that the seventies replica shirt is much trendier than the dayglo, sponsor-ridden rag the team now play in if you can back it up with background knowledge from that era.

But many blokes now simply cannot afford to go to games at all, never mind take his kids; so the youth of today grow up watching Liverpool on *Match of the Day*, and want a shirt with 'Fowler' on the back. The local club thus loses another potential supporter, which poses the question of where the next generation of supporters are going to come from.

With pay-per-view, there is even the likelihood that thousands of young kids will start swearing allegiance to Inter Milan or Real Madrid, and we might see the Evertons and Man Cities of this world feeling the pinch because – make no mistake – come the Super League, they will be coming to a television near you. All of this is relevant to the national side because it is a factor in the break-up of the game as we now know it, and if people cannot afford to go to their chosen side, they will certainly not go to Wembley to watch England. The FA are encouraging the takeover of our game by big business and corporate hospitality, while we sit back and do nothing about it. Euro 96 provided the classic example of this indifference to the wishes of the average supporter as, despite the clamour for tickets from all over the country, thousands of them were being given to banks and fast-food chains to give away as prizes to people with little or no interest in the game.

Let's face it: club football in this country is where the real passion lies. Passion generated by people who would give almost anything in support of their club. Once that passion is instilled and nurtured, it is lifelong. It's not faceless but real and on your doorstep every single week if you want it. Those who see nothing but a fast buck from a television screen as

25

the bright new future for the privileged few might well stop and think what will happen to the thousands of fans outside the top ten. They won't start supporting United, City, Rovers, and so on, but will continue to follow their team in the second division north or whatever they intend to call their revamped League structure when they impose it.

As for following the national side, surely all the cheap seats will have been removed to allow more advertising space, and the players will soon be carrying their own endorsements, negotiated via agents who will be providing the next celebrity fan to come out of the woodwork with free tickets and an invite to the after-game party. Meanwhile, the real fans will be in the nearest pub, where they can cause as much trouble as they like totally outside the control, or the interest, of football. Football down the pub? You better believe it, mate. It's nearly here and it'll be all they'll let you have unless something is done.

One of the beautiful things about football is that if you sit ten fans in a room and ask them a question, you'll get ten different answers. The following three views on the subject of the national side we've received while researching this book come from three fans, each from a different part of the country.

ENGLAND? NOTHING TO DO WITH ME

Me, I couldn't give a fuck about the England team. The whole thing is run by a load of old tossers in suits that know nothing about the real fans. They are so far removed from us that it isn't any wonder that the game is in such a mess. They sit down there in London selling the game off to the sponsor with the biggest wallet without ever asking us how we feel. When was the last time Sir Bert got on the train on a Tuesday night, travelled to Oldham, paid out of his own pocket for a crap plastic seat giving an awful view and ate half a warm pie washed down with a cup of Bovril? Fucking never, that's when, and they tell us what we want when they haven't got a fucking clue. Arseholes.

I love my side. I'll watch thirty to forty games a season following Vale all over the country. I take days off work, spend hours arguing with the wife and spend hundreds of pounds a year, and I love it. It's fucking great. Usually! When do you think the last time one of those pricks from London came to Vale Park? Maybe when we beat Spurs or Everton, when the 'big' clubs were in town perhaps. I've only been to watch England once at Wembley, it was about ten years ago, and it was fucking boring. I'll never go again. If I want to watch them I'll go down the local. The Stadium is still shit; I went down for the Anglo-Italian final, and I tell you Goodison Park is better than that place – better view, better atmosphere, better everything.

The England side don't represent me any more. I bet the first thing that most of them do when they get the call up is ring their agents and see just how much more money they are worth. They're just a bunch of money-grabbing bastards ready to quit your club as soon as the chequebook comes out. The only loyalty shown in football is from the fans, and we plough our hard-earned money into this game and get no respect from those that run the thing. When England have a big game, I've got no chance of getting a ticket; I don't know the players or the sponsors or someone at FA HQ. And that is why Vale are what matters to me.

Ask yourself how you feel about the England side. You love it when they win, but most of the time you couldn't really give a shit. Were you devastated when they failed to beat Norway? Bollocks, you probably finished your pint and continued your game of pool. It's the same as watching Manchester United on Sky. You really want them to lose when the match is on, but once the game is over and they have won again, you couldn't really give a toss. It means nothing. Football has become so greedy and the England set-up is the worst of all. They have their grubby little hand so far down your pockets that they could pick the fluff out of your toes and they would have the other hand up your arse if they thought there was any loose change to be found up there.

AN ENGLAND FAN

In exactly the same way as someone would follow West Ham or Leyton Orient, I follow England. The England national side are my team.

Being brought up in the East End of London and having a football fanatic for a father, I found myself spoiled for choice as regards watching football during my younger years because my dad was, and still is, a fan of football rather than any particular side. As he was once a well-respected non-League player, I would often find myself cheering on my old man from the touchline at various grounds around southern England and, as with most players during their career, he found himself representing many different sides. So I guess it was hard for me to form any real kind of loyalty except that shown to my father.

Whenever the opportunity arose to take in a profes-sional game, Dad, Mum and I would all go off together – the original family supporters if you like – and take in the Hammers, Arsenal, Fulham, anyone. Dad liked to study the game in order to improve himself, I suppose, and I'm sure that rubbed off on me although despite my many afternoons in the local park, and much to my dad's disappointment, I am about as talented with a ball as synchronised swimming is exciting.

We never missed the chance to watch the national side play at Wembley. Without fail, we would travel up on the tube with a crowd of Dad's mates, and while they would take in a pub, all of us kids would run around outside and scream our heads off before going to the game and screaming our heads off some more. We'd get home around midnight. Brilliant. The first time I ever sat in a pub was before an international with my dad and his mates, and they proceeded to get me off my face, after which I spent most of the game with my head stuck down a Wembley toilet, much to everyone's amusement.

As I grew older and started work, I had the money to start taking in matches with my mates. Dad was past the playing age by then and had become more involved with our local non-League team on the social side, but rather than stick with one particular team, I still continued to pick and choose games. I had grown used to the big-game atmosphere and still enjoyed football for football's sake. I found myself travelling all over the country, watching games and visiting grounds, meeting supporters from different clubs, and enjoying football for all it is worth. There is so much bad press surrounding football fans, it amazes me. Football is great, watching football is great and football fans are great people who love to talk about the game. Admittedly, there are some people who follow the game for all the wrong reasons, and the sooner we get rid of them the better, but it is nowhere near as bad as the media make it out to be.

For me, watching football is, I imagine, very different than it is for most other supporters. As I said before, England are my team, I love the English game, and the national side represent the game for me to the rest of the world. I view every player I see on the pitch as a potential squad member which, I am sure you will appreciate, is fantastic. And as a result, I am able to view every piece of skill and enjoy it in a way that most others can't. I find that I am able to gain huge enjoyment from games without that win-at-all-costs mentality that comes from supporting a League side, because they're not that important to me. The obvious disappointment shown by my Tottenham-supporting mates when Robbie Fowler scores a peach of a goal from twenty yards out at White Hart Lane is, to me, a beautiful sight, although I do wait a few minutes before mentioning it to them.

The majority of football supporters I know and meet throughout the country view the whole England set-up as a disgrace. A set-up with bad management, a (sometimes) useless manager, awful tactics and bad team selection. At times, I would agree with them, but these are exactly the same problems that I hear them moaning about week in and week out when they talk about their own team. It's no different really.

Going to Wembley remains a great experience for me because it is my home ground and, despite what anyone says, it is by far the best stadium in this country. The movement that calls for a new national stadium has got it all wrong. Wembley is the home of English football, and the aura that surrounds the place is awesome. With England being such a small country, the argument for a more central location seems pointless because, leaving aside the obvious cost involved in building a new ground, football fans travel the country week in and week out to support their team. Moving from London will just mean all those from the capital having to travel: pointless. Access to the stadium is another argument which always crops up. Well, I'm sorry, but three train stations within one and a half miles, and parking for around 10,000 cars and coaches, kicks that into touch.

One of the most enjoyable aspects of watching the national team is that I get to see the best players in the world. I've seen Marco Van Basten, Cruyff and Zoff play over the years, and despite the fact that most of the games are friendlies, the players still view the opportunity to play on the hallowed turf as one of the highlights of their careers, the ultimate privilege. As a result, they do tend to lift their game and put on a genuine display of their talents which are often a joy to watch. The visiting support is another unique factor with

Wembley matches, and I must say that I find the different way that other countries view the game fascinating. It's such a shame that the English support can't be more hospitable to those who visit. The majority of the sides that come to Wembley have no hooligan element or intentions at all, and are mostly made up of family groups or those living and working in this country.

When I travel abroad with England, I go with a small group of other England-only fans, and we find that it's much easier to make our own arrangements and travel independently whenever possible because we get to see much more of the host country and have more freedom to move around that way. Mostly, when in Europe, we use the rail network and will stop off in other countries and cities on the way. Some of us even treat away games as our holiday time from work and, as is the nature of football, we get to visit places the average bloke would never think of coming to. I've been to Albania, Iceland, Australia, Africa – all over the place. Of course, there are problems sometimes, but they're not that much worse than the ones most people have when travelling abroad. The local police sometimes get a bit heavy, and trouble from rival fans can be a bit of a worry. This only usually happens on the day of the game, or more often, during the few hours surrounding the match, and there are rarely problems during the days before and after games.

It's just like over here really: if you want to avoid trouble and you have your head screwed on, it isn't that difficult. There'll always be some other idiot ready to occupy the locals for you anyway. Some countries are different, of course, due to their own hooligan problems, and it's to these more volatile matches that we tend to travel with the official party. In places like Greece and Turkey, it saves an awful lot of hassle when the police are there to see you in to the stadium and then back to your hotel afterwards, although sometimes they don't seem that happy about protecting you themselves.

One of the other benefits of being abroad with the national side is that it's much easier to spend time with the players and officials because they seem to be a lot more relaxed than they are in England. I've had the odd beer with some of our top players, talking about great games and memorable moments, and that's a fantastic thing because it really opens your eyes about life as a player. They're not all in it for the money; they really do care about the game and are very proud to pull on the England shirt despite what the papers say sometimes. Some have a far greater understanding of the supporters than others, but they all see the rubbish we have to put up with at times, and many are as frustrated at the way the game is run in this country as we are.

Following England has given me some of the greatest moments and experiences of my life. I cannot understand why, when there are so many football fanatics in this country, so few follow the national side in the way that my mates and I do! I realise that many of the games lack the competitive edge that League football brings every Saturday, but the game remains beautiful whenever and wherever it is played. It's quite worrying to see that the crowds at Wembley are on the decrease, when at League level they are rising. Maybe that has something to do with the quality of opposition sometimes; I don't know. One thing that does keep people away is that Wembley is way too expensive, and I don't really enjoy sitting in a half-empty, not to mention half-open, stadium and having to pay a fortune for the privilege. Maybe the FA could forge closer links between the clubs and the national side in order to generate the interest. I don't know all the answers, but I do know that the majority who ignore England don't really know what they're missing.

* * *

A FAN'S RANT

England. Make sure you say it in a hushed voice, when there are positively no social workers, *Guardian* readers or, God forbid, absolutely anyone from the 'England-is-to-blame-for-everything' industry within earshot. England has a problem, and it exists for everyone who hates the English (i.e. everyone). It's as if it's some dodgy aunt, chained up in an attic and never to be mentioned.

In this country those who tell us the errors of our own culture are virtually an industry in themselves. We don't like the EC – so we're 'little Englanders'. We celebrate VE day – we're glorifying war, colonialism and the lack of appreciation for other cultures (not celebrating the defeat of fascism in Europe, apparently, but I digress ...). We are told to make allowances for those who make no effort to live by our laws or who do not wish to use our language as their language. One funded body of superannuated bastards after another have convinced us, the English, that we are indeed to be ashamed of ourselves.

Of course, all the world's troubles are down to us. We've fucked up the Irish, stolen the Welsh's water, made the Scots the most balanced nation on earth (i.e. with a chip on both shoulders), and saved the French's arse twice, for which they have never forgiven us – as their current 'rush-to-bend-over-for-the-Germans' stance certifies. In fact, you name it – India, South Africa, the Middle East, Cyprus, acid rain, slavery, Bosnia, Ethiopia, Taiwan, Hong Kong, Vietnam, the ozone layer, Sky TV, those little tubs of milk you get at motorway service stations and can't open, Jeremy Beadle, yes, YES – it was us.

Lancaster Gate have swallowed this bollocks hook, line and sinker, even to the extent that our national team doesn't even wear the colours of red and white any more. Now if the Germans, who (let's be generous) have a

33

somewhat dubious history, can wear a fucking great Teutonic eagle and a sodding great yellow/red/black stripe across their chests as if they're going all the way to Poland, what the hell is going on?

Our second strip for Euro 96? Grey. Fucking grey. Again, is this Lancaster Gate thinking they might upset some minority group somewhere? Oh, and let's leave our flag off and put those nice little lions on there – and just to be on the safe side, we'll change the name of the country to 'UMBRO'. That couldn't offend anyone.

Well, I'm sick of a bunch of apologists running football. Football is tribal and we bloody like it that way. We understand, we belong. What the fuck is the England team, anyway? Why should I go to Wembley and support an extension of some blazer-wearing wimp's idea of what our country and our football is about? Even rugby, an appalling middle-class mess of a game, has learned to belong to this country and benefited hugely from it. But football can't do it – not those nasty working-class types on the terraces. How the hell can we be seriously asked to be ambassadors abroad when English football represents every clichéd sell-out of our country we can think of?

Despite what I've said, it's not all Lancaster Gate's fault. They are just a symptom of something that runs far deeper. I'm just your average Labour-voting, white, heterosexual, able-bodied bloke. I don't particularly like the royal family, but I don't mind them that much as they're a bit of a laugh and are probably good for a few quid from the tourists. I'm just a normal bloke who does normal things – girlfriend, work, footy, bit of cricket in the summer and so on. But I'm mad as hell about what's happening to my country. I have an almost overwhelming sense of loss about my identity and culture, and I believe there are millions like me, but we have no voice, no platform. Except, once in a blue moon, a group of us get together, one thing leads to another and all of a sudden we have the joy of reminding everyone we still exist. Don't fuck with us.

I make no apologies for what I'm saying. The only England that means anything to me ran down a street in Turin smashing everything in its path in retaliation for being teargassed by a bunch of cowardly Italian paramilitaries when we were doing sod all. We did this in retaliation for days of grief, petrol bombs and kickings, despite repeated cheek-turning and offers of friendship on our part. We were pushed so far – then, wallop.

It makes me sick when everyone goes on about the lovely Irish fans, and the good old Jocks with their bagpipes, everyone being jolly and dancing with the locals. We'd love it, but everyone wants to have a go at us, those mad English people. Everyone hates us – face it. We're never going to be some cuddly group of funny people to the rest of the world. Our history goes before us. Do they owe us respect? Yes. Do we get it? Do we fuck.

This is the point. With England, we think the team is detached from us. However, we have something in our control: we can remind those who 'want to know' that, if need be, we're still those mad bastards who fight like fuck and don't give up until we win. If I'm running with an England crew made up of the Forests, the Citys, the Uniteds, the Athletics, the Rovers, the Hotspurs, the Palaces, the Countys and even the Alexandras, we know that just for once an England that means something to us is all around us – something we can believe in, fight for, get hurt for, wreck for, live for and die for.

I have no solution to offer, except to say that if we were able to support a national team that went some way to mirroring and celebrating our nationality, things could well improve. Until then, don't bore us with it all. Half-full Wembleys will be the norm, and the circus of fear and loathing that surrounds the far more important away trips will continue. Turin *was* a gas and, all together now – 'Two World Wars and one World Cup, doo-dah, doo-dah'.

Chapter 2

Watch Out, The English Are Coming

When talking about European club competitions and international fixtures, two words go hand in hand, 'England' and 'violence'. During the late seventies and early eighties the spread and reputation of the so-called 'English disease' was at its height. As English club sides dominated on the field, the fans left behind a trail of destruction on the terraces and streets of Europe, culminating in the death of thirty-nine fans, mostly Italian, at the 1985 European Cup final between Liverpool and Juventus.

That match, played at the Heysel Stadium in Brussels, Belgium, and the disaster that took place that day, led to a total ban from playing any competitive football on European soil imposed on all English club sides. At the time of the Heysel tragedy, Eddy was working with a Scouser who took great delight in telling me that he and his lovable Northern chums were going to Brussels to kick the shit out of those wop bastards. He came back a broken man, almost unable to speak about what he had seen in the stadium. He told me that there had been trouble the night before and during the build-up to the match, and said that once they were in the ground and saw just how bad the segregation was, it was only a matter of time before the Liverpool fans were going to make their move, the consequences of which proved disastrous.

He also told me that he would never watch football again. Yet, over ten years on, he still attends most games, home and away, including European matches. The fact that he is still involved in the odd bit of trouble is much more worrying, to me, although he assures me it's only at the big games. Many in Liverpool tried, as ever, to blame everyone and anything but their own supporters for what happened that night. But while, admittedly, the Belgian police and UEFA must take some of the blame for holding a potentially volatile fixture in such an old stadium, that still doesn't excuse the fact that their fans charged across a terrace to give the Italians a good hiding. The National Front and even Chelsea fans were also blamed for the trouble as Liverpool tried to divert attention away from themselves.

Liverpool fans, during their reign over European football, left their mark on more than one occasion prior to Heysel. In 1977, Liverpool fans raided shops and fought with St Etienne fans in France. In 1978, some Liverpool supporters embarked on a '500-mile rampage' through Europe, involving fighting, theft and assault, as they made their way to and from a fixture with Borussia Moenchengladbach in Germany. In 1979, eighteen Liverpool fans were arrested as the two sides clashed again. Further incidents followed in subsequent years, too.

The reputation English football earned itself in the seventies and early eighties wasn't all down to the Scousers. Manchester United fans were up to no good as early as 1974, when supporters damaged cars and smashed windows as they fought in the streets of Ostend, Belgium. They also had trouble with St Etienne in 1977: thirty-three fans needed hospital treatment after fighting broke out on the terraces. In 1974, Tottenham fans rampaged through Rotterdam when playing Feyenoord, and then fought in the stadium, resulting in seventy arrests and 200 injuries.

Back in 1975, the problem of the English football fan abroad was made plain for all to see. Beamed live into the living rooms of the nation, Leeds United supporters rioted in the Parc des Princes in Paris during their European Cup final defeat against Bayern Munich. The catalyst for the trouble in the stadium was the poor refereeing along with a 2–0 defeat, but for some days before the game, the Leeds fans had fought with the locals, rather than the German supporters, and many were known to be raiding shops and 'bagging' (swallowing) jewellery. UEFA were so sick of Leeds that they banned them from all European competition for four years.

This warning was far from effective. England's reign of terror continued, as in 1980 West Ham United became the first English club forced to play a match behind closed doors, following running battles in Spain with the local police. The event that sparked it all off was the death of an eighteen-year-old Hammers fan, allegedly run over and killed deliberately by a local coach driver. There were twenty-six arrests, and West Ham fans were said to have pissed on the Castilla supporters that were housed on the terrace below them. UEFA also fined the club almost £8,000.

It would be easy to go on and on, but what is listed here merely scratches the surface of what the English fans were up to on the Continent during those fateful years. Surprisingly, however, the relevant history is somewhat longer than this. The first major incident instigated by English fans came in 1965, when British soldiers serving in Germany fought with supporters of SV Hannover when Manchester United were the visitors. The fighting spilled onto the pitch after battles on the terrace got out of control.

So much for England's offensive abroad. What about the incidents of violence against English fans and players when on their travels? These go back even further.

In 1946, the Wolverhampton Wanderers travelled to play Malmö, Sweden. After the game, 'hundreds of angry supporters' pelted the Wolves team coach with stones as they left the stadium. Chelsea suffered the same fate in 1965 while, and after, they played at Roma: players were struck by missiles as the crowd rioted. In the same year Arsenal's match with the Jamaican national side was suspended; the riot squad had been called into action following brawls between the players and trouble in the crowd.

Nor were the eighties any happier for the English fan far from home. In particular, 1980 proved to be a bad year for following your club into Europe. Fifty Manchester United fans were rescued by riot police with dogs as thousands of FC Nuremburg supporters surrounded them. Before a game with Salonika, in Greece, Ipswich Town fans and players were stoned. Many other incidents where English fans were the victims could be listed.

As you can see from the accounts above, Europe has been a bit of a battleground, as far as the English are concerned. Of course, trouble at League fixtures in this country has been with us almost since the game began, but we were not the only ones to have had such problems. After reading what follows, you may think the phrase 'The English Disease' is somewhat unjust.

As early as 1913, crowd trouble at football matches in Ireland was rearing its head, when players from the Scottish national side were attacked. In 1919, at the fixture between Glentoran and Belfast Celtic, the crowd invaded the pitch and attacked players and officials. Bottles and stones were thrown and the stadium suffered from vandalism. At the same fixture in 1920, there was a repeat of the violence – this time a more serious outbreak, as four people received gunshot wounds. In the same year there was trouble at the Oban Rangers vs Millwall Athletic match, and fighting between rival mobs at the Cliftonville riot. Most of this kind of trouble in Ireland can, of course, be put down to religious differences, and the fact that Ireland was in a state of near (or actual) civil war around this time. The Unionist/Republican divide continued during the seventies, too, as sectarian violence flared up once more.

All this begins to look somewhat tame, however, when you look further afield. If you want serious crowd trouble, there is only one place to begin: South America. Far and away the worst incident we came across anywhere occurred in Peru, in 1964, when the national team took on Argentina. Following a disallowed goal, the crowd erupted, and during the mayhem, frenzy and panic that followed, 318 people died and 500 more were injured. Yet, in Argentina, the problems and consequences surrounding that match were soon forgotten by those intent on causing trouble. Just four years later, at a fixture between River Plate and Boca Juniors, 74 died and 150 were injured as Boca fans threw lighted papers onto the fans below, sending them into a panic. Many other incidents, involving fatalities, throughout that continent could also be listed.

Not a pretty picture. And, as far as European fans' behaviour goes, the picture isn't much brighter. In 1967, as the two Turkish sides, Kayseri and Sivas, met, 44 were killed and 600 injured. Rioting fans used pistols, bottles and knives at the game, and the trouble spread back to Sivas itself, where cars were overturned and set on fire. Things got so out of hand that the Turkish Army were called in to restore order. The USSR, not known for its tolerance of those who misbehave, also suffered football violence on a massive scale. The worst incident occurred in 1982, when 69 died and 100 were injured as fighting between drunken fans of Moscow Spartak and Harlem caused a crowd barrier to collapse.

Before Heysel, in fact, almost every European country had some experience of crowd violence. France, Germany, Spain, Austria, Portugal, Belgium and the now fractured country that was Yugoslavia have recorded incidents dating back to the early fifties, and in Italy (as in Ireland) we go back even further. In 1920, the referee was shot dead as the crowd ambushed the police and stole revolvers at a match between Viareggio and Lincques. In the fifties there were two incidents involving Naples fans; 217 of them ended up injured. Naples have had a history of disturbances ever since, including riots, pitch invasions and, once, having 2,000 fans storm the dressing rooms in order to attack both officials and players. Such incidents as these were unheard of in Britain, yet English fans' reputation as the worst hooligans in Europe, if not the world, remained the accepted view at home and abroad.

Trouble at home wasn't confined to Continental nations in the pre-Heysel period. Over the months leading up to that night, English League football was experiencing traumas of its own. The famous Millwall riot at L*t*n was broadcast all over the world, while trouble at the Chelsea vs Sunderland League Cup tie resulted in a proposal to erect electric fences at Stamford Bridge. On 11 May 1985, a youth died during fighting between rival Birmingham City and Leeds fans, and on the same day 56 people died in the Bradford fire, with 200 more seriously injured – an incident completely unrelated to violence, but adding to the chaotic and tragic atmosphere of that time. The government, spurred by public outcry, were at last forced to be seen to be doing something. But in reality, over the time leading up to the Hillsborough disaster, the violence continued and very little was achieved in combating the hooligan element.

These horrors on the domestic front, added to disruption abroad and culminating in Heysel, left UEFA with no option but to ban all English clubs from European competition. What was surprising, however, was that the national side, despite the recent history that had surrounded their fixtures on the Continent, were exempt from any ban. The history of the England side abroad is a long and not very distinguished one.

Chapter 3
History

Large-scale disturbances involving England fans abroad began in Turin, during the 1980 European Championships. With trouble on the increase at games in Europe involving English club sides, the imminent arrival of the England contingent had been cause for a great deal of consternation among the Italian authorities, and their response was a massive media campaign warning the Italians of their impending doom at the hands of the England hooligans. As a result, both the Italian police and the country's own hooligan element were all over the English fans during the build-up to the tournament, treating many of those fans appallingly.

At Turin, everything came to a head. During the game against Belgium, Italian fans taunted the English following a Belgian equaliser. The English, many of whom were drunk and angry at their treatment, responded by kicking it all off. The Italian police and military stepped in quite quickly and broke up the disturbance with baton charges, and with teargas – which promptly blew back onto the pitch, holding play up for five minutes. When the game restarted, Tony Woodcock scored what was apparently the winning goal, but this was disallowed for off-side and it all went off again. As a result of this, 70 people were taken to hospital and the FA were fined £8,000 the very next day.

With the legacy of Turin still fresh in the minds of football enthusiasts in England, the national team went to Spain for the 1982 World Cup with the threat of exclusion from all football competitions ringing in its ears. A concerted and intensive security campaign had been put in place to deal with any potential trouble. Prior to the tournament, the English authorities had indulged themselves with a campaign to deal with the hooligan element back home, and the FA had put forward a ten-point plan to deter trouble, including such ideas as the return of corporal punishment in schools and the reintroduction of the 'riot act' to deal with trouble at football matches.

The English fans were due to arrive at Bilbao, and here the locals employed a different approach, adopting an attitude of extreme politeness and declaring that they would be delighted to welcome the English fans and play host to them during the tournament. The local Basque police, well known for their intolerance and their ability to deal with almost anything as regards civil disorder, made it clear that they were utilising a 'wait and see' approach to the potential problem.

The fly in the proverbial ointment was the Falklands War, which was still underway as the tournament began. Certain elements of the media at that time believed that as we were still at war, the British teams should be withdrawn from the competition while other elements were, with all-too-obvious intent, busy reminding all and sundry that Spain was allied by history to the cause of the Argentinians. Another aspect of this problem was that Argentina had not been excluded from the tournament, and the possibility of the two nations meeting at some time during the competition was very real.

While the English supporters, in particular, adopted a gung-ho, task-force mentality of their own, much of the Spanish population had shown a fierce anti-British sentiment. It is true to say, however, that the Basques, in whose region the English fans were residing, are traditionally anti-government and oppressed and were, as we've said, strongly supportive of the British cause. This was of great benefit during the early stages of the competition.

Meanwhile, the swell of patriotism among the British as a result of the Falklands conflict meant that the National Front enjoyed something of a renaissance among the English. Many were only too willing to join in with the NF's right-wing doctrine, and the adoption by the FA of a mascot, Bulldog Bobby, which bore a striking resemblance to the logo of the NF publication *The Bulldog*, did little to deter the fans from this. With all this simmering away, in the build-up to each game the police and military were all over the English, with riot teams and teargas highly visible at all times. But there was little trouble, save for the odd skirmish in the local towns, and these usually involved drink. The main problem, for the English fans, was the ticket allocation. Many had travelled to Spain with no tickets in the hope that they would be able to buy them on the streets, and while this was indeed the case, the prices were exorbitant. So many a tout was 'relieved' of his tickets by angry English fans, who would willingly have paid, had the price been reasonable.

During the early stages of the competition, there was only one real incident of note, and that took place at the French game when the police completely overreacted to a minor altercation which involved only a few fans and in which a French supporter had been slightly hurt. The resultant baton charge by the police even attracted condemnation in the local press the next day – but its effect on the English was far more dramatic, with many adopting a siege mentality. But the fact remains that in Bilbao, despite the warnings and the influx of journalists desperate for a story, there was little in the way of trouble involving the English, and the locals were both surprised and pleased that they had been host to what the mayor called 'a nice bunch of lads'. Following their success in the early phase, the England team, closely followed by the contingent of fans, moved to Madrid. It was here that things began to take a definite turn for the worse.

The Basques' sympathy for the English did not, of course,

hold in Madrid, where there was a groundswell of anti-British feeling among the population – particularly as the Falklands War was now over and the English fans were revelling in 'their' victory. An added problem was that many of the English fans had little or no money left while, at the same time, food and drink prices had been hiked up outrageously. The local hoteliers were, in some cases, putting up both prices and the number of people per room in an effort to extract as much money as possible from fans. Complaints meant only one thing, eviction. And meanwhile, the fans resorted to begging, bumming or stealing.

Sadly for the police, the first game England faced in the second phase of the competition was to be against their old foe, Germany. On the back of the Falklands victory, another meeting with Germany was heaven-sent for many of the English fans, who went to town celebrating and drinking. The police, far from happy with the situation in any case, went on the offensive and adopted a provocative strategy to deter any hooligan element, but other problems were surfacing. The Spanish locals were protesting against the Thatcher war machine, and the English were becoming more vocal with the 'You'll never take Gibraltar' songs. Finally, it all came to the boil. Outside the Bernabeu Stadium, the police began indulging in indiscriminate attacks on the English contingent. The German fans were largely absent during this incident, but it is known that a number had been with the English during the day and that the two groups had been drinking together quite happily. Similarly, inside the stadium the problems were not with the Germans but with the Spanish, who were continuing to provoke the English with anti-English chants and abuse. Despite some minor offs in the ground, it was outside that things took a more serious turn when a group of Spanish fans laid a Union Jack across the road for cars to run over, and the flag was then burnt. During the offs that resulted, many of the English took a hiding at the hands of the Spaniards, and at least four were stabbed before the evening was over. So the English media, turning their attention from the English group, went to town on the Spanish police and thugs, and many of the English supporters staying outside Madrid read the news stories and became aware of the incidents and stabbings for the first time. Many fans then left Spain, but those who remained were fired up. The central factor in this unrest, and one that was widely reported, was that no Spanish supporters had been detained during any disturbance – something that told its own story.

With the next game being against the host nation and the very real possibility of mayhem looming, the English supporters decided that the only possible course of action was to stick together. But their forming of a united front merely attracted the attention of the Spanish supporters, who were happy to have a go at the English in the surefire knowledge that the police, who were also well up for it, would leave them alone. Following a serious disturbance outside the ground on the evening before the match, when the police went on the offensive and baton charged the English supporters, the English ranks were considerably subdued during the game. Unfortunately, this did not stop the Spanish from hurling missiles down on them from the upper tier while the police stood by and did nothing except arrest those who complained. Following a few small disturbances outside the game, largely due to the elimination of the England side from the competition, the English fans returned home to face something they had previously never imagined: widespread media support. Such was the level of provocation and abuse suffered by supporters at the tournament, the British press was unanimous in its condemnation of the Spanish, and a number of questions were even asked in the House of Commons about the level of brutality faced by British citizens at the hands of the Spanish police. Following an enquiry in Spain, even the mayor of Madrid announced that he was 'ashamed to be Spanish' as a result of police behaviour, but FIFA, UEFA and even the FA were strangely silent. It seemed, for a while at least, that the sympathy of the English public and the media were with the followers of the national team.

This sympathy vanished following incidents before, during and after a European Championship qualifier in Denmark, in September 1982, when English supporters misbehaved in the worst possible way. With the threat of a total ban still hovering over their heads, the English indulged in an orgy of vandalism and crime in the build-up to the game and widespread violence in the period surrounding it. Despite a huge police effort and concerted moves by the Danish supporters and the general public to welcome their 'visitors', the behaviour of some of the English supporters was simply appalling. Before the game, Danish fans attacked groups of English supporters drinking in bars a number of times, but certain English groups also wrecked bars in which the Danes were drinking – finding, however, that resistance was stronger than they had envisaged. Within the stadium, minor skirmishes took place throughout the game, but the main problem centred around a late – in injury time, no less – goal by Jesper Olsen and the fact that all but some plainclothes policemen had left the ground to be deployed outside. As the final whistle blew, the Danish crowd went wild and so did the English but not quite in the same manner. Approximately 500 English fans went for it in the biggest possible way as the Danes celebrated their result, and on the unsegregated terraces, it was mayhem. While the bulk of the Danish support did a runner, a number of plainclothes policemen did not, and these took the English on in a number of exchanges.

The disorder then spilled out into the area surrounding the stadium, where the English systematically wrecked everything to hand while the police were in complete disarray. It is clear that the English were the major players in this mess; there were, in fact, almost 100 arrests. But there were a great many Danish supporters who had come to the game intent on taking on the English, and this was widely commented on in both the Danish and British media. The cries for a ban were getting louder and louder after this event but again, UEFA did nothing except voice concern. Of greater significance, however, was the fact that as Denmark had proved, groups were starting to see the English as potential targets rather than as opponents to be feared and avoided. This was not commented upon widely at the time.

In November 1983, England and its travelling fans descended on Luxembourg for a match which was to decide the fate of England's qualification for the 1984 European Championships in France. Despite an elaborate police operation, a 4–0 victory was not enough to secure qualification for the English. The English fans went to town, running riot and causing damage worth thousands of pounds. Despite this, UEFA merely warned the FA that unless the government succeeded in stopping English fans from travelling abroad, it would be forced to act. However, following the tragedy of Heysel, even UEFA was forced to concede that enough was enough and after years of threats and warnings, all English club side participation in European football was suspended indefinitely. Strangely, despite all the problems, no ban was imposed on the national side but the actions of UEFA, together with the difficulties of getting there because of distance and cost, led to a fairly peaceful 1986 World Cup in Mexico, including the infamous game against Argentina. Even concerted efforts by elements of the British media who were desperate for stories failed to stir up trouble that time.

With English clubs still banned from European competition, and trouble at home on the increase, the possibilities for disorder in the 1988 European championship were immense. With the tournament being held in Germany, and with a team which had performed reasonably successfully in the Mexico World Cup, it was clear that huge numbers of fans would make the trip and that among that number would be many up for trouble. That England went to Germany as the undisputed champions of thuggery is beyond dispute, and UEFA made it clear that any chance of their readmittance to European competition would depend entirely on their behaviour at the tournament. However, the legacies of both Turin and Spain were still fresh in many memories and revenge was uppermost in the minds of some. Nevertheless, the German police were confident of their ability to control these fans. At a friendly fixture in Dusseldorf in September 1987, they had searched and breathalysed all the English fans before they entered the stadium, and there had been very little trouble before or during the game and only a minor disturbance immediately afterwards. Yet while confident, the German police force did make it widely known that they would resort to any means necessary if things got out of hand. What follows is our account of the tournament exactly as the two of us experienced it.

EURO 88

In 1988, we attended the European Championships which that year were held in what was then West Germany. We were able to do this because Dougie was serving with the Royal Air Force then and, as luck would have it, was stationed in Germany near the Dutch border. The fact that accommodation, food and duty-free drink was readily and freely available meant that there was no shortage of willing houseguests, so four blokes suddenly found themselves at Heathrow awaiting a trip across the Channel and into the relative comfort of Dougie's cellar.

For these four, this was to be their first time abroad watching England, and it was strange to note that upon arrival, they had adopted that cocky, swaggering attitude so beloved, and possibly expected, of England fans abroad. However, once they were transported from a scrupulously clean and efficient German airport (the exact opposite of Heathrow, in fact) to a little piece of England in the middle of Europe, they quickly reverted to their 'normal' laddish behaviour.

Now for those who do not know, Forces camps abroad are fantastic places to be. They encompass all that is good in England together with the values enjoyed in the services but lost by civilians (loyalty, pride, respect, etc), as well as enjoy all the benefits of the host nation which, in the case of Germany at that time, included a better standard of living, not to mention great beer and excellent food. It is also true to say that the mix of European peoples, with their respective characteristics, make for great social events and in a small community which included all the elements of British society (including the rigid class structure maintained within Her Majesty's Armed Forces) plus some Dutch, Germans, Italians and the odd Belgian, it was a great place to be. With Euro 88 about to start and an English team that had the distinct possibility of reaching, at the very least, the semi-finals (and no Welsh or Scottish involvement), it was a brilliant time to be English and abroad.

The excitement surrounding the competition was rapidly developing towards fever pitch, but come the start of the build-up to the game in Stuttgart against the old enemy, the Irish, things started to look a little different. The hype leading up to the match concentrated not on the game, but on the differences between the two sets of supporters, to such a degree that the German people identified the Irish as the loveable, happy, Guinness-drinking rogues and the English as the scum of Europe. All the years of trouble and the negative publicity that accompanied it were wheeled out once again and the legacy of Heysel was examined in great detail at every opportunity. The success of this media campaign was quite astonishing and even for those who had lived and worked in the country for some time, the change in attitude of the German people toward the Forces was significant and clear to see. It was soon apparent that they had begun to distrust anyone English and any show of loyalty towards our own club sides was greeted with disdain and as proof that all English males were the stereotyped hooligans they were expecting. To be realistic, coming from a nation which still puts almost every nationality into a stereotyped pigeonhole, we really didn't have that much justification in complaining about this. But remember, this was the first time we had personally experienced resentment of this nature, and it is not very nice.

That apart, it was clear that many of the English supporters positively revelled in their position as the lepers of Europe. Certainly, the five of us found a great deal of satisfaction from scaring the shit out of shop workers merely by opening our mouths. Was it the fact that we were English, with our Southern English (not 'Cockney') accents, that was causing disquiet, or were we simply playing up to it all along? Anyone who travels with their club knows that they will occasionally be viewed with suspicion even these days, but here we were in a different country at the height of the 'English Disease' era and with all the connotations that bears. We were very unwelcome invaders in a foreign land, and the Saturday game mentality, where the events of the previous afternoon could be forgotten on the Sunday morning, was replaced by something else. We were there for three weeks and we would have to live with both the performance of the team and the performance of the fans.

The closer the first England game got, the more wary of the supporters the German population became. The adoption of that siege mentality so beloved of England's opponents ensured that away from the sanctuary provided by HM Forces, any Englishman was going to be under the watchful eyes of the German Politzi. As anyone who has ever been to Germany will know full well, the Politzi enjoy quite a high profile among their people, and as anyone who has had the misfortune, or stupidity, to get up to anything they shouldn't will also know, they do not mess about either. During the build-up to the competition, they quite happily made it known that they would adopt a softly-softly approach to the tournament but would not tolerate any trouble, in any form, from anyone. For most people, that would have been enough of a warning to let us know what the score was but here we were, five blokes who were, shall we say, up for it, and threats like that simply made the whole thing more exciting.

For Dougie, it was a strange time indeed because here he was, at home as it were, doing a job with a great deal of responsibility in a position where he was highly respected. Suddenly, he was in a position where he could escape all that and go back into that childish environment we all call fandom. But should any of us get into trouble, the consequences would be severe for him because the military police had made it quite clear that once the Politzi had finished with any serviceman who broke the law, they would take their turn. In true Forces fashion, Dougie was fully accountable for the actions of anyone staying in his house, something he made quite clear at great length to the four lads sleeping in his cellar!

Come the day of the Irish game in Stuttgart, our anticipation was at its height. The sun was shining, we would win and more importantly, we would take the piss out of the Micks and the traitor Charlton. Our journey to the city was tremendous, a thrash in a hire car down an autobahn full of English supporters giving it the big'un to everyone they saw, including us. It was brilliant. The service stations were something else, full of English lads at the height of excitement, singing their hearts out and meeting new faces: awesome. Our arrival in the city of Stuttgart was greeted with the sight of hordes of policemen in semi-riot gear, but not much news about what had been happening in and around the city regarding the fans.

There had been a number of arrests over the previous two nights, but all of these had involved German locals, while the Irish had been busy downing as much beer as they could – which is fair enough. Actually, the Politzi were well on the case and the provision of a tented city had given the English a place to gather in numbers, and they were pretty happy really. We were actually quite relieved about the whole atmosphere and went to the stadium to enjoy an English victory. Wrong! As we all know, Ireland won 1–0 and we were gutted. Our anticipation was replaced by anger and fear – anger at the result and fear that it would all go wrong and we would be out. After the game we hung around for a while but nothing of consequence happened, so we headed home with the Dutch game only a few days away. The day after the Ireland match, the British papers were full of reports of 'the battles of Stuttgart' which had not really existed, and we began to take seriously the rumours of the press paying people to stage trouble which, up to then, had been dismissed as pure fiction. If this was what they wanted then we were convinced that they only had to wait a few days and they would get them in any case. But it was clear to us that this provocation would not help although the German press was, to say the least, mildly surprised at the way things had been reported across the Channel.

Dusseldorf was something else because the build-up to the Dutch game was to provide much of the ammunition levelled at the England fans after the tournament. Without the benefit of our accommodation, those living in tents were surprised to find that Dusseldorf had provided little in the way of a welcome for them. The result of this was that the English gathered in or around the main railway station, basically living out of the left luggage lockers, and on the night before the game, they came under attack from local supporters and a German mob who had travelled up from the German game against Denmark. This, as we were told when we arrived, was a massive off and completely foxed the Politzi who hadn't been expecting everything. By all accounts, the English stood and did the business and ended up running the Germans ragged until the riot

Politzi got hold of things some hours later and arrested over 90 English fans and 40 Germans. This had obviously fired up the English lads and on our arrival the next morning, the Politzi were all over the place keeping a very wary eye on things. Those who had seen off the locals were still well up for it but this time, their prey were the Dutch who, having failed to show at Wembley the year before, had warned our lot that they were coming and would be kicking it off again.

The atmosphere was fantastic and the place was really buzzing in the way it does when things are getting really hairy and you expect it to get worse. We kept hearing about little offs involving German fans around the station and were told by the Politzi that they had detained large numbers of German fans travelling to Dusseldorf to take us on but we were still waiting for the Dutch because then it would really go. But it didn't, because they didn't show up, again. Even though a little mob of cloggies had steamed through one of the England car parks just before the game and had scratched a few cars and slashed the odd tyre, which was very big of them, they didn't have the bottle to take anyone on, which proved to us once and for all that the talk about them had been complete bollocks.

After the game, the English fans were gutted, not to mention very frustrated, and there were loads milling around looking to kick it off either with the locals or what Dutch we could find, but with the amount of Politzi around the ground, it was pretty much impossible. All we could do was piss off home but really, we knew it would be all over after the Russia game because we were already out. Again, the press went to town on us and told the fans back home that Dusseldorf had been all but levelled by the English fans while certain sections of the government were demanding that the England team be brought home in shame as a result of the fans' activities. Not quite the truth and certainly not the way we saw it, nor was it the view of the German police or media who again were slightly incredulous at what their colleagues across the Channel were reporting.

We didn't really know what to expect in Frankfurt. We knew England were out and we had also heard in the German press that the local fans were really looking to kick it off with us. Still, the Russians weren't a risk and so we knew where the threat was. However, when we arrived it was clear that plenty of England fans had gone home but it was also clear that among those that remained were an element intent on trouble. Indeed, there had been some trouble in the city on the previous night but again, the Politzi said it was nothing serious although some press boys told us it had been outrageous . . . hmmm. Again, the problems were with the German locals who were getting really loud by this time especially as England had been so crap – something that wasn't helped by probably the most gutless performance of all time against the Russians. Rumours were flying about saying that a German neo-Nazi group were in the area looking for it but we didn't see them. All we saw was a few locals getting a good running by a load of West Ham. However, from what we heard it really went off in the city centre that night because about 150 English lads were nicked, mostly for fighting and vandalism. All we wanted to do was get home: we had seen and had enough.

The fact remains that what happened involving the English fans in Germany was bad, but not as bad as the British press made it look. In all, 381 English fans were detained but few were charged, and while that looks a lot, the total number of detentions was in excess of 1,200, with over 800 of those German. This was something that received little publicity in the English media. However, it remains clear to us that most of the incidents during that championship involved a great deal of provocation and this has been largely ignored.

Certainly the incident at the railway station in Dusseldorf involved the English coming under attack, which showed, if nothing else, that the Germans were well up for it.

Similarly, the worst violence of the entire tournament took place in Hamburg, when the German supporters rioted and took over the city following the 2–1 victory over Holland. While there were no English involved, an Irish bar was wrecked by a German mob and the Irish lads, who had been drinking peacefully outside, were given a right hammering. Still, that wasn't really newsworthy over here so you may not know about that. What is clear though is that the Germans were wankers intent on having a pop at every foreign group they could find, particularly the English. Mind you, on most occasions they did the off at the first sign of any real resistance or retaliation but at least they had a go, unlike the Dutch or the Danish, so in the warped way these things are perceived, they had earned a result of sorts. The English football supporters' mentality of 'stand firm and fight' was never more evident than at this tournament.

Sadly, as a result of the violence in Germany, and the fact that the media had convinced everyone except those who knew the truth that it had been the English fans' fault, the FA withdrew its application to UEFA for the post-Heysel European ban to be lifted. It didn't take a genius to work out what the answer would have been, and English football did not need any more kicks – it was already lying on the ground. However, what was more irritating was that UEFA failed to take action against Germany based on the behaviour of the German supporters, who had been intent on having a pop at the English, and everyone else for that matter; and that was a scandal. UEFA, supported by the Politzi, who were still baffled by the way the English fans were being treated by their own media, merely stated that the disturbances were no worse than on any normal Saturday in the Bundesliga. If nothing else, this succeeded in spelling out a clear message to football fans throughout Europe that 'the English will always provide the scapegoats'. With clubs still out of Europe, the next major hurdle in the battle for reinstatement was the World Cup, Italia 90.

England's World Cup group contained Albania, Sweden and Poland, three nations not renowned for their domestic problems but possessed of police forces who are more than capable, and certainly willing, to keep a lid on things. However, in the aftermath of Euro 88 and the wrongful condemnation of the English fans, the travelling lads were under a great deal of scrutiny from all sides. While the Albania away trip to Tirana went off peacefully, largely because that country believes in suppressing its own population, never mind a load of potential hooligans, the subsequent trip to Stockholm provided a few problems. Groups of England fans were travelling without tickets, and at least 500 were allowed into the ground purely on police advice and in an effort to avoid trouble. The journey to Katowice, however, provided a number of serious problems, mostly involving the local police getting stroppy, but as a result of a 0–0 draw, England, together with their travelling fans, had qualified.

Italy beckoned and England were seeded and drawn to play in Cagliari on Sardinia, conveniently keeping the potential hooligan problem penned in on what is a beautiful island, with all those in authority hoping that we would be knocked out and would go home. Sadly, the last day of the domestic season had been littered with incidents throughout the country, but the main problem occurred in Bournemouth. Leeds fans there went on the rampage on both the seafront and in the town centre, causing widespread damage, and 120 people were arrested for rioting, looting and assault. This very volatile fixture undoubtedly caused the mayhem; the local police had been complaining about it since it became clear that Leeds would be promoted if they won.

Despite this unrest, UEFA threw the FA a carrot and on 18 April, stated that if the English fans behaved, they would let the English clubs back into European competition – so it really was all to play for. The main problem lay in the other teams in our group: Ireland (again!), Egypt and, gulp, the Dutch.

When news of the draw came out, the government went on the offensive against the hooligan element; the sports minister, Colin Moynihan, became particularly vocal and labelled all English fans as potential hooligans. He then went on to state that together with the English, the Dutch would be a major threat, despite the evidence to the contrary provided by all of the previous meetings between the two teams. The English fans intent on trouble, as a result, put the word out that the Dutch would provide their main target.

The government then set in motion a series of measures aimed at stopping convicted thugs from travelling, primarily by making it all but impossible to buy tickets. While this was an almost decent idea in theory, the Italians announced that they would give England only 7,000 tickets, and the England Travel Club announced that you could get a ticket from them only if you agreed to join the club and be vetted for your previous record. To those with previous convictions who were intent on travelling, or even those who just preferred to make their own way, this was not an option. The Italians then announced that no one could have a ticket unless they also had accommodation, as it is illegal to sleep on the streets in Italy. So, the FA did the obvious thing and decided to pass tickets to tour operators and get them to set up hotels, travel, the lot; and this was what they did. Sadly, what they didn't do was to tell the tour companies to charge reasonable prices, so they set out to rip people off. Inevitably, no one bought the tours, and 2,000 tickets were returned to Italy. The Italian officials then announced that they would sell them at the gate, wrecking all the anti-hooligan measures at a stroke. Black-market tickets for the England games were also apparently widely available for seats all over the stadium, and this caused at least one serious incident. This happened when rumours that some of these tickets were on sale in a local bar led around fifty English lads to steam down there in the hope of getting hold of one, and if you get fifty English lads abroad and frustrated, then you have a potential problem. As a result of the ticket allocation mess, the local police were now faced with groups of English fans of whom they had no knowledge, nor any idea of where in the stadium they would end up.

During the build-up other mistakes were made which should also be examined. While it would be very easy to make fun of the Italians for their well-known reluctance to become involved in any form of potential aggression, it is true that most of the mistakes in question involved decisions being reversed. In January, the mayor of Cagliari announced that alcohol would not be on sale anywhere in the city for seventy-two hours surrounding each match, but by May, this had been reduced to 'on match day only', due to pressure from local bars. There was also a great deal of publicity surrounding the Italian decision, supported wholeheartedly by the British government, that it would charge and sentence all offenders in Italy. In truth, this is an excellent deterrent in its own right, because one thing that any potential hooligan fears above all else is the thought of being locked up in a foreign prison. However, this plan was soon amended so that any England fan would be charged in Italy and tried in Britain. By May, however, the Italian authorities were announcing that they would deport all but the most serious offenders without charge.

All was not doom and gloom, however. The locals were going out of their way to boost the group, saying they were proud and happy to host the English fans; and in truth, many English supporters were so angry at 'our' sports minister giving English citizens such bad press that hooliganism was the last thing on most people's minds. The Italian police, the Carabinieri, were also upbeat in their approach and seemed confident that they would be able to keep the balance between friendly and oppressive policing. But in Sardinia, at least, they would be proved wrong.

The group games themselves are history and well documented, but it is the off-field happenings which are of the most concern here. It is true to say that to a large extent the games in Sardinia were tarnished by a number of incidents, mostly minor, involving England fans. But it is a fact that, once again, most of these incidents involved provocation from local youths and the Carabinieri. On 9 June, 60 English fans were detained after running battles with locals in Cagliari, which began when a group of English fans came under attack while drinking in a bar. Just a week later, on 16 June, the night of the Holland match, England fans came under attack from a group of stone-throwing Italians as they were herded to the match by the Carabinieri. While trying to get away from this group, they came under repeated abuse from the police, who used rifle butts, batons and eventually teargas to keep control of the English fans. They refused, however, to deal with the real cause of the incident: the local youths. Horrifically, those who were detained for complaining or reacting were made to kneel in a garage forecourt to be photographed by the world's press; and outrageously, the British authorities never said anything by way of condemnation about this humiliation.

Four days later, in the northern port of Olbia, a group of 25 England fans came under attack by approximately 500 Italians, who had come on to the streets to celebrate their country's victory over Czechoslovakia. With typical English nerve (or stupidity, depending on your point of view), the English took this mob on. They then came under attack from the Carabinieri, who called in the riot police, who eventually fired warning shots over the heads of the English fans. Despite the uneven numbers and the fact that they were attacked, of the 23 arrests, 22 were English, which says much about the way the police dealt with that incident.

As we all know, England won their group and so the team, together with their fans, travelled to Bologna to take on Belgium. And it was surrounding this match, that what seemed to be the worst incident of crowd trouble involving England fans at Italia 90 took place. As a result of the high accommodation prices and the alcohol ban in Bologna, a large number of English supporters were staying 80 miles away, in the resort town of Rimini on the Adriatic. On the night that Italy beat Uruguay 2–0 to make it to the quarter-finals, groups of Italian supporters moved down to the seafront to begin their usual highly vocal and passionate celebrations. Sadly, much of this celebration involved taking the piss out of a large group of England fans, who responded by hurling bottles and anything else within reach. The so-called 'battle of the waterfront' had begun.

ON THE WATERFRONT

We'd been drinking all day in this bar and had been having a great time and a good laugh. It was all totally good-natured and there had been no trouble at all. The locals were having a laugh with us and we settled down to watch the Italy game against Uruguay with them. Of course, we were cheering Uruguay because the last thing we wanted was the spics to get through, but when they had won, well that was that really, it wasn't exactly unexpected. As soon as the game was over, the locals were out on the street going mental. Fair play to them, at least they were having a good time, and we joined in with the old 'England, England' stuff and it was all pretty good-natured. Anyway, a bit later on, this mob turns up and starts giving us the biggie and things started to get a bit nasty. I don't even know what happened really, it must have kicked off at another bar or something, but within seconds it all went off right in front of us and there was bottles flying everywhere.

Well, we lobbed everything we had but there were loads of them and we were driven back into the bar. I mean, there were only about 15 of us and about 100 spics. The barman wasn't going to let us in at first but after a few choice words, he opened the door and we were in and pretty safe. Their mob kept throwing stuff and the windows came in but they wouldn't come down and take us on; they need about 20 to 1 before they have a go at the English. Well, then the police turned up and they were seriously mob handed. The locals all did a runner and the police came into our bar and started giving us loads of grief – but fair play, the old barman stuck up for us and the police went outside and left us alone. After about five minutes, they came back in and told us that they'd take us back to our hotel for our own safety so we got in their van and we were off.

The trouble was, the cunts took us to the airport, and there we were with about 50 other English lads surrounded by riot police who looked like they'd take great pleasure in kicking the shit out of us at a second's notice. Well, as you can imagine, we were all going mental. Not only were we getting deported, but all our stuff was still in our hotel and there was no consulate there or anything. After about two hours of shit, they stuck us on a plane and we were out of there – that was it. As you can imagine, the plane was mental and when we got back to Gatwick, the press were all over us giving us hassle and all that, but it was crazy. There were so many people there who'd just been caught up in it, including us, but that was it. I didn't even have the money to get home from there and it took months to get my stuff back. I'll never forgive those police for that, never. And that bastard Moynihan went on telly saying that we deserved it! Fuck him. We get attacked, deported and treated like scum. For what? Because we were drinking in a bar in Italy and we were English, that's all; and that's bollocks.

It is clear that on that night in particular, the Carabinieri lost it completely. If they wanted to send a message to the hooligan element, the only one they sent was that they were wankers. When the trouble started, they systematically grabbed every Englishman they could find, took them to the nearest airport and kicked them out of the country. Their attitude was clearly along the lines of, 'Don't let a little thing like guilt get in the way, or give anyone time to get belongings, just get them out.' Two of the more famous in a catalogue of cock-ups by the Rimini constabulary involved a guy on holiday, out buying cigarettes, who was deported – leaving his wife and kids in their hotel room – and another bloke deported for driving a UK-registered car, although strangely, they flew him home and kept the car there. Neither of these two had anything to do with football: they were merely tourists.

Eventually, as a result of that one incident, a total of 238 people were deported in what was the largest peace-time deportation in Italian history. Almost all had left passports, clothes and money in Italy, and the vast majority were innocent of anything other than being English. The government, and in particular Colin Moynihan, were beside themselves with glee. This was just what they wanted! Moynihan even went on record to back this deportation of British citizens, who in almost every case had been attacked and who had been given no access to anyone from the British consulate. Thankfully, in the only positive thing to come out of the whole incident, Moynihan's career went on a downward spiral from that moment, as even Mrs Thatcher realised that he had gone too far. The reaction in this country was initially disgust at the fans' behaviour and then, when the truth began to emerge, disgust at the Italians and the Tories for letting it happen unopposed. It was, quite simply, an outrageous episode.

Despite all this, the team beat Belgium (fairly luckily, it has to be said) and then Cameroon in a superb quarter-final match in Naples, and then faced the old enemy, Germany, in a fixture that was as high profile as you could get: a World Cup semi-final. But surprisingly, the German fans had been busier than the English on the hooligan front, and were responsible for one of the most serious outbreaks of trouble at the tournament when their fans went on the rampage in Milan. Five Germans received two-year jail terms, in fact. However, despite the England team's spirited performance – perhaps the best by any of ours for years – the game was lost on penalties, but went by remarkably peacefully, probably due to the emotional turmoil and the aftermath of the Rimini incident. Back in England, however, things were not so clear-cut. On the final whistle, fans all over the country spilled onto the streets in a

show of despair, anger, rage, pride – call it what you like –
and there was a massive outbreak of violence. In Worthing
almost every German car on the seafront was damaged and
in Bournemouth, the police fought running battles with local
youths. Unbelievably, as a result of the defeat and the troubles
on English streets, three people died and around 600 were
arrested.

The fallout from Italia 90 was considerable. Despite the
hysterical rantings from Moynihan, it was clear, and becoming
clearer even to the British media, that the vast majority of
English fans at the tournament had behaved themselves. The
Italian authorities, coming under increasing attack from both
footballing and civil liberties groups in this country, came out
and congratulated the English fans on their behaviour. They
then admitted that out of approximately 10,000 fans, there
had been only 66 arrests and of almost 400 deportations, many
of those were totally innocent. On 25 July, the Italian authorities
announced that all possible criminal charges and all
deportation orders against those in Rimini had been annulled,
in a triumph for common sense. Italia 90 proved that much of
the fear surrounding England (as opposed to English) fans
abroad was hype, and what did occur almost inevitably
involved an element of provocation. This was something that
had been evident in Euro 88, even if it hadn't been widely
reported on, but such was the positive response from UEFA
that not only were Manchester United and Aston Villa allowed
back into European competition as a test, but England were
invited to bid for the 1998 World Cup. This bid was eventually
withdrawn, but only in favour of an application to host Euro
96, a bid that was ultimately successful and proof that the
bad times were apparently over.

Chapter 4
Into The Nineties

After Italia 90 and the successful return, under trial admittedly, of English clubs to European competition, the travelling fans enjoyed a relatively quiet 1991, despite having to qualify for Sweden in a group which included Turkey, Poland and Ireland (again!). Most of these games passed off relatively peacefully, although seventy English fans were arrested in and around Wembley when we played host to the Irish in March. By the time the European Championships of 1992 began, trouble involving England fans had been rare and things were looking good on the supporter front. While Mr Taylor was optimistic for the competition, the government, having learnt much following Italia 90, watched nervously, unsure of the stance they should adopt with regard to the potential disorder of its citizens.

Having learnt much about that potential over the years, the Swedish police began swapping information with their British counterparts very early in the build-up to the tournament. The police in this country also went on the offensive, and announced that they would be sending a squad of 'constables' to travel with the expected 5,000 England fans and work alongside the Swedish police. While some would be undercover, a number would adopt an overt role, calming situations and offering advice to fans where it was needed.

The Swedish authorities announced that they would provide beer tents for the English fans where alcohol, at greatly reduced prices, would be available. This would also enable them to keep an eye on the fans who would, as a result of the cheap booze, undoubtedly stay in one place. The British government and the FA were totally opposed to this idea and campaigned vigorously for the Swedes to change this plan, but the Swedes insisted that they would be able to keep control.

Worryingly, there had been two major incidents of crowd trouble in Sweden at the end of their own domestic season, when first Djurgarden fans attacked their Gothenburg rivals with stones and bottles, and then supporters of AIK Stockholm invaded the pitch and rioted at Norkopping, where twenty-two fans were arrested. Rumours were rife that the Swedes were up for it, a situation not helped by the fact that the Swedish police were told by their high court that their favourite tactic of mass detentions and arrests as preventative measures was illegal and could no longer be utilised. The police at home in England also went on the offensive, and approximately twenty known hooligans were prevented from leaving the UK to travel. Plenty arrived, however, in Malmö for the start of the tournament, which for England began with a fixture against a Danish side who had only come into the tournament at the last minute following the start of the war in Yugoslavia.

The police in Malmö, in addition to laying on a beer tent, had adopted a softly-softly approach to the English fans, and this ensured that the build-up to the game was very much trouble-free. However, after the game, the fans returned to the beer tent and things went seriously wrong.

The following account came from an interview with a gentleman from London who we met in The Torch, a pub near Wembley Stadium, prior to England's friendly against Portugal during the build-up to Euro 96.

* * *

MALMÖ

We'd been hearing little rumours all day that something would happen that night. But by around eleven, nothing had happened, so we just carried on having beer and loads of laughs like you do when you're away. Anyway, this carried on until about midnight, and the local police were all relaxed and everything and suddenly, we heard this whistle and everything went mental. Apparently, these two guys had got on the roof of the tent and that was the signal for it all to go off. Well I've seen some stuff in my time but never anything like that. It just seemed as if this group of lads went on the rampage and sort of sucked everyone else in. The police were completely lost, they didn't have a clue what to do and just fucked off for a while. A load of lads were just lobbing stuff around, cans and that, and then some of them went into town smashing cars and windows, that sort of crap. There must have been about 200, I suppose, and the locals were nowhere, it was just a riot I suppose. Eventually, the police came back in mobbed up and they really laid into everyone to try and get hold of it, but it took them a fair while to calm things down and I didn't see them arrest anyone either.

As a result of this incident, only eight people were arrested and charged. The Swedish police later admitted that they had experienced serious trouble restoring order and could not spare any time taking people away while the violence was going on. In the looting that ensued, over £8,000 of goods was stolen from a jeweller's and a clothes shop was ransacked. It was also reported that another group of English fans became involved in a serious confrontation with a group of about sixty Lebanese armed with clubs. This trouble led to the banning of the English from the beer tents, which merely led to groups of supporters wandering the streets followed by vanloads of what were now extremely wary policemen and local fans.

The trouble in Malmö led the FA and the British government to adopt an 'I told you so' stance, while UEFA began making noises about a return of the ban. Following the Turkey game, England travelled to Stockholm to play the Swedish team, as they needed a result to ensure qualification, while the fans travelled knowing that their every move was being scrutinised by all and sundry. This did not deter them from playing up, however, and more fighting took place in the city centre: groups of England and Swedish fans began baiting each other, and eventually it all kicked off again. It was widely reported at the time that the signal for the start of this trouble was another whistle. Whether true or not, the fact remains that about 100 people became involved in the violence, of which fifteen were injured; but it was clear to all that the locals instigated the trouble, having apparently grasped the concept of football violence with both hands, even if they didn't have the sense to realise the possible repercussions.

England, of course, lost the game against the host nation and returned to England with their tails very much between their legs, while the fans began to make their own way home. As the English left their campsites, they were all screened and photographed, and these photos were compared with pictures from earlier in the tournament. Another five English fans were detained as a result. After the tournament, the Swedish police announced that they were satisfied with the behaviour of the English fans: after all there had only been 122 arrests. The police then declared that the trouble was no worse than they experienced with youths on a normal Saturday night. However true this statement is, it ensured that neither UEFA nor the FA would take any further action against the English supporters and the threat of the ban being reinstated was lifted. This lightening-up process was, in part, aided by the fact that after the English left, German fans went on the rampage in Gothenburg, attacking Dutch fans with bottles and fireworks. This left only one thing on everyone's mind: with the World Cup on the horizon, would we qualify? The fans were desperate for it; after all, who in their right mind would not want to spend the summer in the States watching football? or even *soccer*!

While all the qualifying international games at Wembley passed off without any significant incidents, trips abroad with the national side once again became littered with trouble. The mass deportations of Italia 90 and the incidents in Sweden left some fans so confident that they would be deported that they saved money by buying one-way tickets. The police also cracked down on football violence and made it widely known that anyone arrested at a football event would be placed on the European Police Organisation database, which links twenty-three countries and lists among other undesirable groups, drug traffickers, terrorists and illegal immigrants. The problem was that you didn't even need to get arrested to appear on this database, as more than one case arose where perfectly innocent supporters were refused entry to foreign lands for no other reason than having been photographed at a game.

The real problems, however, were with the team, not the fans. They were still playing badly, and qualification for the World Cup was looking decidedly remote. As Watford fans, we hold Graham Taylor in a special place in our hearts, and yet even we are forced to concede that this was not the best campaign in the world, and Taylor's future was looking anything but rosy.

In April, the Dutch came to Wembley and took away a point. This was potentially high risk from a spectator view-point, yet the Dutch hooligans again failed to show, proving once again that their club and country are two entirely different things. So, apart from a few minor skirmishes, mostly invol-ving rival English groups, the game was peaceful. In May, however, things were to take a turn for the worse when the team, and the fans, embarked on a minor tour taking in first Poland, then Norway – two massively important games for both players and supporters.

The following account came from an Ipswich Town fan.

* * *

POLAND AWAY

A pretty hefty mob, mostly over twenty-five-year-olds, had travelled to Katowice. I arrived with some Newcastle and Sunderland fans travelling via Poznan and Wroclaw and the general impression was that the Polish fans were mental and well psyched up for the game, it was really looking hairy in Katowice where the match was being played.

The Polish hooligans seemed to come in two different types, either scrawny teenage kids, some of whom followed the local GKS Katowice side and carried CS gas cannisters which they would casually spray in people's faces after initially greeting them, and then there were the skinheads. The skinheads were well up for it: very aggressive and wearing those green flying jackets turned inside out. The Poles had had a go at the English the night before and had got a pasting, but on the day of the match there seemed to be thousands of them and the English hardcore totalled only about 400. This didn't stop the English charging them as the Poles were marching up to the hotel; they panicked and scattered, then the police baton-charged the English allowing the Poles to regroup. In the centre of the boulevard ran the trams and under the tracks there were large rocks the size of tennis balls. There must have been about 1,500 Poles and many started to throw the rocks at us. There was no way we could have stayed there under that barrage, so we did a runner up to the hotel. The police, instead of charging the Poles, steamed into the hotel and started whacking the shit out of anyone they could get their hands on using rubber flexible truncheons. Some people got really badly hurt.

Once things had calmed down a bit, the police decided that they wanted us to go to the stadium so they arranged for some trams to take us down. The Poles were waiting and started bricking the trams, every window was put through. I am sure the driver was in on it, as he just seemed to stop in the right place, the bastard. A few lads wanted to get off as there weren't that many of them at this stage, but no one made the move. I got hit on the head by one rock, but those by the windows had it worse and there was a fair bit of blood around.

At the ground the skinheads were waiting for us, about 150 of them. By now loads of the English were raring to go and it was charge and counter-charge for about ten minutes as the police just about kept us apart.

Inside the ground, it was electric. The fans on our left came from Poznan, a nicer city than most in Poland; they were much better dressed and actually wanted us to move back so that they could throw things at the Poles on our right! Those on our right came from Lodz and Wroclaw, I think, and they looked really nasty. Throughout the match they were hurling bottles, cans and bits of the plastic seats at us, which was a real shit as I didn't get to see much of the match because I was too worried about getting hit by something.

When England scored we went mad and the missiles came over in their hundreds. Most of us had had enough by now and started to rip up the seats before we charged at the mob that had been throwing the missiles at us. They did a runner but the police soon sorted things out. The newspapers reported that the English were well behaved during the match, and so we were apart from this incident.

They had two different type of police on duty, riot police in grey with shields, and a smaller detachment of police that looked like commandos, wore black and carried pistols and stun guns. Thankfully, the commandos were pretty easy on the English after that ruck. The skinheads were going mental and seemed to be attacking everyone else, no matter where they came from. Three battles erupted – one along the side, one where they were attacking the mob on our right and one with the police who got a good kicking and were in serious danger of losing control. It was fucking mental, pure soccer warfare and I have never seen anything like it anywhere. It seemed as though everyone in the stadium was involved. The police started to appear in numbers, but it wasn't until the commandos steamed in that the mobs did a runner; the commandos obviously don't fuck about because the skinheads were off and out of the stadium along with anyone else who had wanted to fight.

After the game we managed to gain some revenge, as it was our turn to brick the trams, one even got tear-gassed, which was nice to see after all the shit we had put up with, but this wasn't their main mob.

We were very edgy as we made our way back to the city. We had no escort and it was dark, then as we got closer the police appeared and for no reason steamed into the back of us. By the time we got back to the hotel, most of us were just happy to stay there and have a few beers in the bar. Unfortunately, they only served us coke after what had happened earlier.

The next day most of the English started to make their way up to Oslo for the next match. At the station there were loads of Poles making their way home and I got talking to one bloke who gave me a Polish hooligan fanzine to look at. It was full of pictures of riots at various football and speedway stadiums and he told me hooliganism was big news over there.

Luckily the lads out in Poland stuck together when it mattered, from Millwall to Middlesbrough. There were plenty of experienced lads out there – it's a fucking good job there was, because after seeing all that I think that the Poles have one of the top firms in Europe. If they could afford to travel away they would cause havoc, if they could stop fighting each other that is! After being in a situation like that with lads from all the different clubs, I could never fight against them back in the domestic league. That's bollocks and means nothing after an experience like this. Looking back it was mad, dangerous and very exciting – I don't ever think I'll forget that one.

Following this game, the circus moved to Oslo for what was now a crunch game against Norway. The home secretary, Michael Howard, busy trying to score political points, had urged the Norwegians to prosecute any English fan in Norway. So once again the fans came under increasing, and needless, scrutiny from the media. However, as is all too familiar, the Norwegian police force came out and joined that growing band of law enforcement agencies by announcing that it would detain and deport or release anyone guilty of anything but serious crimes. After all, why should they be saddled with the expense? Michael Howard was incensed (again), but while the game was notable for a devastating 2–0 defeat, it is widely remembered by the fans for a serious, and totally needless, incident in a bar.

OSLO

There were about fifty or so blokes in this bar in Oslo and it had all been a laugh, when these two coppers walk in and try to arrest one of the lads. Well, of course we all start to give them a bit of grief because we weren't having that and all of a sudden it started to get really nasty. The coppers did a runner and the bar was wrecked and before we knew it, the police were all over us and it went right off. The wankers ended up nicking everyone they could get their hands on and the bar was totally fucked. 'Course they couldn't charge us with anything because they didn't know who had done what, so in the morning they just let us all go. Stupid really. If they'd left this geezer alone then nothing would have happened.

In all, eighty-three England fans were detained during this

incident, which resulted in over £100,000 worth of damage to the bar itself. Quite why the police went into the bar to arrest anyone – an action which was obviously going to cause unhappiness among the English fans – is unclear. But when the police released all of those concerned, their action left the British home secretary in a rage. Before the dust had settled, the England team had travelled to the USA to take part in a tournament involving the US, Brazil and Germany, and if Graham Taylor thought things couldn't get any worse, then the 2–0 defeat by the Americans convinced him otherwise. Meanwhile, the US had been keeping a wary eye on the English fans' behaviour, and had been busy plotting anti-hooligan measures of their own. In a country where muggings, rapes and murders are almost routine, the hysteria caused by the possibility of a few hundred football fans arriving was difficult to understand; but the Americans made it clear that not only the normal armed police but also the National Guard, including armoured personnel carriers, would be brought into play to control the English supporters if the team qualified.

Quite why they became so concerned about the English is unclear. After all, hundreds of thousands of English people visit America every year without causing too much of a problem. Still, maybe they had heard enough over the years to know that English hooligans often indulge in massive sieges, among other things. Funnily enough, if they'd only bothered to look down the road, they would have seen 20 people getting killed and over 100 injured during celebrations, after Colombia beat Argentina 5–0 in a World Cup qualifying match. Yet they didn't seem too concerned about that, and I don't remember too many incidents like that in the middle of London or Birmingham.

More pressing business was at hand, however. First we still had to qualify for the US and in October, England travelled to Holland, desperately needing a victory to make it but eventually losing 2–0. It was almost all over for the team and the supporters were not doing themselves many favours either. Dutch domestic football was experiencing a seriously rough patch at that time and it had got so bad that PSV Eindhoven had been forced to call off a game at half-time after receiving two bomb threats which the police took very seriously indeed. With their fans on home ground and with so much at stake, this was a massive fixture and the atmosphere reflected that. Thousands of English made the trip and, despite the usual 'Oranje' neutrality, it was felt sure that the Dutch would show this time. After all, they were at home. The Dutch police adopted a very aggressive approach to the fixture and at least 140 English supporters were arrested in Amsterdam before the match, with most of them alleging police brutality. In Rotterdam itself, a group of English fans were drinking in a bar when it came under attack by a large group of Dutch skinheads, resulting in another serious incident where the English fans took the grief and many were arrested.

In all, over the two days surrounding the game, over 1,100 English supporters were detained in both Amsterdam and Rotterdam – an all-time record. However, of these, only 49 were actually arrested, 18 of whom received on-the-spot fines for minor offences. This fact tells the real story, although the Dutch police maintained that the large number deported escaped charges because the police could not prove which person had committed which act. At home, the English press went to town again, but many of those who were in Holland protested that they were innocent (shades of Italia 90, perhaps) victims of wholesale police brutality. Certainly, if you examine some of the film footage of the events in Holland, it is hard to argue with that, and one of the more bizarre incidents involved a party who were taken off a ferry, held in a car park for three hours with no refreshments or toilets, and then taken to the ground so late that they missed the kick-off. What makes this incident so strange is that the party were all members of the official England Travel Club! On a more important note, England were all but eliminated unless Poland beat Holland, and Taylor's by now crestfallen team hammered San Marino in Bologna. But the way the team had been playing, even the latter wasn't cut and dried. In the event, while England won 7–1, Holland got the result, and we were out.

The American dream was over – something that was not made any easier by the fact that the Irish, with their team of old hacks and an English manager, had made it. The next serious competitive match for the England team would not be until 1996, when England were to host the European Championships, the first major sporting event in the home nation since 1966 and confirmation that both UEFA and FIFA had accepted that the hooligan problem had been brought under control.

With England set to miss USA 94, Graham Taylor did the decent thing and resigned in November 1993. While the FA embarked on a search for a successor, the fans had another problem on their minds: a friendly fixture against Germany in Munich. Strangely, it was only some time after the announcement of this fixture that someone noticed that the proposed date, 20 April, was the anniversary of Adolf Hitler's birth, and to anyone with an ounce of sense, the thing to do would have been to change the date. It was obvious to all that this game would be a magnet for neo-Nazi groups throughout Europe, and that the security problems would defy belief. So of course the Germans refused to change the date, an offer to play the match at Wembley was refused and, eventually, after thinking about it for a while, they decide to change the venue, to Hamburg. Within weeks, this game was cancelled, the victim of increasing fear of problems with right-wing groups. So the Germans then made the monumentally ridiculous decision to stage the game in Berlin, in the very stadium used to hold possibly the greatest ever Nazi propaganda stunt, the 1936 Olympics. The FA finally realised that they were being made to look like complete idiots by their German counterparts, especially as they had taken so long to complete the search for a new manager, to the consternation of the British press; and they decided to pull out of the fixture, to the collective relief of the English fans who, after all, were the people who would have had to put up with all the crap should the game have gone ahead.

With Terry Venables finally at the helm, the national side embarked on a rebuilding programme fairly early on in 1994. A morale-boosting win at Wembley against the European champions, Denmark, followed by a 5–0 thrashing of Greece and a scoreless draw against Norway, were enough to convince the England faithful that maybe, at last, the team had turned the corner.

England began building up to Euro 96 and the squad, under Venables's guidance, held a series of get-togethers, while the fans sat at home, twiddled their thumbs and wondered about the ticket allocation methods the FA would employ. All this was, of course, to change in February 1995 when England, buoyed by the growth of the Premier League, travelled to Ireland for an apparently friendly fixture against the Republic at Lansdowne Road, Dublin.

The reputation of English football supporters reached an all-time low that month. The violence during this game was so extreme that it was abandoned after a mere seventeen minutes – a fiasco that was broadcast on television all over the world, to the massive embarrassment of those at Lancaster Gate. With Euro 96 on the horizon and the 'hopeful' claims that they had the hooligan element under control, Dublin could not possibly have come at a worse time for the FA. Ironically, the usual scapegoats for violence at England games – the extreme right-wing – were instrumental in this outbreak of violence; but, tragically for the FA, government intervention almost certainly lifted the blame from them in this instance and laid it firmly on the shoulders of the ordinary England fan. This may seem a bizarre statement, but if you examine the facts, it is a hard case to argue against.

With the peace process in Ireland in full swing and the full weight of political might behind a peaceful and successful resolution, the governments of both Britain and Ireland were suddenly shown, in no uncertain terms, that there was an element of the English population prepared to demonstrate their opposition to any possible break-up of the Union and they were prepared, and able, to do it in such a dramatic and high-profile manner. No government could possibly be seen to lose face to such groups and it seems clear to us that huge influence was exerted over the media in an attempt to deny both Combat-18 and the British National Party (BNP) any more publicity to further their aims. By the Friday morning, any mention of far right involvement in the riot was largely unreported in the press and the full force of condemnation fell on the English football hooligan we all know and hate. Football hooligans were a soft and easy target, whereas the far right's involvement threw up many complicated issues.

So the far right's instigation of that riot is undeniable. It is also well known that certain political organisations have targeted football over the years in order to recruit support for their beliefs. Thankfully, due to the influx of foreign talent, changing attitudes to racism and the fact that many of the best and most respected players in England are black, that tactic will never again be as successful as it was in the seventies and early eighties. However, the fact remains that when a small number of extremists in Dublin influenced people and caused havoc, this may have been a symptom more of the frustration felt by many Englishmen against the loss of their cultural identity than of support for right-wing political ideology. Sadly, for many, football still provides the one and only platform where they can show their patriotism and national pride.

However, while it would be easy to discount this incident as political, and therefore unavoidable, it is clear to us that this trouble could have been avoided quite easily, at a number of points leading up to the match. It was widely reported at the time that the police in this country, and the National Criminal Intelligence Service (NCIS) in particular, had provided their Irish counterparts with information on a hardcore element intent on disrupting this game. The information included names, full travel arrangements, even photographs of the alleged ringleaders. If the English police had this information, why did they not act to stop these people from travelling? The argument that they did not have the power is ridiculous; one has only to look back to incidents during the miners' strike to prove that the police can obtain the power to basically do what they want.

However, this information was supposed to have been passed on to the Irish police, who then failed to act on it. Did they believe that they could cope with an invasion of supporters containing this hardcore element? If that is their argument, then how can they explain their response following the trouble that had been breaking out all over Dublin for up to three nights before that game? Was this normal for Dublin in midweek? Not very likely, really.

Another factor in this mess was the method of ticket allocation chosen, which was dire. Quite why the Irish made tickets available in the first place is unclear, because at the time they made great play of the fact that they could have sold the game out to their own fans three times over. So why didn't they? There was no real need to give the English any tickets. It was, after all, a friendly, and it is almost certain that the FA would have preferred the option of making tickets unavailable to English fans, but if they had adopted this option, then the English fans would have caused uproar in this country and many would have travelled anyway. The England Travel Club admitted after the event that it had sold tickets to 'known troublemakers' and then tipped off the police that they had done so. Their reasoning was that they did not have the power to refuse tickets to anyone without a conviction for hooliganism. But if that is the case, how did they know these people were 'known troublemakers'? It also makes one wonder why we have the club at all. It is supposedly there to screen the supporters to stop troublemakers travelling but it is apparently unable to do so. A number of other selling ploys contributed to the problem. It is well known that tickets were on sale outside the ground, and people were able to pay at the turnstiles; it has also been reported that stewards on the gate would let anyone in for a £10 note. What is not so widely known is that there was supposed to be a buffer zone of ten rows of seats between the two sets of fans, yet the Irish FA allowed tickets for seats in this zone to be sold to families, as they believed that the presence of women and children would have a calming effect. It has also come to our attention that the Irish FA were selling tickets for the English section to their own supporters in an effort, perhaps, to fill the place. There were other blunders. It is clear that the stadium, with its wooden seating, was totally unsuited to this fixture and that the arrangements for segregating the fans, and in particular the placing of England fans in an upper tier, were naive in the extreme. And in the television film of the incident, it is obvious that there were very few of the Garda in the stadium when the violence erupted immediately after the Irish scored. In fact, if you examine this film, it is clear that the Garda were not only unprepared for what was happening, but that they took an age to get into the thick of things. Certainly, much of the footage showing English fans getting battered was taken long after the bulk of the Irish support had left the stadium. It is also clear that while the trouble began in the upper tier, all the handiwork by the Garda took place on the pitch and in the lower tier.

The following account was sent to us by an Irishman who had studied in London some years ago, working as a builder to finance his education. He often found himself working alongside a number of Millwall fans, and this has given him a long-term interest in the hooligan issue.

DUBLIN

On the night of the England match, I had walked across O'Connell Bridge, where many of the English contingent were keeping busy stopping the traffic and making some of the loudest noise ever heard in Dublin. To say that some of the content of that noise was colourful and anti-Irish is an understatement, but it certainly was interesting.

Inside the ground, the atmosphere was electric because the English fans had generated an atmosphere like I had never experienced before. It was awesome and the Irish added to that. But as soon as the game started, so did the trouble. There were lots of missiles being thrown down from the upper tier, which was a bit stupid because there were more English down there. Well, as soon as the Irish goal went in, the real trouble exploded, and my memory of what happened is most vivid and somewhat amusing. Over the tannoy came the announcement, 'Would all Irish supporters please remain in their seats.' As some of those seats were airborne by this time and many of the rest were lying nearer the centre circle than the architect's original plans would have had them, this would have been worth seeing! Some minutes later, the announcer then issued the following gem: 'Would all Irish supporters please leave by the nearest exit.' A bit ironic as by this time most were half-way down Lansdowne Road! In my own innocence, coupled with curiosity, I stayed behind and watched developments from a position further down the stand from where the English fans had basically been left to get on with it until they calmed down a little. At this stage, I decided to leave and passed many of the Garda who were only now making their way into that section of the ground, something that was greeted with sarcastic cheers from the Irish supporters, who were now pouring out of the ground. It is also true to say that by this time many of the English fans who had been involved in the trouble had also left.

In the Irish papers, the Garda received much praise for how they had dealt with the incident in the circumstances, although the two days of violence leading up to the game should have given them fair warning. But the fact that there were no deaths in the ground is not due to the Garda and certainly not to the FAI. It is due more to the quick thinking of the Irish support in that area and the fact that the English fans were aiming their anger at the pitch and not across the stand, which is most unlike the games at Wembley, where the Irish supporters are often attacked. On national television, pictures were shown of our police force batoning many of the English supporters, but these pictures were taken some time after the trouble had ended and, it is suspected, a considerable time after the ringleaders had left.

At the end of the day, while it is clear that the English hooligans were at fault for causing trouble in the first place, it wasn't too difficult to forecast that this would happen and that things should have been far better organised than they were. The blame for this, in the opinion of many Irish fans, rests squarely with the FAI who, in their attempt to remain tightfisted with regard to paying for security within the ground, jeopardised the lives of many.

Leaving aside the poor stadium, ticket allocation, policing and crowd control, there are a number of other points which need to be reiterated about this game. While the injuries in the ground were serious enough, it is clear from the above account that had the English supporters not concentrated their aggression towards the pitch but across the terracing, fatalities could well have occurred: this area was filled with families who did the off as soon as things began to get out of hand. The fact that this occurred at all is proof enough that this whole incident was perpetrated by people who wanted to make a statement, far more than they wanted to hurt anybody. This wasn't a mob looking for a ruck; the whole thing was down to people who wanted to be seen wielding power, and that is exactly what they did.

One final and very interesting point. As we were researching this book, a number of Irish fans told us that prior to the violence, the atmosphere in the stadium was the best they had ever experienced at football. Strange, that: the line between passion and hostility may be finer than we thought. After all, the atmosphere inside a ground will usually be more intense after a violent incident has occurred, either on or off the pitch, making the desire to win even stronger.

After the events of Dublin, the media went mental, and to a certain extent this was justifiable. Massive publicity was given to the BNP and Combat-18 for all of two days before something happened which made them shift the blame to football fans in general. All the old historical stuff was trotted out and once again, England and its supporters were saddled with the 'scum of Europe' label so beloved of the tabloids. Various Members of Parliament, and even the former England captain, Alan Mullery, went on record to say that England should withdraw its application to host the tournament. And the former L*t*n chairman, David Evans MP, began his routine spouting of 'all football fans should have ID cards', although no one took any notice. However, something strange did happen. Someone at UEFA used their head and avoided a knee-jerk reaction, making it clear that Euro 96 would definitely go ahead as planned. Even when Chelsea fans became involved in violence in both Belgium and Spain during their Cup-Winners' Cup games, FIFA and UEFA stood firm, and the vast majority of decent fans in this country breathed a collective sigh of relief. Football would indeed be coming home.

More meaningless home games followed against the likes of Portugal and Croatia, all carefully chosen to avoid any possibility of crowd trouble, which may well have put the tournament in jeopardy. There was also a potentially risky trip to Norway, scene of previous trouble, which nevertheless passed by peacefully. Finally, the tour to China and Hong Kong came up – a tour driven more by the need to strengthen trade links than to boost team spirit, and one that gave the media more ammunition than it had ever had to attack and criticise the England team. After all, the fans had been on their best behaviour so they had nothing else to moan about.

Then, finally, Euro 96 was here: the greatest tournament in this country since 1966, and with all of the old enemies, both footballing and supporter, coming to our shores. The fears about crowd trouble were very real ones, particularly when the draw put both Holland and Scotland in the England group. The possibilities for the tournament passing off trouble-free were apparently remote and the media went to town on so-called 'intelligence' and interviews with foreign 'hooligans', all telling the English that we were scumbags and that they were coming for us. The FA, meanwhile, did little but very cleverly shift all the responsibility for anti-hooligan measures onto the shoulders of the police who, after all, couldn't really refuse to accept it. (While we will examine the police and their tactics elsewhere, even we have to admit that they were dumped on here.)

What the FA didn't do was to involve fans in the build-up to the tournament and cultivate the goodwill that is there in almost every group of fans. This was a big mistake because, as we have said on many occasions, that is the best way forward in the battle to rid the game of crowd violence. Euro 96 gave the FA that opportunity, and they didn't take it. The football grapevine was meanwhile full of rumours about who was doing what and with whom and what group were linking up with which firm to deal with whoever and where. All of this was, for the most part, complete bollocks, but it was very interesting nevertheless. Similarly, reports of groups from Holland and Germany coming over to carry out a bit of scouting and make the odd contact with their English 'counterparts' were flying about, but the reality of these events is certainly open to interpretation. However, Euro 96 came and went, and was it a success or what!

PART TWO
The Nationalist Debate

***

Chapter 5
Nationalism

When one looks back at the history of the English supporter and their trips into Europe, it is all to easy to become blinkered by the view that here are nothing more than a bunch of right-wing, racist, bigoted thugs. The events that have accompanied many of these 'expeditions' over the seasons have indeed done little to dispel these impressions but while we will look at the political influences elsewhere, there is one issue that gives us most cause for concern and that is the immediate link made by many people between supporters of the national side and racism.

Sadly, England is a country where to many it is a mortal sin to tell people that you are proud to be English. While it is not only acceptable but is positively encouraged for the Scots, Welsh and Irish to hail the land of their birth, for us to do so is seen as being not only offensive, but positively racist. Why, for example, is it fine for someone from Glasgow to say quite openly that they are not British but Scottish when for an Englishman to do much the same would be frowned upon? The Welsh are happy and rightly proud to display the red dragon just as the Scots and Irish happily show their respective national flags but the English usually parade the Union Jack. Why? Similarly, the Scots and Welsh have their own 'national anthems', 'Flower of Scotland' and 'Land of my Fathers', and yet the English do not, having only the dreary 'God Save The Queen' when 'Land Of Hope And Glory' would be far more acceptable in the English sense as opposed to the British one. Any mention of a St George's day celebration brings forth sharp intakes of breath while St Patrick's day or St David's day celebrations and even Burns' night parties are the norm, while New Year's Eve has been hijacked by Hogmanay. The English as a nation seem embarrassed to indulge in any expression of pride in their country and its achievements as if they were shameful; and yet there is no objection when the Scots and the Welsh take the opportunity to show their individuality for all it is worth. It is easy to understand why both the Welsh and the Scots take these opportunities when you examine their history, because they have been persecuted and oppressed by the English in the past. But the past is what we are dealing with, and just because the English were seen as the persecutors and the oppressors should not mean that we should be embarrassed about our own history. There was a positive side to what we did, too. Why do we sit back and allow this to happen in any case? Is it because we, the English, have allowed the politically correct movement to make any show of national pride shameful? If that is the case, we should be ashamed of that. As a nation we have much to be proud of, and we have a right to show that whenever we get the opportunity. After all, the Germans don't seem too bothered about celebrating the land of *their* fathers, despite their past.

We, as Englishmen, are also faced with the situation that people who are born in this country usually adopt the heritage and culture of their foreign-born parents, or even grand-parents, and immigrants who settle here also maintain their own identity. This is not a complaint, far from it. The exact opposite is true because we can be proud to live in a country which has such a diverse range of cultural groups and that those groups have been embraced by the English nation. But we should not forget that the largest cultural group in this country is the English and yet we are not allowed to show, nor be proud of, our own identity or history.

At this point, it would be very easy to launch into a long diatribe against the dreaded PC movement because we have, over the years, witnessed the destruction done to the English culture and spirit by a small group of highly motivated individuals. This constant attack on the English sense of identity provokes a reaction from some who want to prove that we are still a strong nation, and for many of them that recognition can best come through sport. However, as this book is about football supporters we need to concentrate on the effects that this cultural erosion has had on the game, because in the case of our national side, they are significant.

We are on record as saying that we believe racism within the football stadia of this country to be an overstated and misunderstood issue, and nothing we have heard or seen recently has given us any reason to change that opinion. However, the spectre of racism continues to haunt the game and therefore, by association, the supporters, and so we need to examine this problem once again. We do this in the hope that bodies such as the Commission For Racial Equality (CRE) will concentrate on the positive issues within football, rather than the negatives, and focus their attentions on the elements of our society where racism really is rife.

In fact, the CRE have some responsibility for the misunderstandings between various cultures, because they are the very people who quite rightly encourage the ethnic minorities of this country to maintain links with their respective cultures, but fight tooth and nail if we, as Englishmen, try to celebrate ours. Surely rather than division, a coming together and understanding of all cultures by everybody would be of greater benefit. Even by labelling certain groups of people as 'minorities', we are emphasising that some are different to others which is, to a degree, racist; after all, we are all British citizens.

The truth, as it affects football, certainly in our experience, is that as supporters we not only accept players of our team(s) as nothing more than players (whatever their nationality, religion or colour), but that we accept fans of our team whatever their background, too. One only has to look at the West Ham team of the mid-1990s to see the progress made by the game in recent years. Here, in an area of the country which traditionally wears its patriotism on its sleeve, is a club which does indeed have a history of racism, but which now has a high number of players of foreign descent within its first team. These players are not only accepted by the East End faithful, they are positively revered. This pattern is repeated for almost any area or team in England due to the influx of foreign players. If, by attempting to expose these realities, we attract one person, whatever their creed or colour, back into any stadium in England, then we will feel vindicated.

In the dictionary we use most frequently, racism is defined as 'hostile attitude or behaviour to members of other races, based on a belief in the innate superiority of one's own race' which, at first glance, seems a pretty good reason to condemn those who hurl so-called racist abuse at games. However, if you substitute 'team' for 'race' you will get a perfect description of most supporters' behaviour towards other supporters or the opposition – and that is where the flaw is in the racism argument at football. People who hurl abuse at players on the field of play do so because they are members of the opposing side, and therefore a different race if you like, or they are members of their own team who are playing crap. The only reason the colour of anyone's skin enters the equation is because it helps to identify who is being abused. This, in the vast majority of cases of so-called racist abuse, is a fact; it may not be a nice one but it is, nonetheless, a fact.

Of course, there are cases of genuine racism within football crowds and some factions among supporters are happy to be known to be racist because it gives their reputation another dimension; it is perceived as another reason or excuse for violence. We cannot deny this and we certainly would not excuse this. However, it is our belief, and one shared by the majority of people with whom this subject has been discussed, that truly racist acts are rarely seen at football matches these days. When they do take place the police and the stewards have the powers to deal with them on the spot.

The tragedy is that these powers are all too rarely exercised. Only recently, the two of us encountered some moron chanting racist abuse at Vicarage Road (this from the fan of a team whose two greatest ever players were black) and, despite supporters all around him giving him abuse, he would not shut up. A friend of ours finally took the initiative and reported this tosser to a policeman on duty who replied 'he's not doing any harm'. After more incredulous protests, he added: 'Best you don't join in, sonny.' Our friend did what the game had asked him to do and the people the game entrusted with responsibility to deal with racist chanting refused to act. However, the fact remains that a number of people acted and acted correctly. That this reaction to any incident of racism happens at all at football is a clear indication of the intolerance of racism among the majority of supporters. Perhaps this fact should receive greater acknowledgement and publicity.

Within the population of this country are millions of people who are proud to be English, and proud of their history and culture. One of the great strengths of England as a nation, and Britain for that matter, is that not all of those people are white Anglo-Saxons; there is a mixture. However, the sad fact remains that for many English people, football provides the one and only platform where they can show their patriotism and national pride. Surely this should not be the case? We recently saw some old footage of England supporters returning from a trip abroad where the local authorities had not been at their most welcoming. During one interview, one person made a statement which really summed up the true feelings of people placed in a provocative situation like those faced by supporters abroad. He said: 'There's only so much shit you can take before you've had enough. No one should be able to take liberties with us just because we're England fans . . . no one.' To us, that isn't the statement of a racist, it's the statement of someone who is proud to be English and pissed off at being branded a racist because of it. A patriot if you like. Yes, it's aggressive and provocative, but at its core is pride, and that is something that is sadly lacking these days in almost every aspect of English society. However, the sad truth is that a statement like that, especially when made by an English football fan, is looked upon as being downright racist and will be widely reported as such by the media. Once again, Mr and Mrs Average will read only what is put in front of them at their breakfast table and the label will stick. Once in place, there is very little that anyone can do about it.

Chapter 6
A Political Football

There are within the English League set-up certain clubs who have an element of support linked to far-right political parties, such as the British National Party (BNP). The extremist right-wing group Combat-18, with their highly motivated support, rely on violent confrontation to promote their beliefs. They are active at various football grounds throughout the country but, thankfully, their number is fairly small and the majority of us do not have to put up with their influence at our own clubs. However, where the right wing exists, it is inevitable that the extreme left wing will also be active, so both ends of the political spectrum are linked in with football. While their activities are not really relevant, or even appropriate, to most clubs, at national level it is a subject which needs addressing.

In our first book, *Everywhere We Go*, we expressed our views, and those of the majority of supporters and players we spoke to, that it is a commonly held and accepted view that black and foreign players provide positive role models and heroes for both kids and grown-ups whatever their nationality, religion or colour. That is and remains an excellent thing. Politics rarely, if ever, enters the equation. At clubs where far-right groups are active, the numbers involved are usually quite small and those individuals will usually be involved with the main firm in any case. Their reputation for violence will often

95

see them heading the mob. Others, who couldn't give a fuck about the politics but do care about the reputation of the club and its violent following, will tolerate them.

However, when England play, it becomes a whole new ball-game for the politically driven cliques, as the little groups from each club will join up with like-minded people from all over the country. When there is political ground to be gained, such as that so dramatically taken in Dublin, or at a major tournament like a World Cup or European Championship, then the numbers are swollen even more by those that do not usually associate themselves with football. When that happens, and it is primarily with the right wing, then groups such as Anti-Fascist Action (AFA) will put together numbers to deal with them in the only way both groups promote: violence. This violence, which really isn't anything to do with football but is political, will be seen as outright hooliganism. Therefore the extremist parties are damaging the perception of the England fan, which is why ordinary fans should stand against these people who damage the reputation of the majority by their actions.

Quite why these groups target *our* game will be explained shortly by one of their own, but as two people whose political beliefs on many issues could not be further apart from each other, we have to say that we do not need them or want them. We go to football to escape from all the day-to-day shit and to escape our problems for those ninety minutes. We do not need, or want, reminding of them by anyone. The same thing goes for the vast majority of people who walk through a turnstile every week. Football needs to be free of politics, so leave us alone.

We include the following views, not to promote any one particular group or preference, but to bring awareness to the problems when the two mix, though if you're in a ruck, the last thing on your mind is likely to be who the other bloke votes for. Interestingly, both the right and the left believe the police are on the side of their opponents.

* * *

ON THE RIGHT WING

Football, for the BNP, is an ideal recruiting ground and political platform. For us, and groups such as Combat-18, there is no better place than a football stadium in which to reach the very people we see as our future and the way forward for this country.

Football is the sport of the working classes, more people play and/or watch football than any other sport. England took football to the world, but now our once-proud footballers find themselves the laughing stock of the game as we trail in the wake of lesser nations. Many of those who attend football in this country are angry young men. Angry at the way this country has been sold off by those that want the fast buck or Deutschmark that is only too ready to buy its piece of England. For many, the game, and their own club in particular, are seen to be taking the same route by paying foreign players more money in one week than most of us will earn in a year, while at the same time leaving our own English talent short of the opportunity in which to develop their skills. How can the English national side progress when its own countrymen are left on the scrap-heap at the expense of foreign imports? It's disgraceful.

For many people the national football side gives them the only real opportunity to display the pride they have in their country. Certain players will find themselves on the receiving end of aggressive chants, but this is mainly because they are seen not to be trying and if only the same amount of pride displayed in the stands could be transferred onto the pitch then we would soon find ourselves back where we belong and able to hold our heads high again.

The game also provides the ideal arena in which to voice our opinions and distribute material to those that wish to find out more about our policies. The majority of BNP supporters are average people, just like you and me, concerned about the welfare of this country. We don't make a song and dance about who we are, but at football we meet a cross-section of society. We believe in taking our message to those people, not sitting on our backsides spouting lies via the media. Those who are interested know where to find us if they require information. And if people do not want to talk to us that is fine; they should just leave us alone or ignore us, not try to drive us away. That way we could all avoid any unwanted confrontation.

At various incidents of football violence over the last few years, the finger has been pointed in our direction. But the vast majority of these incidents simply involved young men, and the BNP got the blame because the game needs someone to blame. However, it is true to say that we have been involved in some incidents at games, but these involved people who are angry with a society that marginalises and pigeon-holes them. They feel it is a society where they, the very backbone of the country, have become the oppressed majority. Violence occurred during these incidents simply as a reaction to the press-ures and frustrations of everyday life in this politically correct country. If by such a show of violence, they are displaying the passion needed to get this country back to where it belongs then I can fully understand their frustration, although I must state that, as a non-violent organisation, the BNP could not be seen to condone such action.

Despite the pressure put upon the population of this country to deny their nationality, while at the same time bowing to the needs of every other minority group, there are thankfully still those who are proud to say they are English. As I have already said, for many, football, and the English national team in particular, provide one of the few opportunities to display that pride. I have travelled to watch the national team play abroad on many occasions and have seen supporters from all over the world demonstrate the love and passion they hold for their country in a way we the English never could, due to those who oppress the flag and all that is English. It makes me sick that we as a nation have sunk so low. Many of those I travel with share these feelings and we are not prepared to stand back and let them take our identity away from us, and that is why we are defensive of our country and its history.

On my travels with England I have personally seen, and been subject to, some terrifying and unjustified provocation and violence, and it would seem that the English have become a target of hatred throughout the world, and Europe in particular. Memories are obviously short. Where would Europe be if it wasn't for the British some fifty years ago? This country throws open the doors to foreigners from all over the world. They settle here, bleed the system, call themselves British, but when their country of origin comes to Wembley they turn up draped in another flag singing about their homeland. That is why Britain will never become integrated, because people like these are only too quick to return to their roots when the opportunity arises, then send the message home that we are a country of racist bigots when we try to show our pride.

Thankfully, there are those that still have that 'bulldog spirit' and will not let liberties be taken with them – unlike our own government who, it would appear, are ready to lie down and succumb to any foreign power that so much as glances in our direction. These English-men are prepared to fight back when they are challenged, prepared to defend what they hold dear to them. It is no good sitting back and taking all the shit thrown in our direction.

Just look at what happened in Dublin. So many people had seen this country sell itself short once too often. Dublin was a proud moment for all those that truly love this country, its history and the Union. Those that were prepared to make a stand in defence of Britain in my opinion should be thanked, because they not only sent out a message to both the governments here and in Ireland, they also sent a message out to the rest of the world stating that certain elements of the English still have the bollocks to fight back when they need to.

Those in charge of the game have made a concerted effort over the last ten years to change its fan base to a more 'consumer friendly, politically correct' football supporter, while at the same time attempting to drive us out. Yet the links built up during the late seventies and early eighties, when the National Front enjoyed great success in terms of recruitment and raising its profile through football, still remain strong at some clubs and once again we are enjoying a high profile throughout the divisions. I think a lot of our new-found popularity stems from the events in Dublin, because people realised that we had not gone away and never will.

We have been proved right time and time again about the influx of foreign players. They come to England, screw the fans for high wages and then quickly return home with a fat bank balance complaining that they suffered terrible racist abuse and could not stay any longer. Many have seen through this facade and have had enough. We will always support our teams because we will not allow them to take that away from us, but we do not have to support all the players.

When Eric Cantona launched his violent attack on a fan of Crystal Palace, it should have ended his career in this country. If an Englishman playing in the Second Division had committed such an awful act of violence he would have been banned for life, yet Mr Cantona remains. The anti-racism lobby were very quick to jump on this particular bandwagon, in order to gain publicity by branding the fan a racist, something which was unproven. What was actually said to Mr Cantona that night we shall never know. If it did have something to do with his country of origin then I wonder why Mr Cantona chose to react in such a manner: is he ashamed of being French? Every player in the country will receive abuse at some time in his career. What is more disgusting is that the football authorities, not wishing to upset any minority group, didn't have the courage to act accordingly. That breeds a resentment that will not go away, and I am sure that Mr Cantona has not heard his last abusive comment following such a despicable act. He only has himself to blame for that.

There are, of course, other extremist groups in this country who have tried to drive us away from football, groups such as Anti-Fascist Action (AFA), Red Action (RA), the Socialist Workers Party (SWP) and the Anti-Nazi League (ANL). But the game should be very wary of them. If these people had their way then every club would have a black man, a woman and a homosexual playing for them. Anyone but a white Englishman. They believe that the setting up of Asian-only leagues, gay-only sides in London, the flying of the Irish flag at Celtic Park, and the singing of Republican songs at certain grounds is fine. Yet they would burn down the clubhouse of a team with a white-only policy, target fans that carry our flag and will brand everyone that stands up and sings 'God Save The Queen' at Wembley a racist Nazi. They have this pathological hatred of people singing 'No surrender to the IRA'. Why? Are they for an organisation that blows innocent people up? Woe betide you if you do not agree with them, then you are the racist they are talking about. Fortunately these people have their heads so far up their arse that they eventually end up fighting each other because we can't all be black, Irish, lesbian, disabled, transsexual, etc, etc.

You may scoff but there is a well-known case that happened in Germany at an Anti-Fascist rally attended by do-gooders from all over Europe where a group of women's rights activists branded every man a potential rapist and therefore an actual rapist. This accusation was dismissed by a leading anti-racist group attached to the St Pauli football club, based in Hamburg, and weeks later the women's rights group bombed the St Pauli offices and two people ended up in hospital. Both were women. So much for sisterhood.

It is said that both AFA and RA have strong connections with both MI5 and Special Branch – something which is backed up by the, shall we say, 'lean' sentences given out to their 'street fighters' when attacking people showing pride in their country. This proves that the government are worried that we have the potential to harness the true feelings of Britain, and there is no doubt that we are getting stronger thanks to our connections at clubs throughout football. Unlike the do-gooders and puppets, we are clear in what we believe: putting rights for whites first. They will not drive us from football, the national side is the flagship of the nation and it is a nation many are still proud to fight for.

ON THE LEFT WING

We would like to start by stating that Anti-Fascist Action (AFA) do not target football but target the fascists that use the sport to promote their political shite. The activities of groups such as the BNP and Combat-18 have gone unchallenged for far too long. The national side and the clubs, despite the increasing powers at their disposal, continue to tolerate this filth within their ranks. Therefore the only option and the only method the Nazi scum seem to understand is to take violent direct action. We are not against supporting the national side, but we believe that it is bollocks that in backing your own team you have to hate all other countries.

It has been shown time and time again that the wishy-washy liberalistic campaigns, such as the Commission for Racial Equality's 'Kick Racism Into Touch' initiative, are just token efforts which achieve little as regards driving these scum away. We believe that the fascist groups should be allowed no platform whatsoever and that means no leafleting, no marches, no paper sales and no meetings. As long as there are fascists active at football, we shall also be active as our aim is to cause maximum disruption to their activities. We will target any club that allows these people to peddle their filth, so where the BNP or Combat-18 are present, we shall also be present.

Unfortunately, these scum have found refuge in football. Most supporters do not want them there, but to sit on your arse and ignore them is simply not good enough. Yes they are intimidating and aggressive, yes they are violent, but they are also cowards. We have proved time and time again that when fronted these shits are the same as all bullies: they get scared and run away to hide. We have hunted them down and driven them away on many occasions, as they can only hide for so long.

These groups were driven away in the early eighties and now we need to drive them away again because the slime has returned. Oldham, Leeds, West Ham, Wigan, Leicester, Newcastle, Carlisle, Man City and United, Stockport, Charlton, Birmingham, Villa, Nottingham Forest, Millwall, Chelsea – all these clubs have had their problems over the years with fascists, and the list is even longer. Ask yourself, how can you sit next to someone who attacks the players of your own team just because of the colour of their skin or their country of birth and ignore it? We need to come together and kick these bastards into touch. If the clubs and the police don't like that then they can fuck right off, because they have had their chance and we have warned them often enough that we won't have it.

AFA will target fascists anywhere in Britain. Although we have been accused of being pro-Irish when joining

Celtic fans in Glasgow and Hibs fans in Edinburgh, this accusation is untrue. As we have said, where fascists are active we will be active and the fact is we believe that Glasgow Rangers have done nothing towards driving the BNP away from Ibrox. As at Hearts, there are sections of their support we know that have links with Combat-18 followers in England, notably the football firm the Chelsea Headhunters. Both BNP banners and Chelsea shirts were in evidence when Rangers supporters went on the rampage at Sunderland.

When Celtic played Birmingham in a pre-season friendly at St Andrews, BNP and Combat-18 followers from all over the country travelled to the game to attack what they see as the pro-Irish support that Celtic have. At that fixture some Celtic fans who were arrested had their cases dropped as it was found that the times of arrest on their charge sheets didn't correspond to the times of the alleged incidents. To us, this is just another demonstration of how the authorities defend the far right, which shouldn't come as a surprise because fascists usually stick together. There has been no greater demonstration of this than the show put on by the fascists in Dublin. The fact that so many known fascists were allowed to make the point would indicate just where the authorities' loyalty lies.

We understand the mentality that surrounds football violence, but what we cannot tolerate is the way that many football firms allow themselves to be hijacked by this filth in order to gain them political publicity. If you are prepared to run with a firm that allows fascists to promote their filth, then you are as much part of the problem and will become a legitimate target for us.

Those that tell you that racism and fascism are not rife at football are liars. Look at Dublin and look at what Eric Cantona and all the foreign players are subjected to. When Paul Parker was playing for Man United last season in a cup tie at Reading, he had a banana thrown at him, something we thought we had seen the last of years ago. Those who witnessed that incident and stood back doing nothing deserve no more than the scum who did that, because he will go and brag to his filthy mates about what he has done and the fungus will spread and become brave again.

The national side always attracts the scum. They show in large numbers thinking they are safe, pretending to show pride in their country by smashing some Pakistani's window and scaring his children. This is the master race we are talking about here, scum that shove shit through the letter boxes of people that have lived here as long if not longer than they have. This filth is active within football and they must be stopped. If you see them distributing their leaflets and stickers, or selling their propaganda, don't just bury your head in the sand, ram their faces in it. It is no good telling the police, they will defend their 'legal right'; it is no good writing to the club as these people are their customers; and as for exposing them to the press, well forget it, the press love 'The Bulldog Spirit' that provides them with so many juicy headlines whenever England play.

Similarly, they have used football as a recruiting machine for too long. We will track them down wherever they are and kick them into hiding. AFA will be monitoring their movements and waiting for the right moment and if one week you see them and the next you don't, then rest assured that AFA have paid them a visit when they least expected it. Then ask yourself what part you played in getting rid of the low life you have tolerated for so long.

As the fascists and anti-fascists continue to fight it out in both the political and football-supporting sense, one of the lesser-known political extremist groups has slipped ominously into the picture. As a result of a loss of direction resulting from becoming a somewhat elitist group, the anarchist organisation

Class War became less active over recent years. However, under the latest campaign slogan 'No racists, No bosses, No cops', launched to coincide with the start of Euro 96, they have again gone on the offensive and have begun to recruit members to oppose any involvement in football which doesn't stem from the working class. This aim originates in the Class War belief that society is divided into classes based on power and wealth, and that that division can be corrected only by the destruction of the ruling classes. Violence being a necessary part of that destruction, Class War target anyone and anything that isn't working class. After all, it's much easier to hate everything these days. The ultimate aim of Class War is not to lead, but to encourage working-class people to solve their own problems rather than be dictated to by the so-called fat-cats that rule big business, including football, and Great Britain PLC. They reject both the left and the right, believing that politics is life and that life is politics. Their newspaper, *Class War*, has expressed views on football that are probably closer to the truth than many of us would like to admit. Certainly, as many clubs have become more and more alienated from the supporters who have funded them for years, their opinions are worth considering.

We would like to state that the opinions expressed below are not necessarily the same as our own, and the account has been kept anonymous at the request of the person who supplied it. Power to the people!

CLASS WAR

Football was once the game of the working classes and the local club was at the heart of the community, the national side the pride of the country – focal points to relieve the oppression many found themselves under. You would stand shoulder to shoulder on the terraces with the people you worked, drank and lived with, and it was ours. Even some of the players knew what it was like to grow up on those same streets and kick a ball around in the same local park, treading in the same dog shit. They became idolised, but they knew exactly where they had come from.

Today, football is business; they don't want the local riff-raff who built up the club any more, they want people to drive up from the Home Counties in their Range Rovers and company cars. People who can spend, spend, spend. The boss, his wife and their children, Nathan and Sarah-Jane – they're the people they want. That is when the boss can't get on the golf course, or the kids have become bored with their horse. A good result means a check on the share prices more than anything else, and watching the right team or wearing the right tie can help close that business deal because football is trendy and in great danger of becoming the tennis or cricket of the next century.

In the streets surrounding every ground in the country, there are people having to survive for a whole week on less money than it would cost to buy a first team strip. They have to put up with their community being invaded every other week, but the clubs don't give a fuck. After all, they're only the people that the club is supposed to be representing. Supporters have become categorised: if you're rich, you watch big games, even an international, and you're welcomed wherever you come from, but if you're poor then you are allowed to watch only when the opposition is also poor. If you can't afford the ticket, then fuck off to Stockport and if you're really poor, then go to Altrincham, but wear our shirt in any case, just to let people know you're loyal to us. Let them know that you are also one of life's winners.

All of this, you might think, only applies to big clubs. Does it bollocks – look at Blackburn or Newcastle! They loved us when they were shit because we're loyal and we kept them going. It is we who pay the wages when a club is on its knees, because we know what it's like. We don't want to stand next to the people who dictate to us for forty hours a week, we want to stand *en masse* and shout our heads off on the terraces that we have paid for year after fucking year. That's what we do to relieve the stress and the tension. But when success comes, it's not us that reaps the reward. They screw us, take the piss and bleed every penny until there is no more, then kick us out into the street like some kind of undesirable, which allows in the new breed of trendy middle-class supporter. Yes, this is your club we are talking about.

The saddest thing of all is that we have allowed this to happen. We let those who run football introduce seats, let them divide us and let them screw us for money. We have let them treat us like shit and then we allow them to throw us out on to the streets. They watch our every movement, make us unwanted on our own doorstep and take our identity away, but we are not without power because the clubs are nothing without their supporters. Clubs may choose their *consumers* carefully, making the choice in relation to the size of their bank balance, but it is for us to drive them out and reclaim what belongs to us. Let them know that we've had enough and start fighting back. We have let them take the piss for too long and now we must take our game back. Just what is the point in our teams having the best players in the world if we are shut out at their expense and the only place we can see them is on satellite TV.

As true supporters, we hold the power because there are more of us than there are of them and when we become angry, they get scared. Look what happened at Brighton: those fans had simply had enough and were brave enough to make a stand and the chairman went into hiding, too scared to face the music and, at the advice of the authorities, he was driven out and told to stay away for his own safety. That's what works. Make them feel unwanted, make them feel uncomfortable. At Brighton they tried to blame it on the Nazi scum that football so happily accepts, but this was bollocks because they were too scared to admit that they were powerless against the anger of the people who they had been screwing for the last fifteen years.

We can and must learn from the Brighton fans and I believe and hope that the anger demonstrated there was only the first incident of supporters rebelling against the blood-suckers that have taken over the people's game. They have divided us for too long. Anger is a gift and aggression their reward.

Anyone want a coach ticket to Lancaster Gate?

PART THREE
Back Home

Chapter 7

At Home

While the media and the authorities, labouring under the notion that trouble is inevitable, go to town on England fans when they travel away, there is little or no acknowledgement that the reverse is true when England play at Wembley. There are a number of reasons for this, of course, and as far as the media and FA are concerned, it is because the stewarding at Wembley is first class and the police do a superb job in controlling the hooligan element. While there is some truth in this, there are a number of other, and far more significant, reasons why Wembley is usually a trouble-free zone for supporters. These factors stood out clearly during Euro 96, and we need to look at them to see if any lessons can be learnt for the future, and for other venues.

The most important thing is that whatever your opinion on the matter, Wembley is, to the England team at least, home. As a consequence, it is revered by players and tolerated by supporters, but the underlying fact is that when England play, it becomes *ours*, the focus for English supporters for those ninety minutes. This, in essence, means that fans have a duty to defend it, if the opposition have a hooligan element, just as they would their own ground. But in truth, the reputation of the England fan abroad, combined with the fact that most 'foreign' supporters who come to Wembley either live here anyway or are shit-scared of what might happen to them, mean that trouble is invariably the very last thing visitors want. The fact that everyone knows this means that unless the opposition is fairly high-profile, or active on the hooligan front, or the match is important, the crowd will almost certainly largely consist of mums, dads and kids while all the geezers will be watching the game in a pub either at home or near the ground.

There are, of course, a number of other reasons why crowds for friendly matches at the national stadium are so small, and to us the most important is that with the exception of the odd performance, England games are meaningless. At club level, we can make our feelings known every Saturday, but the fact that England games are infrequent means that there is very little we can do to influence the thoughts of the FA or the manager. We just have to live with what they do and leave any whining up to the media who, with few exceptions, seldom disappoint in that respect.

As we noted earlier, there are also huge numbers of supporters who could not give a toss about the England side because they want nothing to do with any team other than their own. If you talk to supporters at England games or examine the flags around the Wembley pitch, one of the questions that comes to mind is how many of the fans are only there to watch *their* lads play. Dougie freely and happily admits that the only time he ever cried with joy at a football match was when the great Luther Blissett scored a hat-trick at Wembley against Luxembourg. What for Luther was the culmination of years of hard work and the pinnacle of a great playing career was shared by every Watford fan who was at that game, but to this day, Dougie couldn't tell you who else scored because it isn't important to him. And if Luther hadn't been playing, the game would have faded into a long-distant memory.

Confirmation that we are not the only people who share these beliefs can be seen not only in the low attendances at England games, but also in the fact that when England play, the local pubs, as we've mentioned, are packed solid. This is in itself a strange thing because it shows that many people do travel to Wembley, only to stay in the pubs nearby to watch the game on the box. But as anyone who has done this will tell you, it is by far the best way to watch England's friendly games. It is also important to note that it isn't just fans from around London who travel to Wembley to visit the pubs on match days, but fans from all over the country. During a friendly against Portugal early in 1996, we spent the evening in a pub full of Southampton and Sunderland fans, less than one mile from the twin towers. They were there because they wanted to travel with their mates, walk up Wembley Way, have a laugh and a drink and watch the game – but they positively refused to walk through the turnstiles.

The usual theory here is that if you mix drink, men and football, it is inevitable that trouble will occur. While this is indeed the case on many occasions, in and around Wembley, when England are playing, it seems that the opposite is true. Quite why this camaraderie arises is not easy to pinpoint, but it does seem to us to be an extension of the 'service station' mentality, where fans only want to mix, talk and have a laugh among people like themselves. A sort of neutral ground, if you like. But while we may be painting a rosy picture of Wembley pubs, it does not mean that these drinking houses are always nice places to be. They do tend to foster male aggression, and the usual 'get-your-tits-out-for-the-lads' type of sexism enjoyed by many males at some time or another. So strenuously avoid taking a woman to one of them on a first date!

The fact that during an England game you can often play 'spot the crowd' does little for the credibility of the English as supporters; but there you go, we have to live with that. However, if the opposition are active, well-known historical rivals or attracting a big support, the crowd's English contingent will be larger and the noise more vociferous, with a far deeper, and more aggressive, tone. In 1988, during the build-up to the European Championships to be held in Germany that same year, the FA invited the Dutch to Wembley. The English fans wanting trouble couldn't have picked a more volatile 'friendly' themselves, while the reputation of the Dutch only helped to fuel the fire.

The account below came during a pint with Jamie, a follower of Tottenham.

HOLLAND

We were desperate for this match because we had been waiting for Holland to visit for some time. At club level we have had a few run-ins with the Dutch, something that goes back to the seventies, when we did the Feyenoord mob over there. I was much too young to remember that, but I do remember seeing the pictures on the telly, loads of Spurs lads coming back from Amsterdam after having the shit kicked out of them in 1981. Three lads were stabbed at that match, so as you can see we have every reason to hate those wankers, and this was a good chance to give them a good hiding on our own ground, especially as we had heard on the grapevine that their main mobs were coming over to set things up for Euro 88. At that time there was loads of trouble at Dutch League games, and in particular with the mobs from Utrecht and Feyenoord. Both these clubs had links with firms in London and that's how we got to hear about it. They were meant to be up for it and coming over to have a pop at us.

We would have liked to have got down to Liverpool Street Station in order to pick off any that had come in on the train from Harwich, but we didn't have the time. Anyway, West Ham should have taken care of that, so we decided to meet up at Baker Street, as most of the Dutch would have to come through there at some time if they were using the train. Some of the lads were able to get into the centre of London early to do a bit of scouting and they told us that a mob of around forty

Dutch had been taking the piss down Carnaby Street most of the afternoon. Nothing had really gone off but they were taking liberties, there were no other England lads around at all and our boys had the right hump.

By half five there were about thirty of us in the bar opposite the Baker Street tube station. A few other lads were obviously there to see if anything was going off – you recognise some of the faces, but who they supported, I wasn't too sure. Word soon spread about what had happened in the daytime and the mood was starting to change, the old buzz was starting to kick in. Someone put forward the idea that we should move into the tube station to see who was coming through, and a total of around fifty blokes moved off. The old bill were all over the place and on every train that came through. Loads of England fans were also passing through the station; some joined us, others continued on, saying that they were going to wait at other stations and pubs along the way. Not one person said they had come across any kind of Dutch mob and we were seeing only the odd orange scarf. The old bill were on to what was happening, and some dogs soon arrived, which seemed to indicate that something was about to happen. Most of the lads were getting restless and wanted to move on to the stadium and wait around there, as time was getting on.

We got the tube up to Wembley Park Station, then walked down to Wembley Stadium Station, as we knew the Dutch were being put in that end of the stadium. The old bill wouldn't walk them up Wembley Way, as that would be too risky. The walk up to Wembley saw a few slaps dished out and flags taken as the odd Dutch fan was spotted, although most of those hit were your family types – nothing serious. Still, the hype around the match, and the fact that the Dutch mob had not been found, had got to some of the lads. They didn't give a toss who they were hitting, they were all fair game anyway. Anyone is at a game like this. There were plenty

117

of lads hanging around and the word was that the Dutch had been brought into Wembley by bus from Harwich as the old bill had been warned that there was going to be trouble at Liverpool Street and Baker Street.

The mob that had been in Carnaby Street had been escorted by the police up to the ground much earlier and were now inside. It was clear that the English lads were well pissed off, and their numbers were growing all the time, especially as many of those milling about had only come up for the trouble and didn't have tickets for the match. There were some Dutch giving us verbal from behind the gates, looking down on us, and we were singing back at them but the old bill were getting a bit heavy as we were getting near to kick-off. As ever, the old bill handled it in the worst possible way. The dog handlers were brought in and the horses started to try and push us back, which of course just triggered it off. Loads of the lads streamed up the steps and tried to get to the gates, and the riot police started hitting out, and it went mental.

Everyone had now turned on the police and they were getting a bit of a hiding until they regrouped, and the dogs were in there. I saw this one bloke with this dog hanging onto his leg go to the floor, and as the copper went in to nick him he got the shit kicked out of him. The dog was set free but wasn't letting go, and this poor bloke was screaming his head off, and there were blokes booting this dog to get it off. In the end it let go: they always scare the shit out of me, but that one was well fucked. The old bill steamed back in and nicked the geezer just to get someone for it probably, and he took a whack on the head and was out cold. There was a bit of a stand-off then and the old bill got it under control, so we moved off to get into the ground, as did most of the other lads. I was surprised that the Dutch didn't have more fans really, they hadn't done badly on the turnout, but didn't seem to have a mob of any kind anywhere. In any case, Wembley is a hard place now to have an off inside. The old bill had them well sectioned off, and unless you are sitting in the sections that are right next to them you haven't got a chance. After the match, the place was swarming with police and the Dutch were being kept in. Some of the lads wanted to go back into town after the game as there were bound to be a few Dutch around the West End and there was no point in hanging around Wembley as we would only end up having it away with the police again. We hung around the West End for an hour or so, but once more the Dutch didn't show and there were plenty of old bill around keeping an eye on us, just in case; but nothing happened. I suppose the mob they had in Carnaby Street are going around saying how they did the English, but really they just bottled it, the tossers.

At games like these, supporters simply have to attend and put on a show and at Wembley, front is really all you can do. The reason for this is, as we have already mentioned, because visiting teams rarely bring anyone capable, or willing, to have a pop at the English fans. In fact, only on one occasion has Fortress Wembley been taken.

Inevitably, that occasion involved Scotland. In 1977, during the Home International fixture, the Scots came to town and took London over lock, stock and barrel. They were all over the capital that year, and the photographs of tartan-clad sweaties taking liberties on the hallowed turf and pulling down the goalposts are a shaming sight for most English supporters. The fact that this invasion was repeated, albeit on a smaller scale, until the English finally got their act together and took the battle to Glasgow, so that the competition was scrapped, still rankles with most Londoners, who remember only too well the hordes of drunken, kilt-wearing Scots staggering around the tube or lying unconscious in gutters. Over recent seasons, there has been a great deal of discussion behind the scenes regarding the possibility of resurrecting the tournament at some stage – something that fills many of the established firms on both sides of the border with glee. For the English, the chance to exact revenge for what was, in effect, total humiliation, would surely be too good to miss; and for the Scottish, the opportunity to build on what has become a legend among supporters would almost certainly be most appreciated, too.

This was certainly the big fear following the draw for Euro 96, when the two sides were drawn together. But as we all know now, nothing significant actually happened at Wembley and the same can be said of every game held at the twin towers for many years now. Before the tournament, if anyone had come out and said that England would play Scotland, Holland and Germany and that there would be no trouble, most people would have laughed. But that was exactly what happened. There were also genuine fears not just that the countries coming to the tournament would import their own problems, but also that mobs up and down the country would indulge in massive campaigns of violence against the many thousands of visiting supporters. There had been a threat, made on television, that the Derby Lunatic Fringe would make an attempt to force the abandonment of the tournament halfway through, for example. However, apart from a few minor occurrences, there were only two serious incidents of note, and they both involved England fans in London. In the end, the tournament was remarkable for the trouble that never arrived.

There are a number of reasons for the relative lack of hooliganism during Euro 96. The main one is that the rival mobs, with the exception of the Scottish casuals, didn't show. Either they had no interest in their national side, or at least not enough to induce them to travel abroad with the team – and there is some evidence to support that theory – or they simply did not have the bottle to cross the Channel. Quite which of these, it is difficult to say, but the fact that they didn't show irreparably damaged what reputation they, and particularly the Germans, had previously built up. They will never live that down with the England mobs. Have no doubt about it, though – if they had shown, as was proven after England were knocked out, then serious problems would almost certainly have occurred, because the England groups were more than willing and ready to kick things off.

This leads on to another factor. Because there had been massive amounts of pre-tournament hype surrounding the so-called meetings between the hooligan ringleaders who were, by all accounts, planning the Third World War. However, as anyone who spent time among the fans or at certain pubs in London during June will know, this was obviously complete bollocks. The evening of the Scotland game, the two of us walked all around the West End and it was obvious that there were mobs from clubs all over England looking for it to go off; but thankfully, no one was talking to each other. At one point, while we were standing on the corner of Trafalgar Square by St Martin-in-the-Fields, it was like the opening scene out of the film *The Warriors*, but no one knew what to do next and it was left up to individual clubs to kick things off on their own. Heaven knows what it would have been like if they had been organised, because that was certainly the biggest potential mob either of us has ever seen.

The following diary of Euro 96 was sent to us by someone we have corresponded with for a number of years. It is fairly representative of a number of accounts sent to us since the tournament ended.

EURO 96 DIARY

At last the waiting was over. We had been waiting for years for this chance to come our way and here we were, with the biggest tournament for thirty years in this country just about to start. All the top targets were coming: the Scots, the Germans, the Italians, the French, the Dutch, even the Turks. The only ones really missing were the Paddies, but we had only just turned them over big-time anyway. All the foreign mobs were making the right noises, they were all coming to turn the English over. Well, let the fuckers come because England were ready and waiting.

The domestic season had really picked up, the casual scene was on the rise again and even the media couldn't cover up all the activity that was taking place. The network was full of the mobs who were going to work every week, who had done who and all that, and it was obvious that football violence was back. We were going to target London because for us it's within easy reach and with it being the base for the England games, it was the obvious place to be. We had taken the time off work just in case things kicked off elsewhere and were phoning around to keep up with the news at the other venues.

We caught a train down to Wembley for the first match with the Swiss. None of us had tickets for any of the matches, except the Scotland game, for which we had four seats, but Wembley seemed really subdued. Most of the fans were your scarf-wearing types and the Swiss had brought over a family following, not the type we were looking for. We wandered around for a while ending up at The Torch. This was more like it – loads of lads on the piss – but still not what we were after. We were told that all the pubs around Wembley were going to be shut at one o'clock, which really pissed us off, so we decided to move off to The Globe, a pub opposite Baker Street tube station, and see what was happening there. This was obviously the place to be. The pub was rammed with pissed-up English lads singing their hearts out. Lovely! The police had swarmed the area and were on the look-out for known faces, so we went into the bar to start drinking, keep our faces hidden and catch up on the news. We were told by some of our acquaintances that the police were taking people out, giving them the full search and photographing them, and were also videoing the pub from across the road. One of our northern contacts told us that the police were trying to track down the Leeds mob, and coppers from Yorkshire were in the pub after they had hit Leeds' usual King's Cross meeting place earlier that day, and had come up with nothing. The only real incident happened when a coach full of Swiss went by and someone threw a bottle at the window. But that was it, so our next move was to find a pub and to watch the match there.

Most of the pubs were refusing to show the match because of fear of trouble, and others wouldn't let you in if you were wearing football colours. What fucking bollocks that is: all the others are allowed to show their colours, but we can't even do it in our own country. This really pissed us off. Later in the tournament, one pub had its windows put through after the landlord had taken our money all day and then asked us to leave before kick-off, as the pub was only open for regulars to watch the match. You see, if you treat us like scum, we will give you what you expect. We ended up in the West End, in a pub full of public schoolboy wankers and for-eigners, but were grateful just to see the game. England were fantastic in the first half, then it all went wrong.

I've never known an atmosphere change so quickly as when the Swiss equalised. After the whistle we left the pub and went straight into Soho, ready to go. Nothing but police around, and our first encounter was with the police photographer. Luckily we were not walking in a group as we would all have been done, but two of the lads were pulled over by the police and searched. They had them up against the wall and their hands in their pockets taking everything out and looking for identity. There's no chance of blagging your way out of that. Then this van pulled up and out jumped the photographer, surrounded by four or more coppers, and the lads had their photos taken pinned up against the wall, looking like real criminals for everyone to see. The way we were treated made me feel sick. After all, we were just walking along and had done nothing. That photographer appeared time and time again, and by the end of the tournament there were plenty of lads ready to kick the fuck out of him if the chance came their way. After about an hour, the fans started to arrive from Wembley but apart from the odd bit of verbal, there was no trouble and we actually ended up in a bar which was full of Swiss. We had a great time talking about football with lads from all over the place. That is how it should be.

The next day, the Germans were due to play their first match in Manchester. We were informed on the news and in the papers that 600 to 1,000 neo-Nazis were coming over to do what Hitler never managed, and rumours were also flying around that the British far right and the far left were going to descend on the match to settle old scores. In reality, it was all far-fetched. There had been the odd incident in Manchester involving Germans the night before, but nothing worth travelling 200 miles for, despite the fact that the press had played their part in building the Germans up to be the main threat of violence in the tournament.

The next night saw Scotland play Holland at Villa Park. There had been the threat of trouble the last time these two had met, but once again both sets of supporters were intent on displaying their better side. The media were giving out hype that English fans were going to attack both sets of supporters, but Birmingham had been quiet so far, even though they were doing their best to start things moving following England's opening match, which they viewed as a disaster. Nothing to write about.

For us, all our attention was on the Scotland match. Everyone thought this would be the one to really start it off, and come Thursday night they were proved right. In Camden Town in North London, following the Holland–Switzerland match, fighting broke out in two pubs. A group of Scottish casuals, believed to be Aberdeen supporters, had started and finished the trouble. At last the first sign: the Jocks would be up for it. We travelled into the West End on the Friday night to suss out the atmosphere and hopefully get our first piece of Euro 96 action. We met up with a few exiled London supporters and scouted around, but again the police had the area covered. We moved around in twos and threes a few yards apart, looking out for each other, but still nothing. We couldn't believe it. Two more lads with us got collared by the police, but that was about it. Trafalgar Square had a few hundred Jocks running around, but no Scottish or English mob was to be seen.

We found a bar, got pissed and stayed the night at our mate's house. The next day we went straight up to The Globe, and it was heaving. Rumours were flying about of small offs and people getting done during the morning and there were a few Villa Combat-18 making themselves known; 'England expects' seemed to be the vibe. Luckily, I was one of the lads that had a ticket, so we headed off to Wembley expecting the action to start any moment, but everyone seemed focused on the game. I didn't fancy getting nicked before the game myself, but I still couldn't believe how quiet the whole thing was. There were plenty of Scots around but I didn't see anything that looked like a mob. We were sitting on the grass bank outside our section when this German comes and sits down next to us. We got talking and he told us that the German hooligans were only coming over for the second part of the tournament. He said that they were sure to qualify and that due to the tickets being so expensive they were waiting in the hope of meeting England or Holland, or hopefully both, and then they were coming to prove that the English were no longer top dog. We would see about that later. He may have been a mouthy German wanker with that stupid haircut and denim shorts but we had one thing in common, he thought the FA were ripping people off as well and he did give me a bottle of beer!

In the stadium there were Scots in our section but it was all just down to taking the piss out of our poor relations. There was this one Scot all on his own, about forty-five, face painted, wearing the football top and kilt and when Seaman saved the penalty his face was a picture. Hundreds of Englishmen taking the piss and laughing right in his face, and when Gazza scored he was off before I looked around, just an empty orange seat. I hope those moments give him nightmares for the rest of his life.

After the game, walking back to the station, you would never have known that England had just won. We were mixed in the Scots and maybe it was all an anticlimax, but everyone was just getting on with it and taking the piss. We just could not understand these people. This was England–Scotland, for fuck's sake, what was wrong with everyone? We headed back to The Globe, but when we arrived, the police had closed it down and were moving people on. At least we were where the England mob were and not with the wank supporters. The pub had been closed because of trouble among England fans, and some were saying it was Chelsea and Spurs, others that it was Forest fans playing up. Anyway, we had to move on. Word was out to meet up at The Porcupine on Charing Cross Road, as this would give us the chance to get into Trafalgar Square if the Scots were going to turn up. The Porcupine was rammed, police were everywhere and the atmosphere was buoyed up by the result and news that actions were taking place all over. The Scots were in Trafalgar Square and were having running battles with the police, so we didn't go in to the pub. We wanted to be able to move if things kicked off big-time. This proved to be a wise move. This was the buzz we had been waiting for, and looking around you could start to pick out the faces we had been looking for all week.

Mobs from all over the country were here – Leicester,

Stoke, Forest, Plymouth, Chelsea, Spurs, Exeter, Middlesbrough and plenty of our lot – which gave us a right
buzz. I would imagine that around 50 percent of the clubs
in the country had some lads in the area at some stage.
We walked the short distance to the Sussex Arms and
things were looking dodgy. Everyone was trying to suss
each other out, who was English, who were Jocks. We
saw a group come up from the direction of Trafalgar
being followed by about twenty police that looked totally
confused. I think they were Burnley fans and they had
certainly seen some action as they were well buzzing
and one had a cut head, but they were laughing and had
obviously had a result of some kind. This seemed to be
the way things were working out. Each individual mob
was out for their own result. We went back towards The
Porcupine just as an off started, which we were later told
was Chelsea and Spurs playing up with each other. This
sort of shit should have been put aside today, as this
was about England and Scotland. It was nothing much,
but the police thought this was the start of it all and came
flying in from every direction. We quickly crossed the
road and it was then we realised just how many different
mobs were here. The tourists had been waiting for
something to happen and were totally engrossed in what
they were seeing, although I think a few were a little
surprised to see the friendly British bobby whacking the
fuck out of anyone that looked like a bloke and telling
them to get out of the fucking way, else they were going
to get a truncheon over the head as well!

With the police preoccupied, this suddenly left the
route down into Trafalgar Square wide open. There was
one mob from Sunderland and a few of the Leicester
boys trying to get everyone together, but it was each man
for himself, really. It's funny that the Northerners were
prepared to fight alongside each other, but the Cockneys
were not, wankers. We made our way towards the
Square with caution. People were coming in the opposite

direction and we didn't know who was who or how many Jocks we were likely to come across. When we made it there were already plenty of English lads around. Most of the Jocks had been forced out by the riot police, and only a few were left. The English were trying to get into the Square to get at them, leaving the police well stretched. We were told that the Jocks had been playing up all afternoon and more came straight down after the match, and they now had about 300 to 400 lads well up for it. I found out later that night that their mob was made up mainly of Aberdeen, Hibernian and Dundee fans, and they had spent the last hour having battles with the police that had provided good entertainment for those that had been following them all day.

The media has always managed to do a good job on covering up the problem of football violence in Scotland. Many of the clubs are well active, week in, week out, just as the English clubs are, and it must be said that they had gained a lot of respect from those that had been watching. Not only had they come down, but they were ready and willing to fight, so fair play to them. It would have been some battle if we had managed to meet up, but the police had taken them down into the tube and got them out of the way. Fuck knows where they went. A few bottles were flying around and slaps dished out, but nothing major, and eventually we got into the Square. Stories were going around about individual mobs having it away with groups of Scottish casuals during the day, and a few lads had been slapped, but other stories of more successful meetings were also coming through. Middlesbrough had it at Charing Cross Road, and another mob were talking about something at Tottenham Court Road. After an hour or so we decided to move on. Things were dead here, and maybe we were missing out on events elsewhere, but as it turned out the action was all but over as far as we were concerned. Still, at last the tournament had got started.

There were a few things about the day that got me thinking. First, we had the Scots to thank for two things. They had the bottle to come down and to a certain extent they went home with a result, and also the team took the piss at Wembley. Secondly, the day was noticeable for the absence of a few of the larger mobs, such as West Ham, Millwall, the Scousers and Rangers and Celtic. Maybe they were up to other things elsewhere, I don't know, but they didn't make themselves known in the West End. Thirdly, the crowd and the atmosphere at Wembley were very different from those at Trafalgar Square. They did sell those tickets very carefully, didn't they? Finally, by all accounts the battles between the police and the Jocks in Trafalgar Square were pretty good, so I was told, yet all you saw on the television the next day were pictures of England fans outside The Porcupine, where nothing very much happened. The friendly Scottish fans didn't get a mention. Everything would now focus on our match with the Dutch on the Tuesday.

We headed into London around midday, going straight to the West End. There was orange everywhere, but no lads. We had not really expected the Dutch to bring a mob, but you never know, it only takes five or ten of them, and you can have some fun if they want to join in. They never cease to amaze me in the way they dress. It's funny, and fair play to them if that's what they like, but it's all very strange if you ask me. One thing is that you can't really get it going with a bloke dressed as a woman looking like the Tango man, and I wouldn't want that anyway. If it's their way of saying they are not into fighting then fine, enjoy the game. We headed to the Dutch bar just off Chinatown, which was rammed and well protected by the police, but there were no boys around. We were refused entry when we told them we were English – another case of them being allowed to show their colours, and the English being refused in

129

every other bar. Going to Wembley was a nonstarter, so we made our way up to The Globe for a few beers. Again, the police were pulling people out and there were a few Dutch coaches that got loads of verbal, but that was all. We watched the match in the same West End pub as before, which was packed again. I can honestly say that I've never seen England play so well in all my life. They were superb. Just to top the night off, they showed the last few seconds of the Scotland game and we got to see the Jocks get knocked out. When the whistle went, everyone else seemed disappointed the Scots were out, but we went fucking barmy. What is wrong with these people? They were looking at us as though we were mad. Later, in Leicester Square, there were plenty of relieved Dutch around and Trafalgar was starting to fill up with England fans celebrating. We left to find a pub but later found that the police had moved in to get the England fans out, and they were really starting to piss everyone off. I mean, if we can't even celebrate a victory like that, what can we do?

The next night saw Germany play Italy. Before the start of the tournament, this game had been highlighted as a potential big one. Rumours that groups such as Combat-18 and Anti-Fascist Action were supposedly up for the Germans, and the Italians had been going around for weeks, but when we got in touch with our Northern mates they told us that nothing was happening and that it would be a waste of money travelling all that way just on the off chance.

Saturday was the quarter-final with Spain. We had hoped that they would bring a mob of some kind over, as they have had loads of trouble in their league this year and had a history with the English anyway, but like everyone else they bottled out. Again, we did the West End and The Globe. For me, the best moment of the whole tournament was when Seaman saved that penalty. We went mad and the buzz around the West End was fantastic that night. The next day we found out we were to play Germany at Wembley in the semi-final. The while country was buzzing and the press were stoking the match up to be the Third World War.

Once again we set off early. Remember, the Germans had done the business in Holland and Belgium recently, and had been giving it the big one about coming over here to kick our arses. Well, now was their chance. Surely they wouldn't bottle out, they couldn't. We did Carnaby Street, Soho, Leicester Square, Trafalgar, the lot. Nothing. We decided to split into smaller groups and keep in touch on the mobiles. One lot went to The Globe, we went up to Wembley. Up at the stadium, there were plenty of Germans around, but no lads, and even The Torch had some Germans drinking in there. I never thought I would see that, so we left. Apparently The Globe was packed, but the lads were keeping their distance because the police were onto everyone, and some of the lads with us today didn't need their photos taken. They said that plenty of the top lads were around and that they heard the police had started on the crowd again in Trafalgar Square after the Spain match. We made our way down to West Hampstead and watched the match in a pub down there which would make it easy to get to Wembley if something did kick off.

Fuck knows how we lost. Once again, the team did us proud, but the second that bastard scored that penalty, we downed our pints and left for Wembley. On the way to the Tube, a vanload of police had pulled up and had three lads pinned up against the wall and were frisking them. They had obviously had the same idea as us, but luckily we passed by unnoticed. The phone rang and the rest of the lads told us they were staying down in the centre and would keep us posted. They also said that the atmosphere was heavy.

I couldn't believe what I saw at Wembley. We were expecting to see things going off big time, but again –

nothing. Maybe it was the shock of defeat or the realisation that the tournament was over, but the English were walking next to Germans as though they were the same. We thought they must be holding the main lot of Germans in to avoid trouble, so made our way up towards that end of the ground going up past the Conference Centre. Wrong, the Germans were gone. Down to Wembley Central Station: nothing. Then the phone rang. We were told to get down to Trafalgar quick because things were now kicking off with the police. I fucking hate the police and they hadn't really done themselves any favours in the public relations department so far during this tournament, so a chance to gain a bit of revenge would be most welcome. There is nothing worse than knowing things have kicked off and that you might miss the lot, but luckily the trains were on our side, although it took the longest forty-five minutes of my life to get to the Square, and that is saying something for a football fan. Things were in full swing. The atmosphere was electric and the riot police were steaming in and out hitting anything they could. Cars were being smashed and kicked and I saw a police car that had been kicked to fuck. Excellent. God knows what would have happened if England had been knocked out earlier. The police made the mistake of forcing people off into the side streets, and you could hear windows going and alarms. It was fucking great, we had the bastards on the run and it proved to them that no matter how much in our faces they are, we will always take them on when we want to, and take the piss. After a few hours, the thing was starting to fade out and when the numbers get low the police usually start beating the fuck out of anyone that looks remotely like a bloke, so we did the off. We had enjoyed our run around and the English had proved their point.

The tournament was over as far as everyone was concerned. Saturday was the last real night of the holiday, and we didn't expect the Germans to bring their mob now, even though they had reached the final. We went into the West End that night just in case, but no such luck. The pictures from Trafalgar Square would be shown all over Europe, in every country taking part. All those wankers who bottled out would see what they would've been up against if they had been brave enough to turn up, and their failure to do so was the only reason the tournament was so quiet. I think that if England had been knocked out earlier, the whole thing would have been the biggest non-event ever. The football was fantastic and England did us proud. If it wasn't for the Jocks having a go and the German game, we would have wasted our whole year's holiday, but those two games made it worthwhile.

Cheers then, and fair play to the Scottish, but to the rest, well wish you were here but you haven't got the bottle so we will have to come to you as always.

See you soon.

Many of those who indulge in violence at domestic football were borne along with the euphoria of the England team's good performance, and this was another major factor in the lack of violence. As our correspondent stated, if England had gone out in the early stages, then Euro 96 may well have gone very flat, as was proven after the Germany game, and the supporters may have started a tournament of their own. But there was another, more important factor in the relative peacefulness, as far as we were concerned, and whether you think the FA were very clever or just very lucky, it was an interesting phenomenon.

We have in the past spent a great deal of time talking about countries who have serious problems within their domestic leagues, but very few with their national side. Denmark is one, but the most obvious is Holland. The famous (or infamous, depending on your opinion) 'Oranje' experience is one of the more intriguing aspects of the Dutch footballing culture, and one which was very much in evidence during Euro 96. They certainly know how to enjoy themselves, and nearly every game is played in a carnival, and, well, orange atmosphere. For many people, this is the way that watching England should be and having been around Wembley for all the England games and watching the crowds and the obvious enjoyment, it is possible that we saw the start of the St George experience at Euro 96 and if so, just how and why did it occur?

It is clear to many, including us, that the arrival of the Premier League heralded a whole new chapter in the growth of football in England. The way that it was marketed attracted a whole new audience to football. The male terrace environment we grew up with was gradually eroded within the top flight, and this process is continuing to this day as the Premier League goes on changing its fan base. The corporate boxes and half-time cheerleaders are all symptomatic of the change in the way the game is being watched. And these developments, coupled with improvements in facilities at stadia and the inevitably increased prices, ensured that certain elements were positively discouraged from attending because they simply were not wanted or needed any more. The Premier League also won its battle to fill the grounds with families quite quickly, and the increasing numbers of women who go to games are proof of this.

All this has meant that the game at the top end is very different from the rest of the professional game, especially in the way it is watched, and this has been a key element in their success in reducing the amount of hooliganism. However, this has a down side. The removal of certain elements within the home crowds has led to significant problems for a number of Premier League clubs, centring on the fact that the new breed of fan simply does not know how to create the right atmosphere. Arsenal, Tottenham and even Manchester United have had to appeal for more noise from the fans – a pretty good indication of how bad it can be.

Now where the Premier League has changed, or developed if you like, the England team have followed, and what we saw at Euro 96 was the result. Whether this was part of some kind of master plan which evolved out of Lancaster Gate is impossible to say. But if it wasn't, the FA were very, very lucky and if it was, then they were very, very clever, because it is obvious to anyone who follows the game that the support at Wembley during the tournament was very different from the support usually seen at home fixtures. Football coming home? In reality, it never left; but what a great slogan and superb marketing device, instantly associating the game with the new breed of supporter. That is not to detract from their performance in generating atmosphere at Wembley in any way, because as anyone who attended games at the twin towers knows only too well, all the England matches were notable for the noise. But we have to wonder how many of those people will turn up for the next home game. If they do, that's great; but if they do not, and we see a rapid return to the crowds of around 20,000, that will be a major concern. Of course, it is important to realise that many people who bought tickets through official sources bought their full allocation and took the wife and/or kids, which may not normally be the case. After all, it was a once-in-a-lifetime footballing occasion. This did, however, have the knock-on effect of diluting the male content within the ground. The cynic, of course, would say that this was part of the FA plan to beat the hooligans by keeping them out – a plan that also included giving away masses of tickets to corporate empires. If that was what they wanted, and still want, fine; but if it continues and we do join the face-painted generation of international fans, it will upset an awful lot of people.

As English football continues to chase its new breed of fan, some of the behaviour emerging from this contingent is beginning to seem rather disturbing. The following opinions came to us via a good friend during Euro 96, and while we must state that these opinions are not ours, we would like to add that we agree with them 100 percent.

* * *

DOWN THE PUB

Just what the fuck is going on? Am I losing the plot or missing out on something here? There does seem to be a rather large number of blokes walking around with inflatable clogs on their heads and others with their faces painted all sorts of colours. Some are dressing up like a bad version of Bart Simpson's mum, some as orange (not red) Indians. Now don't get me wrong. I like a laugh as much as the next man, but there is a time and a place for everything and to me, dressing up like a complete prick is not part of going to football.

I love being a bloke. I love being English and being an English bloke is the dog's bollocks because we are different from the rest. The sweaties can wear their kilts (which to me are only a small piece of fabric away from a dress and personally I find that a bit scary) and the rest can paint their faces, dress up in silly costumes, wear their scarves around their heads and wrists and can then stick them up their arses and sing their national anthems as far as I am concerned but don't ask me or the English to join in. I remember in Frankfurt during Euro 88 watching the lads get stuffed by the USSR. All the supporters were taking part in the Mexican wave but whenever it came over to the English section, we just gave them the old wanker sign. I mean just who the fuck do they think we are? The girl on the PA system kept asking us to join in, but bollocks, the rest of Europe are welcome to make themselves look like wankers, just leave us out of it.

Here I am, eight years on, and the Championship is here in England. I couldn't get any tickets so I watched all the games in London with a load of mates down their local. All the foreign supporters are doing their dressing-up bit – fine, no problem – but what I saw on the way home following the Dutch match made me sick with anger and embarrassment. I was on the train back to

Watford and it stopped at Wembley Central. Loads of English got on and among them was this bloke and his bird and they came and sat right next to me. They had obviously been to the game. She was talking complete bollocks about football and the match, going on about what player she liked, that sort of stuff, and the pair of them had their fucking faces painted. Now this bloke was in his thirties, not a little kid but a bloke, I wanted to wring his fucking neck. What is happening to the English football fan? Is this the future following of the national side? Will we all start dressing up as women or, worse still, Morris dancers? Please no.

What made me angry was the fact that these people had tickets and were keeping the real fans away from the ground. They should be banned from football, not encouraged. If you want to dress up like a wanker, then follow a wanker's sport like basketball or American football, and if you want to paint your face then go to the circus with all the other clowns. We're in danger of losing our sport to these wankers and I think it is the duty of every England fan to tell these prats to grow up, get a life, or fuck off.

What has happened to the traditional football fan and the traditional songs? Why have we suddenly adopted 'Swing Low, Sweet Chariot' as a song? It's bollocks. I'll tell you why, it's because all those that attended the England games got their tickets through corporate packages, that's why. They're not the sort to follow their side to Shrewsbury on a Tuesday night, and d'you know why? Because they haven't got a fucking side. They're there because football's trendy at the moment. That song is a public schoolboys' wanky, head-up-your-arse rugby song. It's nothing to do with us, but these bastard trendy, designer fans have dragged it into our game.

Football is busy developing its own class system, and it is dividing the support of the country. The average supporter that travels the country every week in support of their team couldn't get a ticket for the Germany semi-final for love nor money, but if you just happened to have a spare £450 on the day, you could buy yourself a nice little hospitality package with beer, meal and match ticket – bargain! One match for the price of an average season ticket. Well, let the wankers have it if that's what they want. Don't they understand that we get that same buzz every week because we support football? We support football all our lives, not just for twenty-five days every other year. The FA must love their designer fans, just the image they wanted the world to see: your average face-painting, fun-loving, boy-meets-girl, loves-football, go-every-week English fan.

Let's see what happens when the crowds go back down to 20,000 for the next friendly, shall we? Then they'll ask where the loyalty has gone. Well, I'll tell you, it's gone down the pub where you placed it, you greedy fuckwits. There's your loyalty and that's where it'll stay. Then we'll get all the stupid adverts telling us, 'There's nothing like being there' and all that bollocks. Well, sorry mate, I need my money to follow the lads to Cardiff on Saturday so you can stick Wembley and your prices up your arse because we remember when we were not worthy. Your true supporters at England games are easy to spot because they're the ones not dressed up like complete pricks, although you won't find too many true fans at the really big games – the tickets would have found their way elsewhere.

When will the trendy bastards realise that we are not like the rest of the world when it comes to following our sport. Losing is not something to be taken lightly and washed down with a pint of Guinness. England expects and it hurts when we lose. We don't want to dress up in bright colours. We like the element of fear and of being different, something that is hard to carry off when you look like Barbara Cartland's worst nightmare. Not only that, but dressing up all jolly can make you look really pathetic when the despair of defeat is written all over your face. I love laughing at people when they look like that, it brings great joy to my life. Kids are best, just as the tears start rolling down their cheeks. Football is a serious way of life. Welcome to the real world, now grow up.

The upshot of this move away from the more traditional type of fan is that while the Premier League has moved on (and that's not necessarily a good thing for many people), those clubs outside the top flight have been left languishing in its wake. The changing fan base, as well as the success of clubs who now enjoy sell-outs, has seen the hooligan problem pretty much solved at the top end, and it is now very rare indeed for trouble inside grounds to occur. However, this has left the hooligan problem firmly in the sphere of the smaller clubs where, as most people know, it has usually been at its most dangerous in any case. It is also true that some of those supporters from the top flight who do indulge and cannot get tickets or are banned will simply adopt a smaller club where they can get their fix of violence. As regards the national team, the same thing will occur; but whereas many could not get into Wembley for Euro 96, they'll have no danger next time, or the time after that. The great worry for us is that the FA will begin to believe that the trouble with the national team has finally been solved at home, but as we have seen, it never really existed in the first place. The real threat, and the real test, will be the next time England travel, because then we will see how far we've come.

Euro 96 was a great time for both football and its supporters and was thankfully notable for the absence of the hooligans but the fact that they weren't there does not mean that things have changed. Sadly, that is far from the case. Football may have come home but the hooligan elements never left.

Chapter 8
Rivalries

For the supporters of the national side who travel abroad, it is clear that above all, the success of the team is what matters. While to the many who have been force-fed images of the English hooligan element abroad this may seem a strange statement, it is a fact. The game *is* what matters. This desire for international success is clearly the reason that, in many cases, club loyalties can be set aside when travelling with England. It is certainly the only time that you will ever see the fans of Bolton and Manchester United, or even Torquay and Exeter, drinking side by side. The advent of the England Travel Club, formed with the express purpose of deterring the hooligan element from travelling, assumes that by having the details of every member on file, any troublemakers can be dealt with swiftly and correctly. This ensures (and also assumes) that those who travel with the official party are responsible citizens and will behave themselves. Thus, the adoption of a neutral stance, as regards club loyalty, becomes second nature and there are many benefits to be gained from this. The opportunity to talk football for sometimes days on end with people you have never spoken to before is a delight, and friendships forged on these trips can often become lifelong.

However, problems do arise. Not all fans travel on the

official trips, for any number of reasons. For example, it is clear that some like to make their own way, knowing that whatever the FA say, they will be able to buy tickets at the stadium. Some are ex-pats and some are banned from obtaining tickets through the FA. This doesn't stop them travelling, of course, because these days it is all too easy to organise a trip yourself or to simply fly or drive anywhere. What it does do is ensure that when England play, there will be hundreds or even thousands of people, aside from the Travel Club, who have made their own way and are outside the control of the FA. In a great many cases, these groups will still adopt the neutrality offered by the England shirt for one simple reason: safety in numbers. After all, you wouldn't walk down the Old Kent Road on a Saturday afternoon in your Birmingham City shirt unless there were plenty of you; and by the same token it would be foolhardy to stroll on your own around the centre of Rome in your England shirt the afternoon of a World Cup qualifier. Call me cowardly if you like, but if I'm walking into the unknown, I want someone, preferably lots of someones, with me. This is acceptable and understandable, and it is the reason why these mobs of England fans gather together on their travels. It also gives them the chance to talk about the game, to find out who is up to what and where, and also to gather information. There are exceptions, of course, and – with the greatest respect in the world – certainly in the eighties, groups of Scousers were usually to be avoided at all costs because they were invariably skint and funded their journey and their drinking through their 'activities', knowing full well that the chance of arrest and prosecution were minimal.

However, there are groups of fans for whom the support of their club and their dislike of a rival, particularly a local rival, is too much even for patriotism to defeat. These groups are invariably from the hardcore elements of their particular club; and as we know, England may be one thing, but clubs remain another. That reputation, so fiercely defended and built up, must be maintained and if members of, for example, the Chelsea Headhunters and the Leicester Baby Squad meet, conflict will result no matter what the location. There will be other occasions when club rivalries surface abroad, of course. Local rivalries are the most obvious, a good example being the trouble during the 1982 World Cup in Spain, when a group of Portsmouth fans attacked Southampton fans in a bar. Certainly, if you have recently taken a hiding and you come into contact with fans from the club that inflicted it, revenge will be sought. It is also clear to most that the influence of alcohol will be a cause of tension because you will always find some tosser ready to start mouthing off, and that in-your-face provocation is difficult to ignore. This provocation, and therefore any interclub rivalries, are more usually found when England play at Wembley than when clubs are on their travels because not only will the number of spectators be greater, but there is rarely that *esprit de corps* that only those who travel with England experience. It is also apparent that the opposition will have an effect on the mood among the England fans: if Germany, Holland or Scotland are coming to town, for instance, all eyes and concerns will be focused in that direction, which would hardly happen if Croatia were the visitors.

However, it should be stressed that the camaraderie found among football supporters in general does tend to lessen tension in most instances, as those famous pub sessions around Wembley on England nights demonstrate. And with the advent of satellite television, they are often more attractive than the ground.

While we were researching this book, we visited a number of the pubs around Wembley on match nights and it took quite a time to get people to talk openly about their views. Sometimes it simply was not possible. While the police around Wembley do a pretty good job of keeping a lid on the England fans, it is clear that the most important factor is the good grace of the supporters who go to enjoy the occasion. However, this should not detract from the obvious risks because there is still that undercurrent of suspicion and obvious wariness among groups in pubs. Sometimes, as the following account confirms, with good reason.

STOKE

I'm a Stoke City fan and follow them with the same group of lads all over the place. Whenever England play at Wembley we travel down to London in a minibus and use the match as an excuse for a piss-up free from the hassle you get watching City – other fans giving you grief, the police, that sort of thing. We always use the same pub and the landlord has come to know and trust us now, and it's easy and safe to park the van there and walk to the ground. We're not into the trouble any more, we've done all that but we won't let anyone take the piss either. I mean, we would rather have a drink and talk about football than fight, and that's why the England games are such a crack because everyone usually puts the club bit to one side. Saying that, though, one of our lads is a really big bloke, massive, he won't go looking for it at all, but he wouldn't shy away either. Still, anyone would be mad to try their luck with him. A good lad to have around.

A few years back, we were playing Argentina. The weather was red-hot and the pub was packed inside and out. As ever, there were lads from all over in there and some were so pissed that there really wasn't any point in them going to the game.

Others were singing and displaying their club colours, you know, the usual crack. There was singing from fans of all the different clubs, but with Argentina being the opposition that day we all had a common enemy to have a go at. We were sitting outside in the sun and had clocked this mouthy Brummy strutting up the hill towards the pub with his six mates, cans of lager in hand, well pissed, when he started giving everyone the 'Who are ya? Who are ya?' shit. Then he hopped up onto the wall and started singing, 'Zulu Army, Zulu Army'. Most people were laughing, thinking, 'Just another pissed-up prat', and singing back at him, when he started pushing past people and putting his face right in theirs, that sort of thing. We realised then that he was so off his nut that he actually meant it, so we just watched him, hoping he would piss off. You could have put your house on what was going to happen because our big lad, wearing his Stoke City top, had just come outside with a full tray of drinks when this twat bumps into him, knocking them everywhere. Our lad is none too happy, comments on his place of origin and politely requests the money for a new round. This twat them starts to give our lad the come on, 'Who the fuck are Stoke then?, Come on, Zulu Army . . .' the same old shit.

Now we know our lad is going to kill him as we don't like Brummies at the best of times but we jump up to hold him back more than anything else. People move away, knocking more beer over, while others move in to get a better view of the massacre about to take place. Our mate then lumps this twat, who falls back over the wall, gets up just in time to receive a boot up the arse and runs over the road to join the other Brummies who, by the look of them, weren't up for it at all. We hold our lad back and the twat starts to get brave and mouths off again as his mates drag him away, the usual 'I could've had him' bollocks. Someone else goes off to get another round in as we calm our lad down.

After the game we returned to the same pub, as we always do, for a few more beers and to pick up the van before we set off home. I, for one, really didn't want to hang around too long and would rather have left and found a pub closer to home as this incident was playing on my mind a bit, but the others didn't seem that concerned. The pub was about half full and after a couple of pints my worries had faded and we had settled in when one of our lot comes in and says he thinks there is going to be trouble as the twat and about twenty other Brummies were walking towards the pub looking like they were ready to go. Instinct tells you to grab anything within reach and the landlord, oblivious of the events that had happened earlier, suddenly saw twelve Stoke fans rapidly collecting his glasses for him, so he vanished, obviously to ring the police. Everyone else in the pub was shitting themselves and it was obvious we were on our own as far as they were concerned.

The Brummies walked past the pub, giving it the once over, and started singing 'Zulu Army, Zulu Army', as a few went off down the side road. Then we heard the alarm of our van go off and one of them returned with a City flag. They then started singing, 'Come on City, come on City', and trying to bait us out, but we weren't moving. The landlord came back down and told us that the police were on their way when one of the Brummies opened the door and shouted, 'Where are the Stoke boys then? We've done your van over, come and have a look you wankers!' He went back outside and about twenty seconds later the roar went up and the windows went through as they threw everything they had at the pub. We could hear the sirens in the distance, so we knew that the place would be crawling with police any minute, and these Brummie bastards were screaming their heads off. But they had used up all their bottles and glasses, so we started to return fire back through the windows, forcing them back into the road. This gave us the chance to get out. We threw more glasses and, with the police bearing down on the situation, they did a runner, disappearing down the side streets. We tried to look as innocent and wounded as possible, but I've never seen so many police and dogs in one place.

The landlord, thank Christ, backed us up as he saw it as an unprovoked attack, although he did tell one of our lads that he never wanted to see us in his pub again. The van's windscreen was shattered, a side window was smashed and there were loads of dents, but the police couldn't really nick anyone as all the witnesses had fucked off. It was a long journey home, and luckily I didn't have to return the van to the hire company either. The thing that pissed us off more than anything was that we were all meant to be supporting the same team that day, but the club rivalry had taken over. In all my days at football I've never had to return home in a van so badly trashed and it was all down to one particularly mouthy twat that couldn't hold his beer or back himself up. So much for the English community spirit.

Chapter 9

The Wembley Debate

On any train journey into London, the two of us pass both Vicarage Road and Wembley Stadium. One remains our favourite place in the whole wide world, but the other – Wembley – never fails to attract a lingering look and a wry smile. It is a special place, and the sight of those twin towers are enough to send any football fan in the country off into dreamland, either reviving memories of great games past or, for most of us, taking us off to fantasy land. Wembley remains not only the home of English football but to many, the home of world football, the grand venue of legends. Players from all over the globe see the opportunity to play on the hallowed turf as one of the greatest experiences of their footballing careers, and a trip to the stadium is a must for every supporter during their life of fandom. The walk up Wembley Way cannot fail to stir even the most acrimonious of old farts, and the sense of history and occasion that surround the stadium is palpable. One can spend hours just reading the graffiti scratched into the concrete walls along that famous walk, scrawled messages and club names from all over the world. It all adds to the aura of the place and builds on that special type of atmosphere that only an old and famous place can maintain. From the outside, at least, it is a truly beautiful building.

Built over just 300 days and at a cost of £750,000, Wembley was initially constructed to house the British Empire Exhibition, and reflected the need during the early twenties for a multipurpose national stadium with the capacity to stage any type of sporting event, be it the Olympics, the Cup final or England internationals. The site was chosen because it offered easy access from any part of the country into what was at that time the sparsely populated area northwest of London. While these days that may seem a strange decision, it has to be remembered that even as late as the forties and fifties, a trip from the East End of London to Wembley was seen as something of an expedition. When finished, the place was seen by many as a sort of national monument, and it must have been a fantastic place to visit. The atmosphere, generated by national pride, must have been astonishing, but it quickly became apparent that Wembley was a victim of its own success: even a stadium of that size was not large enough to accommodate the vast numbers who wished to attend given events.

The very first sporting event staged at the stadium, the famous 'White Horse' Cup final between Bolton and West Ham on 28 April 1923, is the most widely known and reported example. Despite its intended capacity of approximately 100,000, over 126,000 spectators paid to enter, with approximately another 75,000 scaling the inadequate boundary walls to gain entry. The stadium was simply overrun with supporters, who ended up spilling on to the pitch where the police struggled, and almost failed, to restore control. From then on, for safety reasons, that official crowd limit was strictly adhered to and tickets were needed for all Cup finals, but clearly, on many occasions, even that figure was exceeded. At the 1982 World Cup qualifier against Hungary, a match that England had to win in order to qualify, people were storming gates and climbing over barriers in their thousands. The terracing was packed solid, with an estimated 110,000 to 120,000 people willing England on. In a stadium where the atmosphere was electric, Paul Mariner scored to secure the victory and the place erupted.

When originally built, the structure of the terracing worked well for the banks of supporters, but when the Taylor report was implemented, Wembley finally became all-seater. And of all the grounds in England, Wembley suffered most from the loss of terracing. Before, the home-end, hardcore and highly vocal support gathered on those terraces by climbing walls and moving where they wanted, and England needed them, to be. Any England international was a noisy and passionate affair, but the loss of terracing, together with stricter steward-ing and crowd control measures, destroyed much of that world-famous atmosphere overnight. Your carefully allocated and controlled seat number designates exactly where you sit these days, so the vocal support has become fragmented, kill-ing the sense of occasion for any game, with the possible exception of the FA Cup finals and the Nationwide League play-off finals.

So supporters began to take a good look at the place they held dear in their hearts, and began to realise that it wasn't that great a stadium after all. Anyone who has watched an international from the lower tier will recognise that in these days of brand-new, spectator-friendly stadia, Wembley, built in the first quarter of this century, has been left behind. It is no longer fit to hold international games with capacity crowds of 80,000 people. We know it looks fantastic on telly, but the reality is much, much different. Awful seating, inadequate toilet facilities, poor-quality and very expensive catering and parking, with dreadful access by road, all highlight the problems Wembley is saddled with. And while this is bad enough in itself, a more significant problem with Wembley is that it is now owned by a public company, so football, along with anyone else who wants to stage an event, has to hire it. That means more money out of the game. We, the paying public, should demand more from those that run football and they, in turn, should be demanding better from Wembley PLC. This of course begs the question of why football in this country owns no real home of its own. When the English Rugby Union side take to the field, they walk out into possibly the best stadium in the country – Twickenham, a huge, all-seater venue, purpose-built for the good of the spectator and used solely for rugby union. This immense stadium generates a sensational atmosphere which gives any game it hosts that sense of occasion so lacking at Wembley. If one examines the structure of the RFU in this country, it is astonishing that a sport which, at club level, enjoys audiences in the hundreds rather than the thousands and stadia which, with a few exceptions, would fail to gain entry to the Vauxhall Conference, can finance such an impressive monument. How is it that football has allowed itself to be left behind in this context? With the continuing debate over the proposed national football stadium, we should be asking the game where our opinions fit into the proposed plans. Wembley may be the traditional home of the English game, but is it really the right one any more? The location of the proposed national stadium is a very important and long-standing debate which has many equally valid and important elements to consider.

With many at Lancaster Gate showing a preference for a Wembley refurbishment at however many millions, we should be asking why this option seems so attractive to them. Turning Wembley into an acceptable all-seater stadium for the next century will be an enormous and expensive task; and where will that money come from? The lottery, perhaps? Maybe even Wembley PLC itself. It is far more likely, however, that a good portion of that money will come from the coffers of the game. If that is the case, perhaps it is cost that is driving the powers that be towards the Wembley option. Admittedly, the tradition and history that surround the stadium do give a certain amount of credibility to that proposal, but with so many games now being played at the twin towers, a trip to Wembley is beginning to lose its magic, even for those from the lower divisions. And with all the other drawbacks we've noted, surely the time has come to end an era, look towards the future and build a bright new home for English football.

The football establishment in England is fragmented – Lancaster Gate, Lilleshall, Bisham Abbey – it's all over the place. Would it not make far more sense to gather all these establishments into one focal point for the organisation of football in England, rather than have them dotted all around London and the home counties? A centre for English football would include FA headquarters, coaching facilities, a rehabilitation centre and even a football museum to bring people in from all over the world. Lecture halls, indoor facilities, the possibilities for the generation of money are endless. The centrepiece, of course, would be the national football stadium: a place to fulfil the needs of the spectator, rather than win some architect a design award, with good spacious seating providing a clear, uninterrupted view, easy access, spacious and clean toilets, catering and other facilities and a design capable of generating atmosphere no matter what the size of the crowd. Is that not an attractive proposition for the game as a whole? Surely there is someone at Lancaster Gate with the vision to see the benefits, both financial and sporting, of owning such a facility? It is normal in the US for many American football stadia and motorsport venues to be built along these lines because the Americans, with their commercial awareness, realise the possibilities of raising revenue from other activities. A midweek visit to the Daytona Raceway in Florida, home of the famous Daytona 500, puts the lacklustre Wembley Stadium tour to shame. Daytona provides a whole day's worth of entertainment, with a fantastic museum, stadium tours and superb catering facilities. The merchandising alone must generate a fortune, and the place is like a magnet to motorsport fans from all over the world. That is how it should be done. With football the largest spectator and participation sport in this country, surely the same lottery fund that awarded untold millions to the opera buffs in and around London could assist football with such a venture, which millions of people would enjoy. Indeed, lottery money has been put forward as an idea to fund the rebuilding of Wembley, but surely with Wembley being a PLC, that cannot be right? With stadium development at its zenith, now must be the time to make that brave decision and leave the twin towers behind. But just where should the game go?

We would all love it if the national stadium were right on our doorstep. Those of us who live in the South already have it, but as football fans, we have to think of the big picture. If you examine the regions in a purely footballing context it has to be said that for passion alone, the Northeast is the obvious place. The fervour and noisy appreciation the fans of the big three of that region manage to cook up would be worth an extra two players on the pitch. Liverpool and Manchester would also be worth considering, while London is in the hunt by virtue of numbers alone. However, football supporters are a hardy breed. We are used to travelling the country in support of our teams, and in these days of cheap and relatively rapid transportation, a trip to Liverpool from London is not that different from a trip to Southend. Common sense dictates that if we are to have a national stadium, it should be in the Midlands. The availability of excellent rail, road and even air links make this the obvious choice as it can be reached within a few hours from anywhere in the country. Indeed, this reasoning has already been used. What is found at the top of the M40 and just off the M6? The National Exhibition Centre, built to take the strain, and some of the business, from Earl's Court and Olympia for the very reasons outlined above. Can football not learn from other businesses and see that change and innovation do work?

There is, of course, another option, less attractive in some ways but proven and successful nonetheless. Keep Wembley, as the largest stadium in the country, for the major Cup finals and larger international fixtures, and take the rest of the England games on the road because there are obvious benefits to be gained from taking the national team out to the League grounds around the country. This option could prove beneficial to the England side in any number of ways, as Germany and Italy, which both manage their national games in this way, can attest. The success enjoyed by these countries would suggest that moving from stadium to stadium has no detrimental effect on the players; indeed, there is the argument that, by playing in familiar surroundings, some of the pressure that a Wembley international brings would be relieved. The Italians and Germans show a great understanding of how important the venue is to the game, and choose them to give their team an advantage. They know that an international friendly against Norway will not fill the Olympic Stadium or the San Siro, so they move it to a venue of a more suitable size. This ensures that the crowd can generate more noise and a more passionate atmosphere: it is far more satisfying to play in a medium-sized stadium packed to the gunnels than it is in a half-empty colosseum. Wembley on a wet Wednesday with 30,000 watching Portugal in a nothing game must be a very demoralising place to be, even for the most ardent England fan.

There are a number of other advantages to be gained from going on the road. By taking the international game around the country, you generate more interest in the game and enable people who would not normally be able, or willing, to travel to Wembley to see the England side. With the recent upgrade in football stadia that has taken place throughout the country, we now find ourselves with some outstanding venues available to the game. Among these, of course, are grounds where the crowd is more intimidating than others. Newcastle, Birmingham, Liverpool, and others of that ilk all benefit from the extra edge given to them by their home crowd. How many times have you heard managers come out with the old cliché, 'Those fans were like an extra player today', or seen referees give the odd 'dubious' decision in front of certain groups of supporters? Hostile, vociferous, rowdy – call them what you will, we have all seen enough over the years to know that these fans do have an effect on the performance of everyone on the pitch. It may not be sporting, but it happens. Can you imagine the effect that in excess of 35,000 Geordies would have on Roberto Baggio if they were screaming down his neck? More importantly, what effect would playing in front of that degree of passion have on the England team? The introduction of that 'home end' identity so obviously missing at Wembley would automatically be present at any ground allocated an international fixture, and that could only be good for the side. With stadia such as Old Trafford, St James Park, and Villa Park, we already have the venues capable of staging any England fixture, and with Wembley no longer the fortress it once was, the England set-up has to examine the opportunities to gain an advantage.

Whichever option is eventually chosen, those that make the decision have to take into account the views of the people who pay to get in, because if the wrong decision is made, they will stay away. While television and corporate money is all well and good, the game will suffer and eventually falter if there is no atmosphere in the stadium. That atmosphere isn't generated by celebrity fans, newspaper prize winners with free tickets, or hordes of school kids: it is generated by those of us who hand over our hard-earned money every time we walk through a turnstile. Football is ours, it belongs to us because we fund it, and therefore the FA have a duty to canvass our opinions and take them into account. The final decision on the national stadium must be made for the good of the game as a whole, not just for the good of those who seek only to take from it. As fans, we want the best not just from those on the pitch, be it at club or international level, but also from the environment we help to fund.

PART FOUR
Travel

———————

Chapter 10

Over Land And Sea

Travelling abroad in support of the national side or your club team is something that every football fan should experience. The feeling of arriving in a foreign city hundreds or thousands of miles from home and then suddenly coming across hundreds of your fellow countrymen, all with the same purpose, is absolutely fantastic. When you are put in that situation, one of the first questions you ask is, 'How did you get here?' because the methods of travel used by the English football fan are many and varied.

The England Travel Club provide what is believed to be the most convenient and safest way in which to follow the national side abroad. With the offer of the complete package deal including flights, transfers, hotels and match tickets, this method appeals to many. One added bonus touted to the Travel Club members by those that operate it is the fact that all those travelling will have been vetted by the FA and any persons found to have been convicted of football-related violence will be refused entry, thus keeping the hooligan element away. The reality is somewhat different. We have been told on a number of occasions that those organising the travel arrangements on behalf of the club have been known to 'make available', through other tour operators, the same packages when seats remain unsold, which does seem to defeat the object somewhat.

Although this has to be the easiest and most reliable method of travel on offer to the supporter, it is clear that many prefer to make their own way; but in either case, neither the FA nor the tour operator can account for the reception given to the fans by the locals. English football has earned its reputation over the years, something we would not and could not deny but, post-Heysel, a lot has been done to improve things although the problems are still with us. However, it is clear that the perception that English fans abroad are fair game is a widespread one and, as has been seen on many occasions, even those on the official tours can become subject to outrageous treatment by the local authorities. Being on an official tour certainly doesn't provide you with a guarantee of safety. After all, it is rare indeed for the local hooligans to stop the coach driver and check if a coach is an official tour or not before they stone the windows. Ask anyone who went to Greece or Spain, or to many other countries, what they came up against and it does pose the question as to why so much of this kind of activity goes unreported by the British media. We genuinely believe that supporters of any other sport would have the House of Commons on their feet within minutes if they were treated in such a fashion. The cost of the tours and the feeling of being ripped off, along with the constant hassle of being shepherded around like animals, keeps many people away from the large groups and forces them into making their own arrangements.

Travelling independently has many advantages, and with it becoming so cheap nowadays this can also save you plenty of money and hassle while giving you the opportunity to plan your own route, have the crack and visit places the main group never see. Obviously, there are some supporters who have no choice but to use this method, notably those with a rather dubious past, but in truth, they would never be seen on an official tour anyway, and will use any route necessary to gain access into a country unchallenged.

The following account came to us from a West Country lad,

and it explains everything you could possibly want to know about making your own way to a place when you may not be that welcome.

SWEDEN 92

There were six of us that had planned to make the journey to Sweden for the 92 Championships. All of us had been done at football by the police and four had served time. Nothing too long, the tops being three months of a six-month sentence by one of the lads. All the press had been going on about was the expected trouble the England fans would cause and the police were saying that they would be stopping any 'known' troublemakers at the ports and airports, as would the Swedish if any did manage to get that far. All this meant was that we would have to plan our journey and find a back way into Sweden.

We had allowed ourselves five days to get there and decided to get a ferry to Cherbourg from Weymouth, travel up through France and Belgium, then go on to Rostock in Germany. There we would catch the ferry to Copenhagen, then another to Malmö, where England were playing. None of us had tickets for any of the games, but we were sure that we would get them as we went and that if worst came to the worst, the police would have left space for us anyway; they usually did. We bought ourselves Inter-rail tickets at Weymouth just before catching the ferry to France, as we thought that would make it difficult for them to have the time to run any security checks on us and stop us from travelling. Once we were on the ferry, we were on holiday and on our way to mainland Europe, so it was time to get pissed. Somehow we all boarded the train at the other end and arrived in Paris at around nine o'clock in the evening, with self-induced duty-free hangovers and nowhere to stay. We planned on sleeping rough that night and after

161

a walk around the red-light district made our way up to the train station. We couldn't have been there for five minutes before the police came up and ordered us to move on. They didn't come across as being too friendly, and let us know in no uncertain terms that they would give us a good hiding if we returned before morning. They also informed us that the French team and the Paris St-Germain fans would give us a good hiding at the first match. Whatever happened to community policing, wankers.

We were going to spend the next day in Paris sight-seeing, but after such a warm welcome and a bad night trying to sleep in a shop doorway, we decided to catch the first train we could and make our way up to Rostock. This would be a long train journey and would give us the chance to catch up on some sleep and have a wash down.

We had to change trains in Brussels and there we met up with other fans making the journey. Most were on their way up to Amsterdam to get stoned and shag themselves stupid in the coffee shops and brothels. This seemed like a fantastic idea and forced us into a difficult decision as to whether we should change our plans or not. Amsterdam is a fantastic place and the thought of being there with loads of other English fans was too much. Amsterdam it was, and so another slow journey and no chance of any sleep.

The city was busy, and finding somewhere to stay for one night would be a problem so we decided to find the nearest coffee shop, got blitzed and the problem went away. That night, we toured the red-light district and two of the lads disappeared, assuring us that they were only paying for a fifteen-minute lie down and nothing else. Well, the 'rest' didn't do them much good as they could hardly walk when they came out, but they were smiling. We found another coffee shop and the next thing I knew we were waking up in the morning down at the train station with loads of other dossers and English pissheads. Luckily, the local police just seemed to want us out of the city and out of their way. Most of the English were heading straight up to Copenhagen, while others were stopping off in Hamburg. For some this trip was seen as an excuse to shag themselves across Europe. Hamburg's Reeperbahn was the next port of call. We had been told so many stories about the city that we had to see it for ourselves – and we were not disappointed. What a place!

I think Hamburg's red-light district is the best in Europe because there is every shape, size and colour of woman that you could imagine to be looked at or whatever. The town was full of English squaddies, some on their way to the football, others just shagging themselves senseless. We met some great lads that knew the place inside out and they told us of a good cheap hotel, where the best bars were, where to avoid and even where to score some drugs. It was fantastic. I saw women do things that night that I wouldn't have thought humanly possible and we got stoned, shit-faced and had a good night's kip. The England Travel Club was never like this. The next day, after we had showered and washed, we made our way to the train station where again we met up with loads of English lads, all heading straight to Copenhagen. The place was crawling with police, as apparently there had been a spot of trouble the night before and they didn't want to see it repeated. Those German coppers look real nasty bastards as well.

We had planned our original route to avoid getting pulled over and deported, so we decided to head to Rostock, as we may have been pushing our luck too far if we stayed with the main group, especially as we would all meet up in Copenhagen any way. This journey would also give us the chance to chill out, relax and take in the sights. Away from the cities, northern Germany is a beautiful country. If it wasn't for the Germans it would be an idyllic place to live, but every place has its drawbacks I suppose; in the West Country we have Bristol City and the Worzels.

The train connections were spot-on and we arrived at the terminal with forty minutes to spare before catching the ferry to Gedser in Denmark followed by the train to Copenhagen. Both ports were hassle-free and we even managed to sort ourselves beds at the Youth Hostel. There we met more football fans and squaddies. The squaddies also knew this place from back to front and told us of an old Army base open 24 hours, 365 days of the year, where you could buy and consume drugs on the premises hassle-free. Apparently it was run by the government, there was a massive all-night market, cafés, bars, the lot, as well as loads of hippy birds from all over Europe. Surely this couldn't be true!! Well, let me tell you now that squaddies never lie, this place was heaven on earth. We spent most of the next day sleeping it all off before returning the following night.

The next day we boarded the jetfoil to Malmö, half expecting to be refused entry into Sweden. All the scare stories back home about the police being heavy-handed and people being turned back proved to be complete rubbish, as we were welcomed with open arms. There were loads of riot police, but they weren't acting up and it all seemed quite friendly. This did, however, provide us with a little disappointment, as first, we had believed all that stuff and secondly, the thought of being turned back to Copenhagen, Hamburg or Amsterdam didn't seem that bad anymore. Still, the football must come first.

We were told where to camp and that entertainment in the shape of a large, cheap beer tent had been provided – bloody marvellous. The local press had built us up to be animals but the local people and the police treated us differently, which was great. The girls were stunning and particularly accommodating. We had no trouble getting tickets because the police were allowing the touts to sell quite openly, as they knew that this was preferable to having us roaming the streets. The French match was terrible – all the matches were terrible, come to think of it – and there was no real trouble, but what did surprise me was the people that were there, because I recognised faces of people that you wouldn't like to see let out of their own homes, let alone out of the country. The English lads were out in force.

I like the odd bit of football violence even now, but it was a shame that things turned sour after the Danish match. I had come to really like the Danes after staying in Copenhagen and the Swedes were really nice as well, but the police had started it all by over-reacting, so what happened was fair enough really. All night things were going off and the locals soon didn't want to know us anymore, which was understandable really. Someone was stabbed, people were getting nicked and beaten up by the police, others were smashing up shops and looting, all the usual stuff. The next morning the campsite was full of stories about what had happened and a couple of us seriously thought about heading back to Copenhagen, doing without the hassle and enjoying ourselves.

Unfortunately, the next match was against the hosts, Sweden, in Stockholm and the Swedes were rumoured to have a mob of their own willing to take us on. We had to be there – after all, we were English and the thought of taking on a load of Vikings in their own back garden was quite appealing and history showed that we did owe them one.

When we arrived in Stockholm a few days later the campsite, an old athletics stadium, was pretty full. Again, getting tickets wasn't a problem as some fans had had enough and returned to England, or gone on elsewhere. We were told that the police were playing up a bit and that the local mob were also out and about, so we pitched our tents and headed off into town. We were getting well pissed in this bar when some English lads came in and told us that things were kicking off back at the site and that the locals were well up for it. They said that the Swedes had attacked the site and that the riot police were all over the place. Not wanting to miss out on the action, we finished our beers and headed back to find that these lads were right. The police were busy blocking off roads and when they found out we were English, they shoved us back into the camp. The place was a picture, with fires being lit, people looking for weapons, others building barricades. It was nuts, just like a scene from *Blade Runner*. A real siege was under way and the atmosphere was fantastic. The whole campsite was pulling together, and I wouldn't have missed that for the world. As more fans returned more rumours spread. They had a mob of around 200, no 500, no 1,000, and the police were going to let them in after what had happened in Malmö, all sorts of rumours, but the night passed and nothing happened. That buzz was fantastic though, I've never known anything like it.

The next day was match day and we lost 2–0. There wasn't any trouble and most of the English support, tired from the night before and pissed off at the football, just wanted to go home. The police were back at the campsite and seemed to be picking people out and arresting anyone they didn't like the look of and so, as we had scored some acid the night before, we just kept our heads down, stayed in our tents and cheered ourselves up by tripping our nuts off.

The next day we returned to Copenhagen, catching up on some much-needed sleep on the way. The Danes seemed a bit worried about the English returning after what had happened in Malmö, and maybe it was just us feeling pissed off at the football, but the atmosphere in the city seemed very different. We were ready to return to England. We came back via Rotterdam without stopping, then bunked the train to London from Harwich before catching a coach home from Victoria, a very long and tiring journey.

That was a fantastic time, though, and the only way to do anything like that really. It was an experience that the six of us will remember and share forever.

Despite much press hype to the contrary and a great deal of so-called intellectual research, the England 'superfirm' does not exist. One of the main points expressed in these accounts is the way in which the England fans will come together when they travel abroad, and the truth is that many of those that follow the national side know the rules inside out, and trust and look out for each other. Even those that avoid trouble like the plague understand that sometimes there is nowhere else to go and you have to stand your corner. They simply know that when the going gets tough, they are all in it together and that, possibly, is where this misconception originates. With very few exceptions, club rivalries go out the window when England fans are abroad; when trouble starts, being English is the focus and all that is foreign is seen as the enemy.

The following is an account of another interesting way of supporting the national side. With Euro 96 staged in this country, bringing fans from all over the continent to these shores, this group of lads decided to head in the other direction.

MAJORCA 96

We had originally planned to follow the England side throughout the tournament, but when we saw the price of the tickets we thought, bollocks. We worked it out that we could get a week in Majorca for not much more than the price of the tickets, with the added bonuses of beer, sun and birds. No contest.

We ended up in Palma Nova and, getting our priorities right, quickly found an English-owned bar with a big screen that was showing every match. Sorted. All the way through, the atmosphere was great. We even supported the Spanish when they played and managed to find a few Jocks and Dutch to take the piss out of as well, but it was all in good fun. England were magic, we pissed the group. Then, in the quarter-finals we had to play Spain and the atmosphere changed as soon as the draw was decided. The British press were stirring things up, and supposedly the local papers had started writing about the English lager louts and making us all out to be hooligans looking for trouble. Now it's not that difficult to find a pissed-up English lad in Majorca, but the police were coming out in force and had started to get heavy-handed since the match was announced, knocking people about and stuff, mainly to prove a point – but all it really did was wind people up and make the situation worse.

On the day of the match, the Spanish were out on their mopeds and in their cars waving flags and being loud, which is great for a while, but after a few beers it starts to get on your tits a bit. The bar was packed and everyone was pissed up and singing. The riot police were out in numbers, tooled up, unhappy and waiting opposite, and it was obvious it was going to happen whatever the result. I remember really hoping we would stuff those bastards.

England were lucky to get to extra time, really, and the pub was bombing along. Then Spain scored. There were a few seconds' stunned silence followed by some choice words, then the realisation that the 'goal' had been disallowed. The place erupted as if we had won. Everyone was pointing at the police and singing, 'You thought you had scored, you were wrong, you were wrong,' which didn't make them too happy but the look on their faces was brilliant. The game went to penalties and the atmosphere was amazing, Seaman saved, and we had won. The place exploded, everyone was jumping on each other, off the tables, beer and glasses were going everywhere and the noise was deafening. It must have been better than being there because here we were in their country taking the piss, a dream come true.

The police were not happy at all. They were getting loads of verbal and then they steamed in, battered this bloke and dragged him out, making his mates slightly annoyed, as you can imagine. Apparently he had given them the wanker sign and that was all they needed to split a few heads. The place was rammed with pissed-up lads and all the birds were egging us on. This was a small part of England as far as we were concerned, and they had just invaded it, the bastards. The sirens were ringing out as more riot police arrived, which had the dramatic effect of sobering most of us up, but we were not going to let them take the piss. The team had done their bit, now it was up to us to do ours, as it were.

We continued to sing our hearts out and front them as much as we could. 'ENG-GER-LAND, ENG-GER-LAND, ENG-GER-LAND' – we rammed that result down their throats. Then they steamed in again. Glasses and bottles went flying at them but this only held them back for a moment, and when we were out of things to throw, they came and battered anything they could get hold of. Even a few of the girls got hit. Still, what do you expect from that lot. The birds were screaming their heads off as only girls can at moments like that, and the police dragged about seven blokes out, threw them in a van and drove off. I was lucky because one of them grabbed me although I managed to get away in the middle of everything, but I hate to think what happened to those poor sods.

After about ten minutes we were told that the police

were closing the bar and that we all had to leave and anyone refusing to go would be arrested – an easy decision to make. We were buzzing, it had been a great night, a great match and a great result, all finished off with a good row. For the rest of the night we moved from bar to bar, slowly getting more and more pissed and singing our hearts out. The police had swamped the area and little things were going off here and there, but nothing serious. The Spanish were meant to have a small mob wandering around but I think that was bollocks, they would have got battered anyway as there were so many English around. Even all the Norwegians and Germans were keeping out. Unfortunately, we had to fly home the next day, which was a shame because the German game would have provided just as much fun, I'm sure.

It is clear that the privilege of following your side abroad does not come cheap, and is often seen by a number of people as just another excuse to rip off the fans. It is our belief that keeping prices down would encourage more to use the official travel packages, and that this would eventually lead to a growing respect for the England fan, as the vetting process would help eliminate some of the unwanted hooligan element. Indeed, it does make you wonder if the FA want the responsibility of the travelling fan at all, as it is much easier for the FA to wash their hands of them when trouble rears its head, and point the finger at those who choose to travel independently. Sadly, it is inevitable that there will always be an element of England support looking for trouble abroad, and where there is a match they will find a method of getting there. Yet by encouraging a wider cross-section of support to travel, either with easier ticket allocation or cheaper travel, the hooligan element would be diluted and a positive atmosphere hopefully fostered. However, travel is not the only problem abroad, and it would be nice if the FA and the government came out in support of the travelling fan when they are intimidated or provoked, as has been demonstrated in some of the accounts we have just read. You shouldn't have to be on an official tour to deserve that.

PART FIVE
The Opposition

Chapter 11

Who Are Ya?

_____

While it is clear that most countries who play football have an element intent on causing trouble, it is also obvious that there are certain countries whose supporters are worse than others. There are many reasons for this, of course. Some nations enjoy a very high standard of football, some a very low standard – but each have that element of passion and pride which can foster confrontation. Similarly, there are countries suffering from economic and historical problems that are reflected in a different kind of conflict on the terraces. For example, while the tension in the former Yugoslavia had been bubbling under the surface for many years, it came out into the open on the football terraces, and finally spilt over into the civil war that wrecked the country. It is vital to remember that for the citizens of many countries, football is all they have; it is basically everything to them. Understanding this is important; but as far as the England followers are concerned, there are obvious foes to contend with and, while this will be examined in a bit more detail, we need to highlight a few of the lesser known problem countries whose fans, as opposed to the local police, have been playing up of late.

Just looking at Europe, it is clear that apart from the more obvious examples, the Greeks have been intent on proving that their fans are up there with the worst and, in fact, the hooligan element has all but destroyed much of the appeal of the game in that beautiful country. Greece may have a small league, but their fans are as passionate as any other and have been only too willing to indulge in violence when the need arises. As recently as November 1995, the fans of Poak Salonika invaded the pitch with two minutes remaining in a cup tie, which they just happened to be losing, and attacked the referee and other fans, injuring over thirty. In fact, Poak have had a pretty rough history, with a two-year ban from European competition to their name after riots caused a match against Paris St-Germain to be abandoned at half time. However, they are not the only club with a chequered past in Greece. AEK Athens, Panathinaikos and Olympiakos all have a long record of crowd violence. Almost certainly as a direct result of this, average attendances at first division games in Greece have dropped from 11,250 in 1988 to only 3,680 in 1994.

Similarly, France have been having their own problems in recent seasons. In 1993, ten policemen were seriously hurt during fights with fans of Paris St-Germain during a game with Caen, although many of those taking part were said to be skinheads and neo-Nazis. Interestingly enough, the Paris St-Germain mob are called the 'Boulogne Boys', and are known for their tendency to wear Millwall and Chelsea shirts. In 1994, Marseille fans rioted after the referee sent off their keeper, and in 1995, all non-League games in and around Paris were suspended when a supporter was shot dead near Drancy. During the 1995–96 season, the two main incidents of note were the arrest of 450 Paris St-Germain fans in Brussels and the closure of the St Etienne ground after persistent crowd disorder among the home supporters.

Spain is another country where the national temperament often spills over into violence although, in truth, the lack of major disorder among the Spanish fans can be put down to the fact that the distances between grounds are often so large that travelling fans are fairly low in number. The Madrid fans seem to be by far the worst, and both the Ultra Sur (Real) and Frent Atletico (Atletico) have a long history of confrontation with each other. Interestingly enough, racism is a real problem among the Spanish support and in 1993, a group of Real Madrid fans were jailed for six months for racist activities at matches.

It would, of course, be easy to rattle on about any number of incidents in countries throughout Europe, but it is clear that they all have problems and some are more diverse than others. As recently as last season, fans of the Bulgarian side, CSKA Sofia, fought on the pitch with fans of local rivals Levski, during which someone threw a snake at the referee. During the Portuguese Cup final against Benfica, a Sporting Lisbon fan was killed when a flare hit him in the stomach. In May 1996, fifteen people were killed as the crowd stampeded following Zambia's victory, in a World Cup qualifier, over Sudan. Even after Euro 96, things haven't improved in some parts of the world. In July 1996 at least twenty people were killed in Libya when security forces opened fire on spectators who had begun chanting anti-Gadaffi slogans. However, as far as the hooligan elements who follow the national side are concerned, the numbers of real opponents are fairly small, and it would be a worthwhile exercise to examine them individually.

Chapter 12

Scotland

When the draw for Euro 96 was made, there was one fixture that stood out above every other game in the tournament. Never mind the actual football: the skill-laden Italians, the workmanlike Germans or even those old historical foes, the arrogant French, would provide that. No – the game on everyone's mind was England vs Scotland. It was on everyone's mind for one reason, and one reason only: the potential for trouble. This situation had not been helped by the fact that in the weeks leading up to the draw, both the FA and the police voiced their very real concerns about the possibility of this fixture occurring, and there were even whispers in the press that the draw would be 'massaged' so that the fixture would – or could – not be drawn out. However, as is usual when the FA say publicly that they would prefer something not to happen (for example, FA Cup replays, snow, etc), England and Scotland were drawn out in the same group. Despite the almost audible gulps from both the FA and the police, the instant reaction from the management of both camps was that this would be a great day out for everyone, a celebration of British football. However, within days the Scottish supporters and certain players were calling this game 'our World Cup final' and the England fans were busying themselves reviving memories of both 1967 and 1977,

179

when the Scots came to town and took the piss.

The reasoning behind the football hooligans' behaviour is all to do with reputation, with the aim being to destroy the reputation of the opposition by humiliation. There are a number of ways this can be done, and one of the more obvious is to travel to the away fixture and put on a show. We have all seen or done it over the years, and there is nothing to compare with the feeling of travelling home, having done the business. Conversely, having someone do a number on you is the most degrading feeling known, and one that will linger for many years – until it is possible to enact retribution. For a League club, the chance will usually come the very next season; but for an international side, the chances are few and far between, so the canker of humiliation will eat away until the chance for revenge comes up.

When this kind of humiliation happens once, it is bad enough; but when it happens twice it is too much. Yet that is exactly the situation that the England supporters found themselves having to deal with. In 1967, during the European Championships and just a year after England had won the World Cup, Scotland came to London and took the place over. The whole city was bedecked in tartan and, following their 2–1 victory, the Scottish fans managed to get onto the hallowed Wembley turf, and ripped it to shreds. The sight of Wembley being overrun was appalling and one which was to be repeated less than ten years later when the Scots got on the pitch again. This time they snapped a crossbar and caused over £18,000 worth of damage to the pitch during their delighted celebration of yet another victory. This happened at a time when the problem of football violence was on the increase, and was a real blow to the pride of the English, who offered little real resistance at the time, despite the huge ill-feeling caused among the general public throughout the capital by the hordes of drunken Scots.

* * *

JOCKS AT WEMBLEY

Whenever the world becomes too much and the pressures of life, such as keeping my job, providing for my kids and finding the money for the next year's season ticket drag me to the bottom of the pit, there is always one memory that brings me around. One day in my life that has made all the struggles worthwhile. A thousand memories of one event that brings with them a glow that only a visit from the Lord himself could match. That day was Saturday, 4 June 1977, a date that saw the liberation of the Scottish nation by the Tartan Army, a liberation that took place in the Auld Enemy's own backyard. Oh deep joy rain on me!

As a seventeen-year-old, I left my mother believing I was nipping out for a packet of Polos while my friends were told that I was personally leading the Tartan Army over the border and into battle. The feeling in my stomach as the night train crossed the border still lingers: 'Fuck me, we're in enemy territory'. I needn't worry that I was surrounded by hundreds of countrymen fuelled by a night on the town topped up with carry-outs and crisps. Sleep? Twenty minutes maybe, and Jesus those toilets. Getting off at King's Cross, the tube, Trafalgar Square, surely we were back in Scotland, everything was tartan. The police had already lost the fight, they were powerless. Thousands had come down without tickets and stories of England fans being 'relieved' of theirs were rife. The smell of the beer in the packed tube was almost enough to get you pissed on its own, and the noise was deafening. You could see English fans going in the opposite direction. We had overrun the place and it belonged to us.

I wouldn't have fancied my chances if I had been a ticket tout that day. Those that wanted to get in just climbed in; tickets counted for nothing. The game was a blur, really – after all, there was no way we could possibly have lost. The English players must have shit themselves as they came out of the tunnel. God, that must have been some feeling for the Scottish boys walking out into that. McQueen and Dalglish scored the goals – surely it couldn't get any better – and then the final whistle and the real party began. I remember holding on to my friend Stevie as if to say, 'No we can't go on the pitch, we'll get nicked' as we watched the invasion take place. Then the realisation struck me – yessss! Here we fucking go, Wembley, no fucker was going to stop this boy. We ran straight into the centre spot for some reason, and just laughed our heads off trying to take it all in. There was one bloke wiping his arse on the turf as his mates took that once-in-a-lifetime photo opportunity. Another was taking a piss, until a copper came up shouting but powerless; the bloke just danced off at the copper with his knob still hanging out of his trousers, piss in mid-flow. Everyone was ripping up the turf and stuffing it in their pockets to replant when they got home and one lad was wearing this massive piece of grass as a wig until one of his mates whipped it off his head and ran off. The chase lasted about five yards before he reached down and just tore out another clump saying, 'Have it, you bastard, there's plenty more'. Pie-crust shoes and tartan flares were everywhere. What a moment, I've never in the whole of my life seen so many happy people in one place at one time.

The police cleared the pitch slowly, but me and Stevie went back onto the terrace and climbed up to the top tier to view the scene. There were plenty of others with the same idea and we just looked on in awe. I remember turning to Stevie and seeing him just staring ahead with a look of sheer bliss across his face as he held his head in his hands. I didn't want to be responsible for spoiling such a heavenly moment so I just bit my tongue and turned away. As we walked down Wembley Way I wanted to turn around and run back just to get a little bit more, but the moment had passed, it was now time to hit the West End.

Trafalgar Square was packed. Scots were jumping into the fountains, climbing over the statues, drinking and singing their hearts out. Again, the police could do nothing, but what was the point anyway? We were only having the crack. The drink continued to flow, but I don't actually remember buying any beer, although I've never been so pissed in all my life. As the time passed, people started to move off and the police moved in and started to arrest anyone they could, so we decided to go up to Soho and take in the nightlife and a look at the porn shops (remember I was only seventeen and this was a whole new world for Stevie and me). What a fantastic time it was, and we decided that we would sleep rough for the night and made our way to Hyde Park. There we met up with a bunch of lads from Stirling who were going over the events they had seen during the day, but the booze had finally caught up with us and the last thing I remember was climbing under a bush, telling myself that there was a God after all and falling asleep.

I was woken up the next morning by Stevie. It was seven o'clock and we had £1.20 between us. I was dreading ringing my mother, she would have known where I had been for the last twenty-four hours and would have seen the pictures on the TV. I rang from Euston and told her I was still in London. 'Don't worry yourself son, just get home safely... It was a great match, wasn't it ... You wasn't one of those on the pitch were you son?' Dad grabbed the phone. 'All right son? ... What was it like? ... We saw the pictures of Trafalgar Square on the television, fantastic, was you there? ... Have you got a piece of Wembley for the garden then?' I couldn't believe it, they were almost proud of me, it was as if their son had been part of the invasion of England. Looking back, that was exactly what it was.

I have had many nights reminiscing over that day. Whenever I meet a fellow countryman anywhere or a mouthy Englishman on holiday, the memories come flooding back. It's something that will live with me forever and can never be taken away. God, I feel happy!

The traditional rivalry between the two nations now began to manifest itself in violence at every Home International fixture either in Glasgow or London, as the English fans, now better organised, confident and willing, took every opportunity to extract some kind of revenge. What follows is an account of one of the more infamous incidents involving England fans and their attempts at taking on the Scots in Glasgow. It was supplied to us anonymously, but subsequent information has proved it to be a genuine account of an attempted confrontation before a friendly fixture in 1987, which resulted in a 0–0 draw.

GLASGOW

Like most English supporters, I hate the memory of seeing 50,000 sweaties swarming all over the Wembley pitch. Those bastards really took the piss in 1977, and the reputation we had built up throughout the world took a serious knockback. I wasn't at that match, but I know a few blokes who were robbed of their tickets on the way up. There was nothing they could do because they were just surrounded and forced to hand them over to avoid getting battered. The police were shit that whole weekend, they were completely overwhelmed and the sweaties were left to do what they wanted, which was basically get pissed and play up. The England support was crap as well. Here we were supposed to be the top of the tree and we were shitting it at home and bottling it at the thought of even going to Scotland, never mind taking them on to get revenge.

When a few of the English firms started to gain links

with some of the mobs in Scotland, they quickly learnt that the sweaties were still full of what they had got up to in 1977; and who can blame them, we had shit it. This was starting to piss some of our lads off. I mean, these were some of the top boys in England and they were going up there and having the piss taken out of them for something that had happened almost ten years previous. This was starting to lead to a bit of friction between the two groups, and even though the English lads were fighting alongside the Jocks, they could see that they weren't really up to that much. As England had never taken a firm to Glasgow for a game against Scotland, there wasn't that much we could say, but it became clear that the only way to regain respect would be to get mobbed up and do the business at the next international. This just happened to be the tenth anniversary of their invasion.

The whole thing was put together by lads from one of the London firms and their links with the BNP ensured that the word was spread throughout the country that the English had to put on a show in Glasgow and gain revenge for the fact that the Jocks had repeatedly turned us over and taken the piss. As we had to get the numbers, it was also made clear that any of the known faces that didn't show would be seen to have bottled it, which was as good a guarantee as you could have. Even though the old bill knew what was going on, and had a few plainclothes coppers with us and loads in uniform, a mob from all over the country gathered at Euston to travel up by train. And if there has ever been a more nasty mob put together, then I would hate to have seen it, but we were all thinking of this as the big one. We had a point to prove and none of us was going to do a runner no matter what. Sometimes it's better to take a hiding than run.

The Jocks obviously knew we were coming because the whole thing had been well planned, but we were told that the Rangers firm were not getting involved due to their links with Chelsea and the BNP. For most of us, though, the politics were left out – this was just the ultimate derby fixture – and I reckon the same can be said of the sweaties.

There were about 300 of us on that train, I reckon, and once we got into Scotland, the buzz really kicked in. The usual drinking marathon had been put on hold, which gave the atmosphere a more dangerous edge: we all wanted to be on top form when we got to Glasgow Central, but we also knew that the filth would be all over us, so anything that went off would go straightaway. As we pulled in, we could see line after line of old bill with dogs and vans ready to cart us off and we knew then that they had cleared away any welcoming committee and, basically, had it all sorted. It's a weird feeling, that. You're sort of relieved to see the law because you know that to a certain degree you'll be protected, but you're also gutted because you can't play up. All we could do really was to get off the train and make as much noise as possible, I mean you might as well let the wankers know you've arrived. I have to admit, I love all that, climbing off a special and giving it the big'un and the sound in that station was deafening.

The old bill obviously wanted us in the ground as quickly as possible, so they got us out of the station and onto the main drag and if we were going to do anything it would have to be soon. The law had done a good job of dispersing the locals, but we could see little mobs of sweaties standing around waiting to see if anything would go off. And Christ, did it go off. At the sight of these little groups, our mob was off through the law and after them. The locals were off like a shot and the coppers were taken by complete surprise, but our lot were lashing out at anything that moved – age, sex, it didn't matter. Some had got themselves tooled up with nuts and bolts beforehand and these were flying everywhere as well. It was chaos. As I didn't want to get split up from the main mob, who by this time were at it with the police, I ducked into a shop and waited for a while until they had all passed. I was with this other lad trying to look innocent when this bloke came up and said something along the lines of, 'You pathetic English bastard!' Well, my mate just lumped him and he went down. 'Time to get back to the others,' we thought, and we ran out and back to the main mob. This copper must have thought we were two mad Jocks running at the English, and tried to get hold of the two of us, but when we explained that we were two English fans who had been attacked in a pub up the road, he told us to get back with the others and we would be taken to the ground with them.

That was that. The massive off we were expecting never happened, but for us, it was a right result. We had fronted it up by going, managed to have a bit of a run around and dished out a few slaps and only a few had got nicked and that was for fighting with the old bill. The atmosphere in the ground was fantastic, talk about hostile, but there was never any chance of anything else going off, as the police were well on top of everything by now and we were happy that we had done what we set out to do.

Over the next few weeks, word came back that the sweaties weren't too impressed with us and were accusing us of taking on old women shopping, but that's bollocks. We took an England mob to Glasgow and they didn't show to take us on, so fuck them.

In 1980, the FA announced that it would no longer make tickets available to the Scots. This caused uproar north of the border. The Scottish Supporters' Club even took the FA to court, citing the Race Relations Act, but lost the case. Then, following riots in Belfast during the Maze Prison hunger strikes, both England and Wales refused to travel to Northern Ireland to play their fixtures in the Home Internationals which, on top of the concern about the inability to deal with the hooligan problem, sounded the death knell for the tournament. In 1984, they were formally abandoned. While both the FA and the SFA have discussed resurrecting the tournament over the last few seasons, the fact remains that the lingering hostility between the two sets of supporters makes confrontation almost inevitable. And until Euro 96, there was little chance that any competitive fixture would take place, although friendlies were fairly regular affairs until as late as 1989.

To those who know the game, it is clear that the Scottish supporters, like the Irish, are held in quite high esteem when they travel abroad. Unlike the English, who get treated like animals wherever they go, the Scottish – with their serious drinking reputation and odd (perverse?) clothing – are usually warmly welcomed by host countries. To be fair, Scottish supporters have been exceptionally well behaved on their travels abroad, despite following a team that has continually let them down and management that has provided, on occasion, total humiliation (remember Ally McLeod and the famous Tartan Army in the 1978 World Cup?). Scottish club sides have also enjoyed a pretty much untarnished image when on their travels in Europe. But this rosy picture is marred by the Scottish domestic game, which is littered with fixtures where violence among the supporters can be quite accurately forecast. Hibernian vs Hearts and Dundee vs Dundee United are two of the more obvious, but Aberdeen, Airdrie, Dunfermline, Motherwell and many other clubs have all had groups of fans active at some time or another. In 1996, Andy Goram, the Rangers keeper, was attacked on the pitch by a Hibernian fan – an act that was widely reported and condemned. What was not so widely reported was that all the stewards were at the other end of the pitch dealing with a serious 'off' in the crowd, and that this was the only reason the supporter managed to get onto the pitch.

There's no doubt, however, that the most volatile game in the Scottish calendar is the world-famous 'Old Firm' derby. With religious bigotry and history both playing their part in moulding the event, plus the fact that the two sides are usually involved in a struggle for some competition or other, the tensions between supporters are obvious, and turn into violent confrontation all too easily. We have talked to a great many Scots over the years, and find it astonishing that the violence which regularly accompanies this fixture goes largely un-reported in England. The clubs involved have, however, staged all-out war against the violent element and, in a city where season tickets for either club are as good as solid gold, the threat of that ticket being revoked for life is as powerful a weapon as anything the local police will ever have. The only problem is that this leaves the pubs and clubs of Glasgow facing a potential battleground on the day of every 'Old Firm' derby instead.

Nevertheless, while Scottish football as a whole does not 'enjoy' the stigma attached to English football, with some justification, things are rather different when the two nations meet. From the Scottish perspective, anything south of Hadrian's Wall will inevitably seem suspect because the Scots have a dislike and distrust of England as a nation. The Scottish Nationalist movement is a strong and proud one, and good luck to them – pride is an important feature of the Scottish race. But as far as football is concerned, the anti-English senti-ment runs far deeper than that.

A great many English supporters view the top six clubs in the Scottish Premier League as roughly equivalent to the mid-table English Premier teams, and any club outside that top six as being little more than GM Conference standard. Many of those same supporters almost undoubtedly view the game north of the border as nothing better than a breeding ground for players for the English game. These opinions are incredibly condescending, and they quite rightly cause a great deal of anger among Scottish supporters who are not only proud of the game in their country, but who have also seen the English game systematically draining their game of its greatest players over the years. It has always been thus. From the professional game's early days, players from all the other nations of the

United Kingdom saw, and took, their chance in England. Certainly, a number of Scottish clubs were reliant on these transfer dealings for their financial security, even though their game suffered as a result. That trend began to slow in the early nineties, and is even working in reverse these days, but south of the border, many have been slow to accept this change, and this ingrained attitude undoubtedly rankles with the Scots. The English do not for one moment acknowledge the fact that the most successful managers in the history of our game, and many of the greatest players ever seen in England, have come from across the border. That the Scottish have a far better record of World Cup qualification than the English is also considered by many to be of little real consequence in the context of international football; to some degree, the English interpret that statistic as luck on the part of the Scots, whereas the English have simply been crap (a sentence of which only half is true, of course). There is little doubt that as a race and in a footballing context, the Scottish have every right to feel just a little patronised.

Chapter 13
Wales

As a result of the League set-up in England, some of the more dedicated followers of clubs in the lower divisions will find themselves having to travel to 'foreign' soil at least once a season – that is, across the border into Wales. Now a trip to the land of the red dragon can be a most dangerous experience for those looking for trouble, as the two of us can testify. Two broken ribs and a bit of wood with nails sticking out of it wrapped round your legs (Dougie) and a fractured skull (Eddy) are testimony to the fact that a matchday at the Vetch Field can prove a bit dodgy. Both Swansea and Wrexham have clearly got tidy little firms, but Cardiff City undoubtedly possess a hardcore that are more than capable of taking on any firm in Europe, let alone the Valleys. But let's be honest here: Welsh football is shit. The crowds are pathetic, and to most Englishmen the game 'over there' takes fourth place behind rugby union, sheep-shagging and inter-breeding. That view may take a bit of a battering after you read what follows, which just might dispel a few myths about your average football-loving Druid.

* * *

THERE'LL BE BLUEBIRDS OVER . . .

As a follower of Cardiff City over the years, I have suffered more than most having to put up with the shit dished out at every game by the English wankers we come across, week in and week out. Sheep-shaggers, Druid-worshippers, dragon-puffing tosspots, etc. Well, for the record I've never seen a dragon except in the Bristol nightclubs; I've never shagged a sheep because their hooves scrape the skin off your shins (so I'm told); and I don't own a white full-length gown or visit Stonehenge every solstice, so you can fuck off.

Being a Welsh football fan makes me hate the English with a passion. They look upon the Welsh as second-class citizens – poor, thick tossers. Well, we don't get many of your firms coming to Wales trying to turn us over because you know you'll get your arse kicked. One thing that really pisses us off is that you all think rugby is 'the game' in Wales. Well, I'm afraid that's rubbish. If you go out on a Sunday morning into the parks of South Wales, you'll see thousands of boys' clubs and pub teams playing football, not rugby, and you'll also see more League club scouts down here than anywhere else in Britain, that's for sure. The English clubs know that there's a wealth of talent down here and our clubs just can't compete with the money they offer, which is the real reason why the Welsh clubs are struggling to survive.

The Welsh FA do nothing to help this, as they're just another load of twats on a power kick, jobs for the boys and free-ticket-around-the-world scam. The Konica League of Wales is of such a poor standard that the coaching is not good enough to see the players filter through, and if a player wants to better himself he has to travel into England and train with an English non-League side rather than stay here and get nowhere. City would die overnight if we were forced to play in a division that was no better than the ICIS Premier League.

The hatred shown to those in charge after forcing Newport County to play in England (in order to regain their League status through the pyramid system) means that they will never be trusted by the fans in this country. Alun Evans and his tossers put forward the argument that by joining the Konica League, Cardiff City would become the Glasgow Rangers of Wales. Fucking yippee! Look at the Scottish set-up; it's a joke. Crowds are down to 3,500 at some clubs in the Premier League, and the low hundreds in the other divisions. Fuck that. With only five clubs in Wales worth talking about, us, the scum [Swansea], Wrexham, Newport and Merthyr, that will really pack them in, attract the major TV companies and pull in the top players! Would it, bollocks. The City fans wouldn't be welcome at most places anyway for fear of trouble, and what is the point of claiming a Champions League entry if you're going to get stuffed 10–0 by Valletta of Malta in a preliminary round?

When I see the money in the top flight, it makes me sick, yet even the poorest clubs in our division look down on us as the poor relations; the English are so fucking pompous. I'd hate to think what would happen if City were to get back to where we belong. When we drew Manchester City in the FA Cup recently, there were 41,000 requests for tickets, and we were getting crowds of 18,000 for games in the third division recently, which shows that the support base is there. How many could match that? Why no one has taken hold of this club I will never know.

At Cardiff, we have a hardcore ready to fight anyone, and at away games, most of the support we have will, at best, stand and fight if it goes off. At home matches, no one will let another club come and take the piss out of us, no one. With the crowds generally so low now, they need us to be there so there isn't that much the club can do about it, really. When the club does well, the hardcore gets bigger. We're proud of our reputation because whenever we play we look upon Cardiff as representing not only the city but Wales as well. Everybody hates the English here, the Tories in particular, and when the big games are on then the boys turn out. The main groups come from Barry, the Rhondda Valley and the Soul Crew from Caerphilly, but the top mob come from Bridgend. For us the games with Hereford, Exeter, Wolves and Birmingham are always violent, but Bristol City and Plymouth are always going to go off.

We hear so much about Bristol City, but to us they're all that we hate about the English. They've always mouthed off about what they get up to and who they turn over – all very easy when you hide behind a line of police. I remember once they were singing 'Aberfan, Aberfan' – well bad, that is, and that really incensed the Cardiff boys and we caused havoc, fucking good job too. We did them in 1974, 1983 and 1989 big time, and not once have they come to Cardiff and had a go. Typical mouthy English twats! Plymouth are a bit different, they will have a go back; they have some top boys down there and there's a grudging respect for each other. There is a story that some of our lads were nicked down there and found themselves in court. When they came out, some of the Central Element [Argyll's main firm] were waiting for them and took them out for a beer by way of saying fair play for coming down and having a real go! The only clubs I can remember coming down here and having a pop are Chelsea and Portsmouth. Pompey were well up for it with a crew of about 300 ready to go in the city centre. The police just about kept hold of that one as it took us a bit by surprise as well, and we think it was because we had gone down there and smashed up the famous old clock, which gave everyone there the hump.

Cardiff do have a reputation and, in truth, we deserve it and have earned it over the years. We love it and we love kicking the arse of the English. We would really love the Home Internationals to restart, but I don't think that'll happen for a while yet. Still, having said that, the most violent games down here are the derby games with those bastards up the road. You will never witness hatred like that shown between City and those jack bastards. It's not like your Merseyside derby where they all get on. What sort of derby is that? It's like the Third World War down here every time we play, an animal's day out with all the lads who would never go to a normal game turning out. In truth, we take the piss every time as we have the numbers to take that shit-hole over. One thing I will say for them is that they will mob up against us, not like most of your English clubs; they will have a go and, as much as I hate to admit it, have won the odd battle. The trouble in the ground is not just with the jack bastards but with the police as well, because they love beating the shit out of all the local lads. I'm sure they treat it as a stress release, a sort of training thing. The surrounding area has its share of trouble – Neath in particular, where it always goes off. On one occasion a mob from Cardiff went along to the Vetch to take on the scum and Newport, when they were playing each other, rather than take in the home game against Notts County. There is so much pride down here that the opportunity to take on both sets of scum was just too much. The police were tipped off by British Rail so they were all over our lads and the jacks were going frantic apparently. There were only about seventy of our lot; that takes a lot of bottle.

Newport was also a big away-day. There was a famous incident when we wrecked a train and cut down the fencing in the ground. They had been expecting it to go off and had erected these fences just in time and had made a big thing of the fact that we would be penned in and easily controlled. Well, they got that wrong because some of our boys took in wire cutters just to prove they could do it. There was also a big off at a Stone Roses concert between them and us once when the singer put on a City shirt thrown to him by someone in the crowd. The locals didn't like that and a fight broke out.

I've seen City cause trouble at almost every ground in England: Burnley, Blackpool, Peterborough, all over. A fair few will have a go back and I'm sure that it's an English/Welsh thing at times. Cardiff fans are very proud of being Welsh, and they do make up the majority of the national following, even when games are played at the Vetch or the Racecourse Ground. The FA Cup matches with non-League sides are always fun, as the local police have no idea how to handle the trouble. We could wreck the places most of the time if we wanted to.

Probably the only bonus of being a Welsh side is the Welsh FA Cup competition which enables us to qualify for the European Cup-Winners' Cup. Over the years we have had some great trips into Europe; playing up and causing loads of trouble abroad is brilliant. We get the same attitude over there as we do in England, only they don't know what we're capable of. We did find it quite surprising that we were allowed to continue in Europe when the English were banned as we had been known to play up before and at internationals with Wales.

Recently we travelled to Standard Liège in Belgium, which was a great trip. We travelled by car, meeting up with loads of other fans on the ferry, getting pissed and singing our heads off. By the time we left the boat, there were five or six carloads heading for Liège and the first bar we could find. We had just won promotion from the third division and had caused trouble at our first three away games – Fulham, Port Vale and Exeter – and the trip to Belgium was seen as another opportunity to show how good we were. With 2,000 pissed-up Welshmen aged between sixteen and sixty, there was always going to be trouble. The bars were all busy and the Welsh pride and passion was in full force. It's always the best part of any trip abroad: the few hours before the match, getting pissed and singing. We had heard that the locals had a mob called the Hell-Siders, and supposedly a few things had been happening already and a few of the locals in our bar were starting to get a bit touchy. I didn't fancy getting arrested or held before the game so I was just about to leave when this prat whacked one of our boys at the bar. That was it: they got the shit kicked out of them and the bar got smashed to bits, windows, tables, bottles, the lot. As we all ran out the police were on their way in, hitting out with their batons, but we had got out although a few were caught and arrested.

The police were not that happy anyway, due to loads of Welshmen pissing and throwing up in the main street. God only knows what they were expecting, but they had the riot gear on and the water cannons and the dogs were out. As it all went off, the bars emptied and we all mobbed up while the police started to get a bit heavy with loads of pushing and shoving, the usual shit, and herded us together, about 700 pissed-up Welshmen singing our heads off in a foreign country – smart. Word had obviously got out to the locals because within about fifteen minutes a mob of around 200 strong appeared at the top of the street; fair play to them, at least they turned up. We were raring to go by now, they were baiting us but didn't seem to know what to make of our firm. As luck would have it, the police just seemed to clear a path and let us at each other. Now whether they thought we were going to get a hiding or not I don't know but they must have thought the local boys were good enough to take us on and give us a lesson. Big mistake! They were well tooled-up with stones and bottles, but once they let it all go, they were fucked and we steamed into them. We ran those fuckers everywhere, a few stood their ground but they got hammered. It's such a great feeling, that, even better when you're abroad. All this went on for about ten minutes before the police got hold of things. They wanted to get us all in the ground as soon as possible and as we had proved the point we were ready to go. Amazingly, there was more drink inside the ground so we all continued drinking and playing up during the match, just like the old days.

When we got back to England, the press were all over us, calling us 'scum', 'animals', etc, as apparently there had been loads more trouble after the match and what we had seen had only been the tip of the iceberg. They still don't understand that we really don't give a fuck what they write about us. WE DON'T CARE, you tossers, because when we got back to Wales our mates wanted to hear all the info, we told it over and over again and can reminisce about having a great time abroad with hundreds of our countrymen while scaring the shit out of the Belgians.

Chapter 14

Germany

It is obvious to anyone with an interest in football that Germany are one of the main rivals to both England and English supporters. There are, of course, other more obvious factors than football involved when one discusses Britain (rather than England) and the German nation. But without wishing to be dismissive in any way about the two World Wars, we are not really interested in them here beyond their occasional bearing on the way supporters behave. Certainly, the English supporters use these historical thrashings as justification for their aggression. In the context of football, however, the clash between the two nations really dates back to the mid-sixties. The 1966 World Cup final was the start of the England/Germany football rivalry, but as far as football violence is concerned, the first recorded incident between fans from the two nations took place in Hannover in 1965, at a match between Manchester United and Hannover. The British contingent at this game actually mainly consisted of British servicemen stationed in Germany, rather than any travelling support. Although there were incidents involving club sides throughout the seventies and eighties, the main rivalry between the two nations began in Dusseldorf in 1987, when England were beaten 3–1 on the pitch, and there was severe crowd trouble surrounding the stadium.

With English club sides banned from Europe as a result of the Heysel tragedy, the German authorities had taken a high-profile and assertive stance with the England supporters to prove that they would be able to deal with any trouble during the forthcoming European Championships. However, these strong-arm tactics backfired when the English fans were provoked into violence by the behaviour of both the German police and sections of the German support. That rivalry continues to this day, but it is clear to us that, over the years, the German people have found themselves with severe football violence problems of their own. As long ago as 1931, a pitch invasion by fans of Hertha Berlin led to the hospitalisation of an opposition player.

During Euro 88 our own experiences proved to us that there were elements among a number of West German clubs who were more than willing and capable of holding their own, should the need arise. The infamous riot in Hamburg, when the Germans overran the Dutch supporters outside the stadium and in the city centre, remains the worst incident of crowd trouble either of us has ever witnessed. However, while the problem of football violence remained at a pretty constant level in the immediate aftermath of the tournament, one of the bizarre consequences of the end of the Cold War in 1989 is that the problem of football violence in Germany became markedly worse at that point. The unification of East and West Germany after the Berlin Wall came down led to a massive restructuring of the game there as the larger, former East German clubs demanded entry to the Bundesliga. Once the restructuring had been completed, the supporters of former East German clubs were suddenly able to travel freely not just within their own league structure, but also in what was, for them, a whole new country. Clubs such as Dynamo Dresden, Locomotive Leipzig and FC Berlin indulged in some horrific outbreaks of crowd violence on their travels, and they were aided in no small part by the total ineffectuality of the police in former East Germany to deal with crowd disorder.

In late 1990, there was an explosion of violence involving

German fans. On the night that English clubs returned to European competition under the watchful gaze of both UEFA and FIFA, Eintracht Frankfurt supporters rioted in Copenhagen. That same month, supporters of the national side rioted in the capital of Luxembourg before the start of a European Championship qualifier. And just one month later, FC Berlin fans were responsible not only for over £300,000 worth of damage to a train, but also for laying waste to the centre of Rostock. It was about this time that some supporters of German clubs developed a particularly nasty little punishment for any opposing fans they happened to catch hold of. Known simply as 'biting the pavement', it involved forcing the poor sod on to a concrete pavement, where he had to bite the kerb. Someone then stamped on the back of his head. At best, his teeth were smashed; at worst, his jaw shattered. Lovely. The worst incident, however, involved a fixture between FC Berlin and Leipzig. The crowd erupted inside the stadium, and the police effectively lost control. In a bid to establish order among the supporters, some of the police ended up firing into the crowd, killing one and seriously wounding three others. Despite this death, the violence continued. During the European Cup quarter-final against Red Star Belgrade in 1991, supporters of Dynamo Dresden fought running battles with rival fans, forcing the police to use water cannons on the fans inside the ground before the referee abandoned the game. With the match no longer an issue, the trouble moved to the centre of Dresden, where widespread rioting and looting took place, after which UEFA banned Dresden from European competition for two years. However, within months of that incident, nearly 800 German fans were arrested, following street battles before another European Championship qualifier in Belgium.

These were just the well-reported incidents from that period. The German authorities did eventually begin to come to terms with and deal with the problem, but they still have work to do. In August 1995, a group of over 600 hardcore German supporters travelled to Belgium for a friendly fixture between the respective national sides and caused severe disruption. It may have been in revenge for the arrests surrounding the game in 1991, but it was a massive invasion in any case, and one in which over 300 Germans were detained by the Belgian police.

Of course, the spread of the neo-Nazi movement is a big factor in German football violence – and something that makes the rest of us uneasy. While not unique to Germany, this movement is growing, and is possibly stronger there than in any other country which, bearing in mind their history, is not too difficult to understand. The spread of this neo-Nazi skinhead movement is an indication that the game is being used as a platform to spread both the group's political message and the cult of violence. This was never more evident than during the infamous episode of the proposed England vs Germany fixture on the anniversary of Hitler's birthday, in 1994, which we've discussed in detail on page 78. In the top ten ridiculous footballing decisions of all time, this one is right up there with the decision to stage the Dublin fixture and Watford's signing of Kerry Dixon. It is, however, inaccurate if all too easy, to say that all football violence in Germany contains a large right-wing element. It's just that what *is* there is very, very dangerous.

The widespread availability of a huge array of weaponry in Germany make their supporters difficult opponents both to contain and confront. This was made patently clear to all who were watching in Rotterdam in April 1996, when Germany played Holland in a pre-Euro 96 friendly. Quite why this fixture was ever suggested so close to Euro 96 remains a mystery. It was always going to be volatile and difficult to police, despite the reputation the Dutch police enjoy as having possibly the best anti-hooligan intelligence network in Europe and a supposed capability of dealing with any form of crowd disorder. In the event, they were obviously totally unaware and unprepared for the 1,500-strong German mob that landed on their doorstep and caused mayhem. The group, who were mainly from the same club, Fortuna Cologne, fought with police on their arrival and following the Germans' 1–0 victory.

However, the main flashpoint came near the end of the game, when the German fans attempted to break out of their section of the ground using metal barriers to break down the reinforced plastic dividers, causing over £15,000 of damage to the Feyenoord stadium. As the Dutch fans panicked and fled, it took almost 150 Dutch riot police with batons flaying to restore order. At the end of it, two people were in hospital with stab wounds from fights with Dutch fans, and almost fifty had been arrested. It is clear that this was a mob intent on trouble, and that they had engaged in some horrific violence during the day. If the aim of the trip was to turn over the Dutch and boost the Germans' reputation for violence this was done with remarkable success.

Before Euro 96, much was made of the possible threat from German fans coming to the tournament, and there was a lot of hype surrounding certain groups, with German hooligans on the television and in the papers telling everyone what they would get up to. Even the German police got in on the act, spreading fear by warning the ethnic minorities of Manchester that if the Germans could not fight with English fans, they would turn their attentions to them. This was an outrageous statement, but it was also a clear warning that the German mob had to come here or they would never live it down; that's the way football violence works. But despite a few incidents in Manchester, the main bulk of the German mob did not, apparently, have the bottle to cross the Channel and take on the so-called kings of hooliganism. This failure to show was as big a dent to a reputation as there ever could be, and one which they will never live down.

Unfortunately, it didn't stop them playing up at home. On the night of the Euro 96 final, thirty people were arrested in Essen and Dusseldorf after fighting broke out, and vandals smashed windows and looted shops in Herne, while in Berlin police were attacked with bottles. And all after they won!

Chapter 15
Holland

It is widely accepted, although not strictly true, that the birth of football violence involving English fans abroad was at the second leg of the UEFA Cup final between Feyenoord and Tottenham in May 1974. That year the hooligan problem was increasing week by week, and that atmosphere, coupled with the importance of this match, led Spurs fans to riot before, during and after the match (which they lost 2–0), resulting in over 70 arrests and more than 200 injuries. This incident sparked off a number of problems abroad in the seventies involving English fans and left Holland with a legacy it has found difficult to live down. The arrival of large-scale hooliganism left the Dutch game, like its English and German counterparts, riddled with clubs who suddenly found themselves with a violent following of their own. And as in other countries, the hooligan problem persists, despite strenuous work by both the police and the Dutch authorities. Ajax, Feyenoord, Utrecht and PSV Eindhoven are probably the most widely known examples of Dutch clubs with organised firms, but there are others – Den Haag being one. Of all these clubs, the followers of the first three are probably the most dangerous groups among the Dutch supporters, and their exploits are well documented. Ajax supporters have been known to orchestrate outrageous incidents of violence against other clubs, including acts that would never even be considered by most groups in this country, such as placing railway sleepers across train tracks to derail visiting specials, and planting nail bombs. It is also not unknown for the mere threat of crowd disorder to spur the Dutch FA into cancelling fixtures.

This type of cowardly act is one thing, but actual confrontation is quite another. Over the years, Dutch supporters have been involved in many major incidents, both in their domestic game and in European competition. Ajax have the dubious honour of being the first club to give a group of English supporters a real hiding, and this is probably the reason why the English regard them as 'fair game'. The occasion in question again involves Tottenham, who travelled to Amsterdam in 1981 only to be turned over. In the main incident, 60 Spurs fans fought with 200 local youths. There were over 30 arrests (of which 25 were Spurs supporters) and two Englishmen ended up in hospital with stab wounds. Another unfortunate first can be credited to supporters of Feyenoord, who brought Continental hooliganism to Britain when they wrecked the ferries that were taking them to Aberdeen for a UEFA Cup tie in 1987. As a consequence of this, and various other acts at home and abroad involving both Feyenoord and Ajax, the Dutch became for many the most notorious supporters in Europe, a label they were proud to bear.

Certain English elements were sadly more than desperate to remove that label. And an opportunity arose when Holland travelled to Wembley for a pre-European Championship friendly in 1988. But while the English fans may have been primed, the Dutch fans simply failed to turn up. This meant that any confrontation would have to wait until the competition proper; but again, in Dusseldorf, the Dutch didn't show. These incidents reveal that while certain Dutch clubs do have that violent element, the same simply cannot be said of the national side. The organised mobs, so prevalent at England and Germany games, are also absent when the Dutch play, and most games are free of terrace taunting. Of course, Holland games are not completely rosy; it's just that any problems that do arise are often not of their own making. This was clearly demonstrated in Hamburg during Euro 88, when Holland were slaughtered by the Germans, and in October 1993, when England were the visitors for a friendly in Rotterdam, when a record 1,100 English supporters were detained over a three-day period. And as we have already mentioned, in early 1996 the Germans visited Holland for a friendly and went on the rampage with little or no resistance.

Quite why the Dutch national fans adopt this peaceful approach when their club sides have such a bad reputation is unclear, but they tend to adopt a refreshingly humorous, carnivalesque approach when supporting their national side. There are almost always plenty of families among the supporters, with their now-famous orange faces, wigs, clothes, etc, and bands playing on the terracing, all so the fans can enjoy the day rather than indulge in any form of violence. Certainly, there are many fans who would welcome the opportunity to watch England in the 'Oranje' style, as it would be a most welcome addition to our game and would make a change from being treated like animals. The Dutch were a source of major fun during Euro 96, with some of the attire being particularly, well, orange, and some of the hats decidedly strange. (As an aside, the ability of Dutch women to look so beautiful painted orange is a curious feat.) However, the potential for disorder involving Dutch League clubs has always been present, as has the threat of serious repercussions for the clubs themselves. During the 1989–90 UEFA Cup competition, Ajax fans rioted and forced the abandonment of their match with FK Austria, and as a result the club was banned from all European competition for two years. As recently as March 1996, Feyenoord faced the very real threat of their supporters being banned from the Cup-Winners' Cup semi-final against Rapid Vienna after severe crowd trouble inside and outside the ground during their quarter-final tie with Borussia Moenchengladbach. In the event, possibly due to the fear that fans would travel without tickets and cause severe disruption around the stadium, the club were fined only £30,000. This had little real impact as a deterrent: prior to the 1996 European Cup final, Ajax fans went on the offensive and fought running battles with fans of Juventus, resulting in four stabbings and nine arrests.

Chapter 16
Italy

As anyone who has experienced Italian football at first hand will know, Italian fans are among the most passionate in the world. They have good reason to be. Serie A is probably the best-quality football league in the world, even if the English Premier League is the best in terms of entertainment and excitement, and the Italian national team has a record up there with the best. Where there is passion on this level, however, there will at some time or another be violence. And within the Italian game, violence has never been too far away.

As with the British game, incidents of crowd disorder in and around the Italian game date back to the beginning of football itself. It would be easy to list any number of riots and major incidents, but it is the background to the problem as it is now which is the real concern. As the English game has its firms, the Italian game has its Ultras, groups of organised supporters who follow nearly every Italian club. Groups such as the Tiger Commandos and The Red Brigade have aggressive names, but in truth much of the violence surrounding these groups comes from a lunatic fringe, and the Ultras are, to a large degree, no more than supporters' clubs. Where the Italian supporter differs from his English counterpart is in the way he views the Ultra as a way of life. The build-up to games begins in the previous week. The groups meet to decide what songs they will sing and when, which players they will support and which they will abuse. They will also choreograph their movements on the terraces, each playing their part on the day.

But despite the fact that the response on the day is so rehearsed, the violent element is indisputably linked to these groups and has been allowed to develop unmolested, because the clubs are aware that they need this vociferous support both at home and away. The clubs themselves have, in the past, assisted their own expansion by supplying free travel to away games and allowing the use of flares and abusive banners within stadia to help create the atmosphere which is unique to the Italian game. However, the fact that these groups have been allowed to grow unchecked has left the clubs with a major problem: the Ultras are getting too powerful within the domestic game and the clubs simply do not know what to do. Unlike clubs in this country, the Italian clubs know that their supporters are vital to their survival and, as a result, there are a number of cases of Ultras influencing the running of the clubs with the threat of incidents or boycotting of games if things are not done their way. One of the biggest football riots ever seen in Italy took place in Florence, when Roberto Baggio was sold by Fiorentina to their big rivals, Juventus. The fans saw this as proof that their club was becoming second-rate, and as a result over 2,000 local people went on the rampage and over 400 were arrested. While, to many, the mere fact that supporters are able to have a say in the running of their clubs is justification enough for violence or intimidation, it is a very dangerous phenomenon indeed for clubs to be held to ransom with the threat of crowd violence and it is certainly something we would never want to see in this country.

The power that the Italian fans, and in particular the Ultras, have over the game was no more apparent than on 5 February 1995, when not only football but all sport in Italy was suspended following the stabbing of an AC Milan fan in Genoa the previous Sunday. Interestingly enough, the fan was stabbed by a member of Gruppo Barbour, a small group of AC Milan fans who identify themselves by wearing British-made Barbour jackets. This one incident was enough to force the Italian game to say enough is enough and demand an end to the problem. Such was the feeling within the game that even the Ultras themselves began to question their role, and representatives from approximately forty groups met in Genoa in an attempt to put an end to the violence. However, despite the fact that a 'code of conduct' was issued, including the banning of knife fights and unequal street battles, the initiative was lost and the game quickly reverted back to the dark ages. In fact, the 1994–95 season was a particularly rough one for the game in Italy: over 200 police officers suffered injuries at games.

At club level, the Italians have as big a problem as the Germans and the English with trouble at games, and this is due, in no small part, to the fact that they enjoy a large travelling element. In October 1995, there was serious crowd disorder at the Olympic stadium in Rome following Lazio's victory, and forty people were injured and thirty arrested at a third division match between Nocera and Turris the same weekend. In May 1996, Fiorentina were banned from their own stadium for one match after home fans pelted the referee with coins and bottles during a Serie A fixture. Such is the concern in Italy about violence at club level that perimeter fences are seen as a necessary evil, despite the tragedy of Hillsborough.

When Italian clubs take to the European footballing arena their reputation for violence precedes them. But, in truth, and certainly post-Heysel, there are few incidents involving Italian clubs exporting violence abroad. It seems that the Italians see travel with either their clubs or their country as a holiday, and much of their travelling support is, like the Dutch, made up of family groups. Indeed, a number of Italian clubs have formed strong and friendly links with other European sides – for example, Juventus and Den Haag of Holland, Genoa and Barcelona, and Sampdoria and Olympique Marseille – which is excellent, and something English clubs would do well to copy. We have received a number of letters from Italian fans who say that they have little or no time for the national side, and this explains why the crowds for internationals in Italy can be so small. Local fans have even been known to boo the Italian national anthem when they play on home soil – a bit strange, but it does explain why no serious hooligan threat travelled from Italy to England for Euro 96 and there was little or no trouble involving them. This, however, is far from the case when teams travel to Italy, and the history of supporters suffering at the hands of Italian fans is long and bloody. As regards England fans, the record starts in Turin during the 1980 European Championships, an episode which still rankles with many for the appalling way the English fans were treated.

TURIN

What happened in Italy was simple: we gave them what they wanted. I arrived the day before the first match with Belgium and when I got to the campsite the atmosphere was really hostile. I was told that the local boys were burning tents by throwing rags soaked in petrol down on them from the bridge at the side of the camp, and that anyone who complained to the police was just getting battered. The bars and the shops didn't want to know us and the local press were really stoking the thing up, making us out to be animals. Some of the lads that had been there for a few days had been attacked when they went out in small groups and some had even been mugged while the police did fuck all. The English papers were saying nothing and making us out to be just as bad, which really pissed us off because they knew what was really going on.

On the day of the game we were well pissed off. The locals had mobbed up but were total wankers hiding behind the police and doing the off if there was the slightest chance of us getting at each other. Once we were in the ground, the police were even worse. They were letting the wops give it the big one and they loved it.

Then they started themselves and went in to nick a few blokes that were pissed up. Well, we had had enough. Word had gone around that people were ready to go when the time was right and this was it; fuck it, this was what they had wanted so they could have it. Their answer was to fire the teargas at us and then baton charge. So what, as long as we took a few out, it was worth it. I wasn't going to take that shit and the same went for most of the others.

Their 'mob' shit out when it came down to it. The rest of the tournament saw off after off, but we weren't going to do a runner no matter what the numbers were, and that tournament set the reputation of the England fan from that day on as number one. If I go away with England and the people of that country treat us with respect, then that's great, but if the police, the people or the media take the piss and want to play don't expect us to sit back and take it. This is England you are talking about. We don't run.

With England's reputation in tatters, the Italians went largely unpunished and continued to inflict violence on teams who came into their country. There are many instances of teams and their supporters from countries throughout Europe being subjected to intimidation and violence at the hands of Italian fans. Certainly, England fans were provoked into retaliation during that competition to such an extent that they were seen as the aggressors, when in truth, media and political hype, together with a need for self-defence, were far more serious problems. However, given the large-scale problems within the Italian game at domestic level, it is astonishing that neither FIFA nor UEFA seem willing to do much about them when sides travel to Italy for European competitions. Even during the build-up to the 1996 European Cup final in Rome (as near a home fixture as you can get), Juventus fans were involved in serious disturbances with fans of Ajax and yet little was heard in condemnation. Could it be that Serie A, the flagship football league in Europe, is beyond reproach?

On the face of it, the assumption that football violence in one country is much the same as in any other would seem pretty reasonable. After all, there are only so many ways in which two people can fight. Yet this assumption is one of the main reasons why the game is still saddled with this problem, because it proves how little those who run the game understand the hooliganism issue. It is different, in some cases completely different.

Take the Italians as an example. They have a massive problem with the Ultras in Serie A, as they do when the Italian national side play at home, yet when Italy go on their travels, the fans behave. There is no logical reasoning for that – after all the Italians have a reasonably large travelling support, and some of the more volatile fans must travel, so why don't they play up? Similarly the Dutch have terrible problems with their club sides, home and away, and yet with the national side, nothing. They don't even have a problem at home; every game is party time. The Germans are a different kettle of fish altogether; they have a problem at club and international level, both home and away, yet despite all the fears their fans didn't show during Euro 96, which almost certainly destroyed any hope they ever had of taking away the mantle of 'top dogs' from the English. None of it makes any sense, because football violence makes no sense.

For many supporters, USA 94 and Euro 96 gave them their first taste of what football could, and should, be like, because they were both largely trouble-free. The philosophy of supporting enjoyed by the Dutch national fans, the Danes and, to a lesser extent, the Irish, is one that the rest of us should aspire to because, face-painting and extreme costumes aside, that is surely what it should be like for all of us.

PART SIX
The Establishment

Chapter 17

The FA, FIFA And UEFA

For those who don't know, FIFA runs world football. The Federation Internationale de Football Associations holds the ultimate responsibility for the world game, sets the rules and runs the World Cup. UEFA (the Union of European Football Associations) obviously look after the European game, and the European Championship, and is therefore responsible for putting down the sanctions on national governing bodies such as the FA, SFA and so on, when, or if, they step out of line. Their power was shown to all English fans when UEFA banned the country's clubs from European competition after Heysel. It is beyond dispute that this ban was deserved, not just because of that night but because of a catalogue of problems dating back years; but the question of UEFA's attitude to English supporters needs examining. Anyone who knows about the game abroad, and looks at the hooligan issue, knows that many countries have serious problems with their fans, but UEFA rarely act against them in the way they did against us. For example, during the 1995–96 season there were major problems in Spain, Italy, Scotland, Bulgaria, France, Turkey, Holland and Germany, to name just a few, but what serious action did UEFA take in any of those cases? None: it keeps a wary eye on the English game at all times and would probably have slapped a ban on us if things had gone wrong at Euro 96, without any hesitation or remorse.

In England, as we all know, the game is run by the Football Association. Never mind any other body, such as the Premier League or the Football League; the ultimate responsibility for football rests with Lancaster Gate. There is, of course, a great deal of mileage to be made from the argument that many of those within the confines of that fine, and very valuable, building are not fit to hold that responsibility; but on the whole, they do a fairly decent job. That may seem a strange statement for us to make, but remember that supporters think mainly about the professional game but that the FA deal with the whole thing, even down to the Sunday morning pub hackers' worst eleven. With players and managers, they are fine – the odd ridiculous fine or penalty here and there, but nothing drastic, unless your name is Jones. With the professional clubs, however, things are different: to a certain extent (and they can deny it until they're blue in the face, but the evidence is there for all to see), the FA are scared of ordering clubs about. Let's be honest, most clubs are run pretty poorly, as you can tell if you look at the number in financial difficulty, but chairmen do not appreciate being told how to run *their* businesses by anybody. So the FA let them get on with it, until they either get deposed, or go under. In a game which is so money-driven these days, it is surprising that the game's governing body has no direct say in the financial regulation of clubs. And then they wonder why people take bungs and backhanders or, even worse, go mental when fans revolt at what is happening at *their* club. Given the financial clout of many clubs (often now publicly quoted companies listed on the Stock Exchange), it is unlikely that this pattern will alter, though they could surely help some of the smaller clubs by providing advice. However, we believe that the main problem with the FA is that they don't seem to like supporters – and travelling fans, even less. No away fans mean no problems, no policing, no crowd disorder, no local authority problems and no governmental problems. Never mind the fact that it is just those people – us – who fund the game and pay their wages: they don't like us and they seem to believe, in their ultimate fantasy, that the game does not need us. If you do not believe us, ask yourself when was the last time the FA did anything specifically for the benefit of the fans? All-seater stadia were forced on them by the Taylor Report and, anyway, the fans weren't consulted, and many did not want them. The Premier League was driven purely by the top clubs wanting more money rather than by the fans. We're never asked, we're never talked to and, however hard we try, they'll never listen because they know that they do not need to. Those who run football are also safe in the knowledge that, as obsessives, we simply have to go. Football isn't like the cinema; it's compulsive. It's a drug to which addiction is lifelong and because of this the FA know they have us all by the balls.

If the FA thought that they would be able to get away with banning travelling fans they would, because it would probably solve the hooligan problem at a stroke. Similarly, if they thought they would get away with pay-per-view, they would. But the dream for the FA, and certainly the Premier League, seems to be to have every game screened live into front rooms. They don't care about supporters because they don't understand us. Have either Graham Kelly or Sir Bert ever travelled to Scarborough to watch a crap game on a wet Tuesday night using money they've slogged for all week and knowing they've got to be back at work in the morning? You bet your arse they haven't. But we do, thousands of us, and we pay for the privilege and allow ourselves to be treated like shit and taken for granted without any redress, because there is no one to complain to. That commitment and passion is something they don't understand, or try to make allowances for, which is why so many fixtures are inconveniently scheduled. You could perhaps contact your club, but there's no solution to gaining redress for an England game. You could write to the FA, and they may even write back, but it'll almost certainly be the most patronising letter you've ever received, and will offer no solution or apology. The only real way you can ever hope to get any response from the football world is to ring

David Mellor on *Six-O-Six* and hope that he will take up the case, which is exactly what he has done on a number of occasions, particularly in the cases of fans treated badly when abroad. For the governing body of the most popular sport in this country to offer no real liaison with supporters is an outrage.

This is due in no small part to the fact that the FA do not really understand the average supporter, and haven't the slightest clue about the hooligan issue. Do you honestly think that the 'suits' at Lancaster Gate have any idea why the Stoke Naughty Forty or the Plymouth Central Element behave as they do? If they did, do you think that the problem would still exist? As we have said before, the key to the hooligan issue is understanding it, and both the FA and the police fail miserably at this because to understand it they would have to talk to the fans, and that seems to be a nonstarter.

The FA get more than the hooligan issue wrong. For years it has allowed the supporters to be bled dry at every opportunity, something that was never more obvious than during the build-up to Euro 96. Here we were, handed the greatest opportunity to build on the game in this country ever available, and the FA almost blew it. Never mind 1966 and all that – that was thirty years ago, and, despite the fact that there are those within Lancaster Gate who can still remember it as if it were yesterday, it's history. The game and the way it is watched are totally different today. The truth is that Euro 96 was a success because the majority of supporters in England wanted it to be. The normally staid English began to adopt that carnival approach to their national team in the same way as the Dutch and the Danes, even if some of the more ridiculous wigs were a bit much. People who were previously indifferent to the game suddenly discovered its attraction and, as a result, the tournament, despite some very lacklustre games, was a massive success. However, it so nearly all went wrong.

One of the major problems surrounded ticket allocation. To serve the average bloke, tickets were made available for

Euro 96 by the FA years in advance to ensure that the 'true' England fans would, and could, get their full allocation – not to mention ensuring that the revenue would start coming in quite early. The first problem arose because whoever set the price structure for games got it wrong. The tickets were simply too expensive. A number of key FA personnel and football pundits, who spent the entire tournament moaning about empty seats as if it were the fans' fault, obviously missed the detail of expense. I doubt that many of those working for TV, radio or papers had the remotest idea of how costly tickets were because they rarely, if ever, have to buy them. The strict allocation methods adopted by the FA to deter hooligans meant that many fans had more chance of winning the lottery than getting tickets, while those who did qualify bought up their entire allocation, in the surefire knowledge that they would be able to unload them at a profit should the need arise. But to follow this course you had to assume that the fans could afford tickets or would buy them that far in advance and, as we all know, this was not the case: the real rush only started once the draw had been made. The problem was that by then, for many, it was too late, and the England games in particular had been all but sold out. However, while the sold-out notices were being put up and the FA were busy crowing that the tournament would be a massive commercial success, the fans quickly realised that despite their supporting the game for years, not all the tickets would be coming their way. Given the atmosphere and the spectacle provided by the crowds at Wembley, this seems an odd statement; but it is a fact. A great many of the people present at England matches were at their very first football game, and many more were there for free; but many who attend games on a weekly basis had no chance.

Before the Germany game, the two of us spent some time walking up and down Wembley Way. One of the more interesting sights was the hundreds of people with their corporate folders, trying to find out where they had to go, intermingled with a large number of Japanese tourists in England shirts, also on their way in to the stadium. The gnashing of teeth from fans without tickets was almost drowning out the singing. All the major sponsors were given a ticket allocation as part of their contract and, in the case of one high-street bank, that was rumoured to be in four figures for England matches. The sponsors then offered these tickets to staff, as sweeteners for major clients or, even worse, as prizes in competitions. Customers of the credit card company who sponsored the tournament were even sent a letter offering them the chance to buy tickets with their monthly statement. A huge number of tickets were also given to clubs and regional football associations all over England as well as to the three branches of the Armed Forces.

The FA had made it clear from the outset that they would only sanction corporate packages offered through two of the more reputable agencies, but the failure of that policy was never more evident than when the police raided a number of ticket agencies throughout London and seized both tickets and people in Operation Potent. The resignation of the man responsible for the ticket distribution caused more problems for the FA, who by now were seriously concerned about the ultimate ownership of many of these tickets. However, the corporate side of football was, and remains, a major factor in the removal of tickets from the hands of the average fans, so that the Germany game was watched by approximately 14,000 people who got tickets in this way, often for free.

Of course, every country coming to the tournament was given an allocation of their own, but only in a few cases were all these tickets actually sold. In the case of a number of countries, in particular those from the former Eastern Bloc, a fair number of those tickets were never returned to the FA, yet remained unsold – one of the reasons why there were great expanses of empty seats at a number of games, despite the fact that the FA was telling everyone that the games were all but sold out. However, many of those tickets found their way back across the Channel and into the hands of touts rather than into the hands of real fans, simply because someone, somewhere wanted to make a bit on the side. And once a ticket lands in the hands of a tout, who knows where it will end up? Even the plans to deter hooligans from buying tickets went wrong. Right from the outset, the FA, together with the police, had made great play of the fact that segregation and security would go hand-in-hand during this tournament, and it set about ensuring that the allocation of tickets to supporters who applied to Lancaster Gate were vetted as far as possible to ensure that the recipients were not major troublemakers. However, what it did not allow for were all the cock-ups we've listed, surrounding the prizes, the overseas allocation, the corporate freebies and the fact that the touts had more tickets than they knew what to do with.

So by the time the tournament started, the segregation plans were almost in ruins. Nor was that all. A further problem occurred when the England team managed to negotiate the early stages and made it through to the game against Spain. After telling everyone that any spare tickets would go on sale the next morning, people from all over the country, including some from as far as Newcastle, travelled to Wembley to queue up in the hope of getting their hands on one. What the FA failed to do was to make it clear that these tickets would be on sale only over the phone to ensure that they would be allocated fairly. Quite how fair it is when someone travels overnight from Newcastle and fails to get a ticket, while his neighbour has a lie-in, makes a call and gets four, is beyond me.

Another flaw in the FA master-plan was their aim of making a financial profit from the tournament. Despite the fact that it is rare for any major international sporting event to make money for the host nation, the FA were determined to buck the trend, and so set out on a course of commercialisation to drag in money in the hope of reaching a £1.5 million profit. However, when the ticket farce ensured that security for the tournament would have to be stepped up to combat the increased threat from the hooligans as a result of the breakdown in segregation, the possibility of any operating profit vanished.

The financial side of the tournament is interesting because, while many of us believed at first that the various commercial deals had been struck by the FA, it was actually UEFA, as owners of the tournament, who were responsible for the wheeling and dealing. It was also UEFA, together with the British government, who were the real winners of Euro 96. The FA eventually broke even, largely as a result of the prize money won by the England team making the semi-finals, but the government took a share of every single pound spent during this tournament, from ticket sales to hotel bookings – even fuel to travel to games. The government will have made an estimated £64 million from Euro 96 in VAT, income tax and corporation tax, and it has spent practically nothing, though there was a small contribution from the National Heritage department. Even the policing, usually a major drain, was paid for by the FA and the local authorities, who staged games for which, as always, the council tax-payer footed the bill.

UEFA did well out of Euro 96, too. Although they paid out an estimated £40 million in prize money, they auctioned the television rights for around £50 million and the sponsorship rights for approximately £27 million. Their total profits would be in the region of £30 million.

UEFA sold the sponsorship rights to a company called ISL, who then sold them on to eleven separate corporations – including Vauxhall, McDonald's and Coca-Cola – for £3.5 million a throw, giving ISL a rumoured profit of £11.5 million. This gave these companies the right to display the Euro 96 logo on their products, as well as acquire a big block of tickets to give away. The merchandising rights were sold to another company, who in turn hawked them on to over 100 manufacturers who marketed approximately 1,000 different products, ranging from ballpoint pens to baseball caps. It is also worth noting that UEFA took a cut out of everything bearing the Euro 96 logo.

There were other big winners, of course. The brewers made a killing with promotions at pubs and off-licences, ensuring that the public spent in droves. Umbro inevitably did pretty well out of the tournament, as sales of replica shirts (even the horrific grey thing) and training kits left profit margins soaring. The fact that Umbro also supply kit for the Scottish side didn't do them any harm, either. Tee-shirt manufacturers made a bloody fortune, as anyone who walked down Wembley Way can tell you; and even the flag makers saw a massive hike in sales. Similarly, the bookies are on record as saying that the tournament drew a record £80 million in various bets which, if nothing else, proves that people have still not realised that the bookie never loses.

The amounts involved overall are staggering, and even a bit scary if your own club is about to go under; but they are worth looking at to see how much money is flying around the game these days.

Money wasn't the only factor in the Euro 96 fiasco. The FA was also involved in the entertainment laid on in the host cities, and this was another area for which they suffered a great deal of criticism. The problem arose when the host cities found that the money the FA had promised for staging these events failed to materialise. In Nottingham, the promise of approximately £100,000 led the city authorities to plan a fantastic array of events for fans who stayed there, but the mere £12,000 that arrived meant that either the local taxpayer would foot the bill, or the events would have to be cancelled. After the FA denied promising any money, Nottingham Council took the latter option. The goodwill of the locals and the visiting fans ensured that things went well, but in many cases it was a bit hit and miss.

Even the opening ceremony was marred. Although the FA spent in the region of £400,000, this is a pittance in comparison to the cost of similar events, and a great many favours were called in to ensure things went well. The RAF certainly provided the services of the Red Arrows on the cheap, as did the Red Devils parachute team, while Mick Hucknall is rumoured to have performed at the expense of his own record company rather than Lancaster Gate. Not the best way to do things when some 400 million people are going to tune in and watch it all on the telly.

It would be easy to pick holes in everything the FA did in Euro 96, but that would be unfair because the tournament itself was a huge success. However, much of that was down to the goodwill of fans and the success of El Tel and his boys. If the fans had played up, as was feared, or the team had gone out in the early stages, things would almost certainly have been very different indeed. The fans, in fact, participated in the festival approach to the whole event that had been adopted nationally. This helped, along with the fact that the overseas mobs bottled out, and that there was a great deal of work going on behind the scenes to discourage the hooligan element. It is also important to stress that while we are happy to have a pop at the FA, the government missed an opportunity to do a lot of good for Britain: while England were the hosts, the whole nation was in the shop window. As we have seen already, the Tories were firmly placed in a no-lose situation with the tournament, and they should have had the foresight to commit money to ensure that things were perfect, rather than leave it to the FA and hope. Football did, after all, provide much of the nation with that elusive feelgood factor in the summer of 1996, and no one would have minded if that had been exploited abroad. After all, the government took full advantage when the team were in the Far East at the same time as a trade mission. If the FA hoped to land the 2006 World Cup, they should have worked even harder to make sure the chance was taken.

Chapter 18

The Police

Among sports, football has a feature which is totally unique, not just in Britain – although it is more prevalent here than anywhere else – but across the world, which many in this country, including the clubs themselves, take it very much for granted. It is that football enjoys a huge level of travelling support. Within the confines of our little island, every Saturday (or Monday or Tuesday, etc, thanks to the demands of television), literally thousands of people will travel throughout Britain to watch their own particular team play, be it at home or away. And of course, the visiting fans contribute to that unique matchday atmosphere. We have a deep respect for visiting supporters and we love travelling to other grounds, for the simple reason that, for us, it's all part of being a football fan. Sadly, there are two factions who are intent on putting that simple pleasure beyond reach: the hooligan element and the police. We have looked in detail at the effect of the hooligan element already, but the police are something else, present at games purely as a reaction to the presence of the other. The legacy of the seventies and eighties is never more evident than when a vanload of 'constables' equipped with body armour are sitting outside your local ground staring at you, tapping their batons on their Doc Martens and swinging their crash helmets from their leather-gloved hands. The general public has a long memory and insists, quite rightly, that they be there, but there is more to the old bill and their relationship with football than meets the eye. Before we look too closely at law enforcement in this country, however, we need to examine the way in which the English fan can expect to be treated when he crosses the Channel. There can be a marked variation in the performance of plods as you traverse Europe and beyond.

As anyone who has travelled abroad will know only too well, English football fans are not often the most welcomed of tourists. It would be easy to condemn the police forces of nations throughout Europe for the way they treat us when we come to town, but things take on a different perspective when you look at it from their point of view.

First, in view of the English fan's history, their presence – and attitude – are hardly surprising. Most countries also have their own problems with football hooligans, and tend to deal with them in a particular way. They know who they are, what they look like and what they will almost certainly get up to and, more importantly, they know what they, as the representatives of the law of that nation, can and cannot get away with. They practise their tactics week in, week out; the fans get to know and understand them; and, as with all footballing nations, the uneasy peace that surrounds football fandom descends, only rarely exploding into a major incident of crowd disorder.

Then, England or an English club come to town. It may be a friendly fixture, in which case the chances are that only a few English fans will travel. But it may be a full international or even a major cup competition, in which case the whole occasion will take on a very different significance. The local press will ensure that the anticipation of a home victory will be huge, but more relevant to us is that they will inevitably, at some time or another, focus on English fans and their historical potential for disorder. By the time this happens, the police will have been in contact with their English counterparts to gather intelligence on known hooligans likely to travel and will put into operation their well-oiled anti-hooligan operation. Or perhaps this country has had experience of English fans in the past, or their own fans will announce their intention of taking on the English fans, or they have an anti-English sentiment within their own culture – in which case the situation will be very different. The locals may well want, or in extreme cases, expect the local police to treat any English fan like scum and beat them senseless at the slightest hint of trouble, or just deport the lot *en masse*. Never mind the fact that in general, the behaviour of English fans abroad has improved in recent years; the fact remains that for the host nation, the impending arrival of the English supporters, still widely regarded as the lepers of Europe, will be a one-off visit and, as such, the local population will be right behind anything that protects them.

After all, who cares if the police batter a few hooligans senseless? As long as they keep the locals safe, it's all right. It may well be that the police want to test themselves against the so-called best and be seen to have done a good job, or they may even just want to bust a few heads, in the surefire knowledge that no one will complain about it and the local fans will back them all the way. There is also the chance that the local police may give the local fans the opportunity to have a pop at the English, knowing only too well that they, as a law enforcement agency, cannot lose because they will simply go in and clean up the mess, all the while discreetly ignoring the locals, of course. This brings into play the element of provocation so evident and well known to any English travelling group of fans. And as we all know only too well, the English will not run from a fight abroad no matter who it is with. In short, the local police know that if things get out of hand at any stage, they can get away with almost anything if they feel like it.

There are, of course, many other factors involved which can come into play and inflame any given situation involving fans abroad. The use of the military to police games is the norm in many countries; and the military, unsurprisingly, do not mess about. Indeed, in many countries, they positively relish the chance to batter a few people with absolutely no chance of anyone complaining. There is also a strong possibility that many of the police or military on duty will be football fans themselves, and if you see your favourite or even national team get beaten, you tend to get a bit pissed off, particularly when the visiting fans get loud. Of course, some police forces, just like some countries, are worse than others, and anyone who travels regularly will have their own experiences, both good and bad. And the ultimate awful encounter? It simply has to be Manchester United's infamous visit to Turkey.

The circumstances surrounding the game are these. In November 1993, Manchester United travelled to Turkey for a European Cup tie against Galatasaray. The Turkish media, not known for its tolerance of anything English, launched into a blaze of anti-English incitement, calling all Englishmen 'barbarians' and printing inflammatory articles about both Hillsborough and Heysel (both well known for their links with Manchester, of course). This press campaign whipped the Turkish fans into a hysterical frenzy, and made it known that the United fans could not expect much in the way of a warm welcome from them which, as it turned out, was something of an understatement. The Turkish police had obviously caught a dose of this frenzy because they arrested people indiscriminately before, during and after the game including, among others, a seventy-one-year-old pensioner. Other incidents of mistreatment included a fifty-one-year-old deaf woman who was detained and made fun of by police, while a local taxi driver deliberately took a disabled fan to the wrong stadium and dumped both him and his helper there. Indeed, such was the level of abuse and provocation, and the total lack of help and protection from the police, that many United fans felt it would be safer to watch the game in their hotel and simply stayed there. Those that did make it onto the coaches were bombarded with rocks and coins, some allegedly thrown by policemen, and on their way into the ground, many

Manchester United fans allegedly had money and belongings stolen while they were being searched. When they were in they were confronted not only by the infamous 'Welcome to Hell' banner, but also by a coffin draped in United colours, and they were constantly bombarded with stones and sticks throughout the game. That was bad enough, but many of the United fans didn't even make it to the ground: some had been put into a van during the afternoon and told they were being taken to the ground, but were in fact taken to the airport and deported.

The game itself was a farce. Eric Cantona called the referee a cheat and had a ruck with the police in the tunnel, and Bryan Robson was struck by another policeman. Meanwhile, back in Istanbul, a mob of Turkish fans laid siege to the Tamsa Hotel, where many United fans were staying, with the result that the police came in again and deported everyone they could lay their hands on – a total of 217 fans – while another six were held in prison. These six were later released and tried in their absence for a variety of offences which, considering they had come under attack and were basically scared shitless, wasn't a very good example of the Turkish legal system. The British media went berserk, not only at the treatment of English citizens abroad, but also at the fact that the British Consulate had been conspicuous by their absence. UEFA banned Eric Cantona for four games but did nothing about the Turkish authorities or the police, and neither was any real complaint made to the Turkish government by their opposite numbers in Westminster. Strange, that.

Galatasaray was almost unique because of the level of provocation by everybody in Istanbul, but many incidents involving England or English fans abroad involve provocation or very aggressive policing and the sad reality is that nothing has ever been done to redress the situation. It would be naive to say that certain groups of English fans do not deserve some of the things that come their way, but it is almost certain that, given a more tolerant approach to policing, many incidents would be avoided – as was proven by the German police during Euro 88. Police intelligence may be one thing, but a little common sense would solve more problems than it causes.

Of course, the English police do not have these problems. With very few exceptions, no one ever comes here with the slightest intention of causing trouble. If you look back to the build-up for Euro 96, you will remember that the Dutch, Germans, Portuguese, French, and so on were all on the television or in the papers saying how they were coming for the English to teach us a lesson once and for all. Did they come? Did they bollocks: they were scared shitless, and with very good reason. However, the British police and their methods to counter the hooligans are worth looking at because they are probably the best in the world at dealing with this problem. They have had a lot of practice.

Now we are not naive enough to say that the police are all complete bastards at football, but during our footballing lives, and while researching this book, we rarely heard anything in the way of compliments for the boys in blue. From the travelling supporter's point of view, be they male, female, young, old, black or white, the police come out of things pretty badly. First, though, we need to take a long, hard look at the policing of football in this country and some of the background to the problems faced by all sides.

Anyone who travels regularly to watch football will know that there are certain police forces whose officers are more zealous in their treatment of supporters than others, just as we all know which police forces will put up with what and more importantly, what they will not put up with. The reason for this is that the police perform very inconsistently at football. At some grounds you will be arrested for singing or chanting; at others, you won't. At some you will be thrown out if caught in the wrong part of the ground; at others, you will be taken round to be with your mates. Similarly, the hooligan elements know that certain police forces will arrest you if you play up during games, while others will just eject you. In some areas, policemen have even been known to give people a good kicking rather than arrest them, while others will just escort you out of town if you play up. The inconsistency isn't all. To a certain extent, the average copper on the beat loves football because they get loads of overtime and possibly the chance to see a game for nothing and, if they're lucky, a chance for a fight which, to be brutally honest, they can't lose. Furthermore, on all but the rarest of occasions, there is no chance anyone will ever complain about them because fans are so used to being treated badly.

It is, however, important to acknowledge that the police presence at football is down to us and people like us. If people didn't fight at football, there would be no need for the police to be there: it really is as simple as that. The good old days when 'there used to be nearly 30,000 people here every Saturday and only two coppers' could, just possibly, return. And while the police have to be ready to deal with public order offences at football, these are vastly different from the ones they face whenever there are major gatherings or demonstrations anywhere else. For example, during the miners' strike, the poll tax riots and the marches against the criminal justice bill, the assembled mobs travelled and were ready to fight the police head-on; but at football, the mobs want to fight each other and the police are there to prevent that. Fans do, of course, fight with the police, as everyone knows; but in most cases that is because there is no real opposition from the other fans and the police are all over them – and therefore a ready-made target. The mobs do not go to football tooled up and looking to fight with the police instead of the opposing mob, and therefore the police are under no direct threat and, in truth, their main role at football remains as a deterrent. However, the police love football: it gives them the chance to be highly visible and effective, and it is a very cheap training method for crowd control procedures. The game also gives the police the chance to wield a bit of power by dictating kick-off times, pub opening hours and so on, as well as enabling them to justify the installation of CCTV cameras everywhere they can get them.

Similarly, the mere threat of football violence is enough to make the government, and particularly the Home Secretary, sanction any legislation put before it. It has also been suggested that the police are able to get anything past the Home Secretary in the battle against the hooligan element, and the spate of dawn raids on fans (remarkably well filmed by the accompanying television cameras for the six o'clock news) during the build-up to Euro 96 were evidence of this.

Undercover officers and infiltration operations are two other things that the police make great play of, but everyone involved with football violence knows they are a complete waste of time. Despite what was seen in the film *ID*, you simply cannot infiltrate a football firm in that way: it takes years and years to work and earn your way into any group, and when the police have tried it, they have come unstuck. For example, the Sheffield United firm, the Blades Business Crew or BBC, sussed the police, inventing a leader whom the police actually went looking for. Similarly, other groups have fed the undercover officers totally false information for months before the police realised what was happening and pulled out. But they still make great play of their intelligence network, and for what reason? In truth, the only real weapons they have are closed-circuit television and the hooligan hotline – basically a channel through which people grass – and there is no real evidence that they use that information in any positive way. After the Dublin incident, much was made of the hooligan hotline and the number of calls received, but what happened to this information? During our research into both our books, we never heard of the hotline leading to one concrete conviction, which must say something. However, while the police happily carried on the policing of football without any real effort to solve the hooligan issue, that issue was suddenly thrust in to the limelight when Euro 96 was awarded to the FA. Certainly, the police felt that the eyes of the footballing world would be upon them, and after a season during which football violence in and around grounds suffered an increase, the police knew that they had a job on their hands during the build-up to the tournament. Looking back, as we can now, Euro 96 was apparently a massive success for the police in this country, and will certainly be hailed as such. For many, the £20,000,000 operation involving around 10,000 officers did what it was supposed to do: it kept the peace in and around the host venues. However, in our opinion the police were simply lucky, and we tend to believe that the lack of violence in and around the tournament was due to a number of other factors.

During the build-up to Euro 96, the papers were full of features telling the public at large that all manner of mobs were coming over here to take on the English at their own game. These 'stories' were usually totally fabricated but were, for obvious reasons of public confidence, countered by the police, who trotted out the usual line that they were in constant touch with their colleagues across the Channel and they had it all covered . . . There were real hooligan threats, of course, most obviously from the Scots and the Germans, but there was also concern about the groups from Italy and Turkey, for example, and the possibilities for violence among the citizens of the competing countries who are resident in England. The ticket fiasco, which we've discussed at length, certainly caused a number of further worries for the police, and there were other, far more dangerous, threats from terrorist organisations such as the IRA and the French extremists, the GIA. Similarly, the presence of right-wing extremist groups from both Britain and Europe were cause for unease, as was the fact that the left-wing anti-Nazi groups were apparently eager to sort out their opposite numbers once and for all.

While certain officers at the National Criminal Intelligence Service (NCIS) were busy with the potential importation of problems from abroad and political concerns, others were involved on a more pressing matter: the last few weekends of the domestic season had seen some serious outbreaks of hooliganism at games. Leaving aside the pitch invasion at Brighton, which in any case didn't really involve violence, there were major problems at Hull City. Here, an organised demonstration against the board after they handed the home stand over to visiting Bradford supporters deteriorated into violent confrontation against visiting fans, both on the pitch and outside the ground. It also went off at Ipswich where Millwall were the visitors, at Coventry during the Leeds match, and at Portsmouth–Huddersfield, where those fighting on the pitch included a bloke with a young kid actually sitting on his shoulders as he swapped a few right-handers. There were also violent incidents at the play-off matches. The Blackpool–Bradford game is one example; there were two pitch invasions and twelve arrests. Even the play-off finals were marred by the tragic death of a Plymouth fan, who was seemingly killed by another Plymouth supporter on the Wembley concourse. But one of the more important incidents, from our point of view, was the outbreak of violence in and around the centre of Newcastle on 5 May 1996. For those who do not remember this incident, it centred around the simple fact that Newcastle had failed to win the championship. That evening, hordes of Newcastle fans spilled onto the city streets to celebrate their season, finally congregating in the Bigg Street market area. Within this element were a number, rumoured to be in the region of 200, who were planning to ambush Sunderland fans returning from their game against Tranmere. But the police had got wind of this plan, and set out to move them on. It was not to be as simple as that: the violence that followed resulted in two policemen put in hospital, and three police vans damaged. And it spread – in Bigg Street, around 800 fans left a trail of destruction behind them, including smashed windscreens, looted shops and all-but-destroyed public lavatories.

The bonus for the police, apart from twenty-nine arrests on the night, was the fact that it had all been captured on closed-circuit television. Within days, the media was full of pictures of those involved and Operation Harvest was soon in full swing. The police, in their attempt to press home the value of closed-circuit television and make their point as powerfully as possible prior to Euro 96, continued their offensive, publishing photographs in the local press and then rounding up the Newcastle mob called the Gremlins in what they called 'a major initiative against the hooligans'. This operation was closely followed by dawn raids, prompted by closed-circuit television photos from the recent Arsenal–Spurs game, on addresses in London, which resulted in six arrests. The FA, of course, were delighted: the police were putting on a real show of force against the hooligan elements, and issuing statement after statement along the lines of 'no stone will be left unturned'. But while we watched all this unfolding, two things didn't add. The first was that the police were obtaining massive media coverage of it all, and in the case of the dawn raids, the film crews were actually there at the point when the doors were kicked in, but for relatively few arrests. Great play was also made of the weaponry seized during these attacks, which is fair enough; but why go on about the books and videos? After all, you can get those from the local library. And as for having tickets for games, that was ridiculous. What is strange about a football fan having a ticket for a football match? The second problem with all of this is that for years the FA have vehemently denied that violence away from the ground is anything to do with them, and yet they quickly came out and supported the police during and following the Newcastle incident. The police did, however, succeed in sending a message of sorts, and certainly the raid in Walsall, where they seized fifty CS gas canisters, was definitely a resounding success.

To counter the obvious worries surrounding Euro 96, the police had at their disposal a number of very useful initiatives and weapons. Following some behind-the-scenes lobbying by the Home Secretary, they now had, for the first time, the full cooperation of all the European countries, which meant that the swapping of intelligence was supposed to be guaranteed. This was rightly applauded as a major step forward, but it was then announced that neither Germany, Switzerland nor Holland would be able to send information about their citizens, due to their respective data protection acts. Despite this hitch, all the police forces of the other European countries made it plain that they would send spotters with their own fans and do their utmost to point them out to the police in this country for them to deal with. And the government made it clear that they would prosecute any offenders, whatever their nationality, in this country, and would make an example of them. These plans were all fine in principle, but the real weapon was the intelligence available to the actual officer on the ground because it was, apparently, considerable.

NCIS, right from the start, made it widely known that they had a database of 6,000 known hooligans at their disposal, including 400 ringleaders. Using a new tool, the 'photophone', they would be able to flash photographs of troublemakers and suspects around the country as well as to the central coordinating centre at Scotland Yard. They would then be able to feed back information on the suspect, including their previous record, fingerprints and even links with known gangs, as well as any warnings for the officers at the sharp end if they were needed. If nothing else, the so-called iron fist in a velvet glove would have a very sweaty palm.

The police had also been busy in other ways, involved in a massive intelligence-gathering operation whereby they had infiltrated pubs, clubs, snooker halls and so on to get information on known troublemakers and people they were seen with. As a result, the police knew where they were, who they were with and, in many cases, what they were planning. These officers were then utilised as spotters during the tournament to pick troublemakers out for special observation. This included the utilisation of a fairly simple, very effective, tactic: plonking two uniformed plods right next to the hooligans to make it plain that they had been seen and would be watched. It also became clear quite quickly that what intelligence the police did gather on organised violence was used in the best way possible. In a number of cases, buses were stopped and the occupants detained, sometimes for many hours, and released only when they could not reach their destination in time. This approach was used in a number of locations, including Barnsley, Darlington and Norfolk.

During the tournament the police also used photographers who ran around dressed like SAS soldiers and protected by up to six plods. A photographer would point out a target in the street, who would be pulled out, searched, questioned and then photographed. The aim, obviously, was to keep track of known faces and where they were seen, but this tactic almost backfired in a big way because it succeeded in seriously pissing people off. Dougie certainly has a vested interest here; he was pulled and photographed almost every time he went to a game and was getting extremely annoyed, not just at the attitude of the officers dealing with him but also at the obvious failure of so-called police intelligence.

ON THE TOWN

On the night of the Dutch game, the two of us were wandering around the West End soaking up the atmosphere and having a laugh on the back of probably the best England performance for years.

By about ten, the law had already pulled, searched and photographed me once, but by then I was so used to it, it was no more than an irritation. However, about an hour later, we were having a last walk around the West End before getting the tube home. The place was crammed with people and, as we walked along, the photographer and his mates walked round the corner and up the road towards us. As soon as we saw them we split up and they walked right between us, but about thirty seconds later, the cry went up 'the bloke in the green baseball cap', which, I quickly realised, was me.

Without looking round, my pace quickened but the long arm of the law grabbed me, spun me round and I found myself surrounded by five or six policemen and was told in no uncertain terms that I was to be searched. My pockets were emptied, not by me I should add, and my wallet searched during which time, the copper found one of my business cards. To his obvious delight, he exclaimed: 'Ah! A calling card!' When I pointed out that I would hardly have a calling card with my name, phone number and address on, he became even more of an arse than he had been before.

At this point, I was spun round and came face-to-face with my old mate and his camera who, up to that point, had been notable by his absence. Now usually, as I have said, this wouldn't have bothered me because the police had always taken me to one side or up an alley out of the way, but this lot searched me right in the middle of the road, with people sat at tables outside restaurants looking on in amusement and I lost my rag. 'For fuck's sake, how many pictures of me do you bastards want?' I was warned that if I swore at an officer again, I would be arrested. I then asked the photographer why he wanted my picture again when he had taken it only about an hour earlier. But again the only response was to be careful about my language.

They then went into the old 'What are you doing in London?', 'Where do we know you from?' routine to which I gave the usual answers and was then told to leave London unless I wanted trouble. At this point, as they had found nothing and totally humiliated me, I took out my notepad and asked the officer in charge for his number. 'Why do you want that?' he asked. When I told him that I wanted it for future reference because I was a writer and was doing a piece on police behaviour during the tournament, his whole attitude changed. He obviously thought I was taking the piss but couldn't take the risk and for the first time, the word 'sir' became involved in the conversation. I was then told to carry on and 'enjoy the evening', but by then I was not in the best of moods. After all, if someone has written a bestselling book about football violence, with their photo on the back cover, as well as having been on loads of television programmes talking about the subject, you would have thought that the police, with all their highly publicised so-called 'intelligence' would have realised at some point during the tournament who I was and what I was doing.

We have heard of other people who were stopped up to twelve times in this way. Quite what happened to these photographs is unclear, but it is almost certain that they ended up on a noticeboard in a briefing room somewhere, and will almost certainly cause those individuals problems when and if, they attempt to travel abroad with the national, or even their own, side. However, no matter how good the intelligence was, the most effective tactic the police had was to adopt as high a profile as possible and flood the area to deter any trouble-makers and show that they were as ready as could be. Privately, though, a number of officers admitted to us that they were concerned that they had not covered all eventual-ities and would not be able to contain things, should it go really manic. Others freely admitted that they were shitting it at the thought of a Saturday night in the West End.

Now as you may know, the two of us are southerners. That isn't an excuse or an apology, but it is the reason why we will, for a while at least, concentrate on what happened in and around London during Euro 96. There are of course a number of other and equally valid reasons why the capital city was the obvious place to be, including the fact that England play there and the place would be a magnet for most visiting supporters. We have to say that for the two of us, who spent almost every night in and around the West End, London was simply superb. The pubs were packed full of fans from all over the place talking football. However, we were convinced that if it was going to go off in a big way, it would go off in London. And, judging by the number of policemen around, that was pretty much their thinking as well.

Come the opening game with Switzerland, the place to be was The Globe opposite Baker Street Station, where it seemed that a number of known faces and groups had taken residence. The police, of course, were in a bit of a frenzy: they really had no idea what would happen in and around Wembley but, as we all know, it was all pretty quiet – hardly a surprise, bearing in mind the opposition. Following the game, groups of Swiss fans gathered in Leicester Square, near the self-declared neutrality of the Swiss Airlines building, and began drinking in the bar there. They were joined by a good few English lads, including the two of us and many of those who had been at The Globe. All was fine, until the police, with the photographer in tow, arrived to piss everyone off. I cannot imagine who ordered two policemen to walk into the middle of the seating area outside the bar and just stand there, but it was a provocative and needless thing to do. They were merely left looking stupid and pointless, but this was an indication of what was to come.

England's next game was, of course, the big one: Scotland. For the police, this was a category C+ game (ie. one in which they expected many serious troublemakers to turn up), and they had gone on record warning the fans of repercussions, should anything happen; but no one had really listened because by then, anyone up for it was certainly ready for it. Rumours were rife as to various groups planning to take on the sweaties on the train down and at both King's Cross and Euston, but these were apparently nipped in the bud by the Transport Police. However, a group of about sixty Aberdeen casuals had come in to London on the Thursday before the game, and had wrecked two pubs in Camden before doing the off. These incidents provided clear evidence that not all would go smoothly. It also became obvious quite quickly that Trafalgar Square, the historical centre of the problems in previous years, would be the focus for both groups.

Come the Friday, the Scots did indeed begin gathering in the square, but the police took the decision to let them get on with it in the hope that by having them in one place, they could contain them and deal with any English groups looking to get at them. As it happened, this was a fairly sensible move and very little happened in the way of confrontation among the fans who, in many cases, were mixing together quite happily in the spirit of the tournament so far. The police, meanwhile, maintained their uneasy stance and sat in the numerous transit vans parked all over the West End.

Come the Saturday, a planned confrontation between two sets of fans in North London was averted after someone tipped the police off, while Trafalgar Square was quiet, with groups of Scottish supporters singing and playing football under the watchful gaze of the law. Loads of tourists milled about, hoping, possibly, to see football violence in the flesh, as it were. Despite an off in Leicester Square apparently involving Middlesbrough and Aberdeen, it was a fairly quiet time for the police and even at Wembley, the atmosphere was friendly, if not a little flat, right up to about half an hour before kick-off. For the bulk of the English, the pubs at Wembley and in North London were the places to be, with The Globe in particular enjoying a highly charged atmosphere. Despite two instances of bottles thrown at Scottish coaches, and a few fairly minor incidents on the tube, there was little real trouble before the game; and even at Wembley, the apprehension among fans of both teams concerned only one thing – the game – and anything else could wait until later. It was clear that the police held the view that there would be a certain amount of trouble after the game no matter what the result and that trouble would be centred in and around the West End. As a result, their whole operation was geared around that region and it was imperative that they contained it as best they could to prove to the two factions that they would stand no nonsense.

If the police had not expected anything to happen until the supporters returned from Wembley, they were wrong: things began to kick off just after the game finished. Almost on the final whistle, a group of Scots who had remained in Trafalgar Square came under attack from a group of about thirty English fans, believed to be Chelsea. The police, caught totally unawares, were unable to contain things initially and the two groups indulged in a serious ruck until police reinforcements forced them apart. This left the Scots groups firmly encamped in Trafalgar Square and, as more and more arrived from

Wembley, the police again took the decision to keep them there and flooded the area with transit vans to effectively seal the square. Meanwhile, the English groups were gathering in and around the area, obviously looking for things to kick off, but the key issue was when. From a personal point of view, it was actually quite a place to be because there were groups from all over England, some of whom had obviously been at it already, as was clear from the bloodstains and bruises; but the police could do little except wait for it to happen or latch on to small groups and follow them around. This standoff went on for about two to three hours and, despite the odd group attempting to gain entry to Trafalgar Square and being repelled by the police, the English groups were forced to stand and listen to the Scots, by now over 200 in number, singing and chanting. The police, meanwhile, were very restless and seemed doubtful that they would be able to control things once darkness set in. After all, they couldn't keep the Scots there forever. At about seven o'clock, an off started just up from Leicester Square tube, apparently between the Spurs and Chelsea, and possibly a spillover from an earlier incident at The Globe, and the police took this as the start of the major confrontation they had been expecting. As they steamed up Charing Cross Road to deal with this incident, they actually ran past the two of us, who had been talking to some lads from Leicester City. It became crystal clear that the police had made a major mistake, because they left Trafalgar Square totally open from the north side. The English groups, realising this, began shouting at each other waiting for someone to start moving; but no one did, and by the time things started to happen, the police had realised their mistake and came back down, truncheons flying, to cover their backs and close things off.

However, some of the English groups had made it down to Trafalgar Square and were now at the walls around the Square baiting the Scots, who responded by throwing bottles and cans out into the police and the passing traffic. Clearly, things were in danger of getting out of hand and the police made a number of baton charges into the Scots to arrest those who had been throwing bottles, which only succeeded in provoking the situation. Things did indeed kick off, but only between the Scots and the police, while the English stood by and watched as the police used batons and CS gas to regain control. Eventually the police, having decided that enough was enough, drove the Scots fans out of the square into Charing Cross tube and away, which enabled the English fans to, in their words, retake the square and remove all the Scottish flags and banners left behind. The English fans began a long period of singing and shouting but eventually, rather than let them drift away peacefully, the police took the decision to clear Trafalgar Square. Using every means available, including dogs and horses, they drove the English fans across and out the square in the direction of Whitehall where, apart from the odd skirmish, things died down on their own as the groups drifted away to catch trains or closing times. And by half past eleven it was all but over. For the police, the operation had been a success because nothing significant had occurred. But for those of us watching from the sidelines, including the hordes of tourists, the police had been simply lucky on a number of counts. First, it was apparent that a number of groups simply did not turn up in the centre of London. There were very few people from the East London clubs, nor were there many, if any, from either of the Glasgow clubs. Similarly, the supposed links between many of the more well-known firms were pure fiction, as indeed was the so-called England 'superfirm'. It was clear that if things had been organised, the outcome would have been very different indeed. As it was, the fans had put the police firmly on the rack for a while.

With the Scotland game out of the way, the next real test for the police in London was the Dutch game, but again, the threat was more imagined than real. The Oranje experience, coupled with the failure of any Dutch group to show, ensured that the largely peaceful atmosphere was maintained through-out the evening, with the exception of an incident in a pub involving Stoke and Leicester fans. Similarly, the Spanish game, even with everything at stake, gave the police a relatively quiet time, although many groups celebrating the result in other parts of the country became involved in trouble. In Enfield, a small mob pulled a traffic warden from a motorbike, which was then set on fire after the warden was badly beaten. In many parts of Spain, English tourists indulged in violent incidents with local youths, and one English man was stabbed. However, the large-scale violence predicted for the tournament had not occurred; but all of this apparent calm was shattered on the night of the semi-final against Germany.

With the country at an emotional fever pitch for this game, the police were always going to have problems if England lost. On the evening that England lost to Germany in Italia 90, it had been proven that the English public were more than capable of going into self-destruct mode after occasions like these. As a result, the police were all over London, ready for things to kick off at any time. At The Globe the atmosphere was especially heavy. Yet as always, Wembley was fairly quiet, and the two sets of fans mingled quite happily. The key to the lack of trouble before the game was that the German groups didn't show, for whatever reason; it was probably more to do with lack of bottle than police presence. With no opposition, this left the English groups without tickets only one real problem, and that was where they could watch the match.

On the final whistle, the atmosphere at Wembley was one of resignation, but in the West End, it was apprehension. Deep sighs and gulping noises were almost audible from the transit vans parked all over London: it was obvious that things were going to happen. Almost on the final whistle, approximately 200 England fans poured into Trafalgar Square and quickly swelled to almost 2,000, who began baiting the police and occasionally throwing bottles and cans. The police had apparently spotted over fifty known troublemakers from all over England in and around the square, but they stood firm until individuals began running out of the mob to taunt them face to face. After a short time, the police closed ranks and attempted to seal off the square to contain the mob. The crowd then surged against them in an attempt to move up St Martin's Lane, but this was repelled by the police lines. Then waves of glass came flying out of the crowd. The police, now in full riot gear, made their first charge into the crowd in an attempt, not only to arrest certain individuals, but to show force. Other groups of policemen, including mounted officers, moved to close off Charing Cross Road, Whitehall and St Martin's Lane, effectively forcing the crowd down Northumberland Avenue. There, widespread vandalism took place, including serious damage to over forty cars and an attack on a Ministry of Defence police patrol car which was wrecked, luckily after the officers inside had escaped. Throughout all this, the media in and around the square had also become a target for many and at least one camera crew had all their equipment wrecked.

Once the police had managed to clear Trafalgar Square, the crowd began to disperse and eventually it became relatively quiet and the cleaning-up could begin. Again, the police, although very unhappy over these events, claimed their operation was a success but a number of people criticised their handling of the situation, claiming that they had actually provoked the trouble with their first baton charge. Unsubstantiated rumours also began circulating that Combat-18 had been paying people up to £150 to start trouble with the police and that a German student had been thrown under a tube train by a group of English fans. However, the police took the firm stance that this was orchestrated violence which was targeted directly at them and used football merely as a cover.

The media churned out massive amounts of newsprint on the problems after the Germany game, but it has to be said that this was hardly a surprise. It was clear to us that there had been almost as many reporters as supporters in Trafalgar Square, and that they were desperate for a story. And there is little doubt that the legions of photographers and camera crews were provocative to some of the supporters. However, there are a few points to be made about the police tactics in the West End, because not everything was as it should be. For those who were there, it was clear that many of the coppers on duty derived a great deal of pleasure from running around waving their batons in the air. In this they weren't admittedly all that different from the many participants and spectators who got pleasure from the mayhem. Indeed, it was even said that the trouble after the Scotland game was the best entertainment in London that night and it was free. Certainly, the number of tourists taking photographs after the Scotland game (in complete safety, of course) was clear evidence of that. But not everyone had a good time; and for those not too thrilled with what was happening, the sight of groups of old bill running up the road laughing as they pulled out their sticks was not a pretty one. Furthermore, a great many people were upset at the thinking behind the removal of the England fans from Trafalgar Square after both the Scotland and Germany games. After all, the police had let the Scots take over and even play football in the square from Friday lunchtime; why not leave the England lads there, where they were pretty much containable, and contented? It was only when the police attempted to move them on that things went wrong and the groups played up.

It should also be made clear that trouble was not confined to the West End. Following the Germany game, incidents occurred all over England as people took out their anger, disappointment and frustration on anything to hand. In Reading, for instance, police were swamped with 999 calls as a mob damaged cars and smashed windows, while in Bedford a mob of 400 youths rampaged through the town centre, a pattern that was repeated throughout the country from Mansfield to Exeter. Sadly, not all groups took their frustrations out on material items: in Sussex, a Russian student was stabbed by a group of youths, who asked him if he were German before attacking him.

The incidents surrounding both the Scotland and Germany games did detract from what was a tournament free of the orchestrated mayhem predicted by the media. But it wasn't all trouble-free, as we have seen. Nor did it involve only England fans. In Manchester, some sixty minor offences involving German supporters occurred and a policeman was put in hospital after Croatian fans were baton-charged by police for not sitting down at their group game against Turkey. Fighting also broke out among Turkish supporters after their cheerleader got the hump when the other fans wouldn't sing during their game against Denmark. In the scheme of things, however, these were minor incidents, and while it is difficult to know what, if anything, the police can do about this sort of spontaneous criminal activity, it is plainly linked to football because few, if any, of these incidents would have taken place if England had not been hosting Euro 96. A great deal of time will obviously now be spent poring over CCTV film, not only of Trafalgar Square but also of town centres throughout England, in an attempt to identify and then deal with the culprits. Despite the apparent success of this operation, and the fact that they have a job on their hands when dealing with football, the police are, in the end, merely reactive in their approach to the hooligan problem and in most cases, can only act when it is actually happening. The responsibility for dealing with it in the long term rests firmly elsewhere.

Chapter 19

The Media Influence

Sport in this country is big news. It sells newspapers and it makes great television. Certainly, in the case of the tabloid newspapers, it is a vital ingredient in the mix. Stand outside any newsagent's on any morning and you will quickly see that the first thing the majority of blokes do when they pick up a paper is to look at the back page. Indeed, for many of the millions who read tabloid newspapers every day, the back page is more important than the front page, and this changes only when sport becomes so important that it makes the switch and dominates even the front-page headlines. And the most important sport of all is football.

This is nothing new, of course. Like any consumer-driven business, the tabloid papers know and respond to the wishes of their customers. They are well aware that we want to read about the game, but what they fail to realise is that most supporters only want to read about their own team and players. The activities at Arsenal, Liverpool or Manchester United are all very interesting to Arsenal, Liverpool and Manchester United supporters but to the rest, particularly those outside the Premier League, they are an irrelevance. However, if their clubs are mentioned, even in a small paragraph stuck away in a corner, it's of far more interest to them than anything else. When Graham Taylor and Luther Blissett returned to Watford, we read every article in every paper and nothing else. We couldn't care less about the latest millions being spent by some Premier League outfit on some second-rate Brazilian; at that time, Vicarage Road was the all-consuming topic as far as we were concerned and it is certain that the supporters of any club outside the big six feel the same way when *their* club makes the news.

To some degree, newspapers recognise this narrow vision and so they focus their attention on the national side, which is of at least secondary interest to most of their readers. Criticism of the England team is common among the vast majority of football supporters, who give the national side a hard time for their own, private reasons, more to do with team selection than anything else. But the criticism of the national side's management has, at times, overstepped the mark, and some of the things which have appeared in the tabloids over the years have been disgraceful and shamefully embarrassing. We accept that they have to sell papers – that is their job, after all – but at what cost? Is there nothing more constructive or positive that could be done? What possible value is there in newspapers printing composed photographs of England players wearing tin helmets or England forwards wearing Geoff Hurst's 1966 World Cup shirt? We are most concerned, however, with another aspect of press coverage: how this affects us, the supporters.

As should now be very clear, most football supporters care only about what is written regarding their own team. Similarly, the stuff written about the England team is only of interest if you follow the national team or are interested in a particular player. However, when the press start writing about the fans, things are very different, because here they can influence the way people imagine supporters to be. Despite the fact that in the vast majority of cases these days, England, and English, fans abroad are pretty well behaved, it is clear that anyone who travels to watch the national side play away from Wembley risks being labelled as nothing less than a fascist bully boy intent on causing mayhem. The events of Dublin in

252

1995, when English fans rioted inside Lansdowne Road and caused the England–Ireland friendly to be abandoned, merely strengthened this image in the minds of Mr and Mrs Average when, as all true fans know, the reality is somewhat different. And the fact that our non-football-loving critics have this perception of football fans is definitely down to the media.

Of all the influences on the skewed perception of the England supporter on his travels, the media must bear the brunt for the way things have gone, because for many they provide the only evidence of what does or does not happen. We will not, cannot and never will deny that England fans have been the best behaved when abroad, but that does not excuse the way that certain newspapers attack and portray supporters in the way that they do. The fact that some news-papers send more news reporters than sports reporters to games does not help, because they feel duty-bound to write something, and 'fifteen lads having a beer and a laugh with some supporters from the local club' does not have the same attraction to an editor as 'fifteen drunken lads wrecked a bar and had a ruck with some locals'. Remember, responsible journalism is fine if you're talking about an MP or a court case – but football fans? No chance.

Of course, football violence needs to be reported, but it needs to be reported sensibly; sensationalising it makes it look attractive, and that is one thing it is not. Television does not escape this attack, either. If you show footage of fans on the rampage, accompanied by commentary about English sup-porters, Mr and Mrs Average will draw the natural conclusion. Yet it is obvious to anyone who bothers to look that the people in the film are far from English; the classic film of the Danish policeman kicking the shit out of an English fan is a case in point. The TV crews know that if they point a camera at a group of blokes, the blokes will start to shout, wave, sing or whatever because people want to be on the TV, and if those blokes are half-pissed anyway, the resultant pictures can be edited to 'prove' anything they, the media, want. It is also true to say that certain elements of the media were not above 'constructing' pictures or scenes when England played abroad in the past, and we have even witnessed reporters bribing fans to play up, and been present when camera crews provoked fans into trouble. We have also met foreign fans who were asked to pose aggressively while draped in the Union Jack, for money, and have seen reports of completely innocuous incidents we were actually involved in blown up into full-blown riots by so-called responsible journalists.

We would not for one moment accuse the press of carrying on like that these days, but press coverage of supporters' behaviour is still occasionally pretty poor because they know that they can really print what they like. And this is because to many people of this country, not just football fans, the media are pretty much untouchable. If the average man in the street is portrayed as anything but a model citizen, there is almost nothing that can be done to redress the balance, and the media know this full well. They also know that by the time any complaint is heard, the story will have faded from memory and any resultant retraction will be almost meaningless to anybody but the poor sap who was wronged. The old adage that today's news is tomorrow's chip paper is absolutely correct.

As football fans, we are a good target because supporters can provide graphic and violent footage or photographs and, let's face it, everyone hates us anyway; but that does not make it right. If you examine the press coverage of the events in Dublin in 1995, some of the photographs were pretty graphic and clearly showed certain people carrying out terrible acts. However, some of these photographs were accompanied by so-called facts that were anything but.

While the people photographed were obviously guilty of what they were shown doing, the additional labels put in as a by-line by some reporter under pressure stick for life, and can do irreparable damage to people's lives and careers. In the aftermath of the Cantona affair, for instance, Dougie took part in a televised debate for Central Television where a former

Manchester United defender labelled Matthew Simmons, the Palace fan concerned, a member of the National Front. This allegation was made on live television without any proof whatsoever, and is one of those things that not only stick, but actually make people think that Simmons got what he deserved. The fact that at the end of the programme, Central made an apology and admitted that there was no proof to link the two made little difference: the damage was done.

The media have a vital role to play in the way the game is perceived in this country and, at times, the way they deal with specific events is exemplary. Certainly, the help given to Paul Merson so that he could recover and deal with his addictions proved that sections of the press really can be responsible and professional. However, there is no doubt that events have occurred within the game where the exact opposite is true, and these should not be ignored. One only has to think back to the ridiculous way the press behaved in the aftermath of the Far East tour, and subsequent events on the Cathay Pacific aircraft, to see that many of them love to rip into people. The treatment of Paul Gascoigne in particular was outrageous; the poor bloke was branded as the guilty culprit without any proof whatsoever and they were allowed to get away with it. The calls for a player who is arguably England's best to be axed from the squad days before the start of Euro 96 were so sensationalist it was pathetic, and were made to look even more so when the truth of the matter started to come out. Events on the pitch showed what it was really all about and in truth, that was all that mattered. People who should have known better than to be critical of the England team's build-up were made, after the event, to eat huge quantities of humble pie. The build-up to the Spanish game saw the tabloid press overstep the mark and the papers were rightly ridiculed by many parties – not least because the game and, to a certain degree, the public affection for it, had grown in stature during the tournament. One tabloid did not learn from this during the build-up to the semi-final against Germany, and continued with jingoistic and offensive rantings that were nothing short of pathetic.

As we have said many times, both the clubs and the FA have largely banished violence among supporters inside grounds, but the fans have had a huge bearing on what has happened, with little or no acknowledgement, and that needs addressing. Similarly, the appalling way in which fans are treated by the authorities when abroad needs a balanced examination in the press. If the English lads play up – fine, hammer them. Put their names, photographs, even their addresses in the papers if you like; but if a policeman or fan from another country is filmed or photographed beating the shit out of an England fan for no reason other than his nationality, the press should highlight that too, and make people aware of what it is really like.

Football fans are people. Some are angels, some animals. The media have a duty to highlight that fact at every opportunity, because that is the only way that the violence surrounding football can be reduced to an absolute minimum. In the two seasons leading up to Euro 96, the FA and the media attempted to keep a lid on the spread of violence among supporters, but it did not work, because the football grapevine took the bad news about the growing problems to every ground in England, and the local press still covered it. The game and the police argue that by giving the hooligan element any amount of publicity it actually fuels the problem, but this is simply ridiculous. The reality is that incidents involving supporters occur week-in and week-out, yet the national press will only report on those that either involve players or have been seen on television. This has the effect of sensationalising crowd disorder as if it were something out of the ordinary when that just is not the case. A good example of this is the incident involving Gary McAllister during Leeds' game against Birmingham at St Andrews in 1996. While the national media rightly put across the fact that the objects being thrown at him were potentially lethal, it ignored the fact that similar missiles were being thrown at the opposing fans, and that incidents such as this happen among spectators with alarming regularity.

The only way to deal with this issue is to confront it head on, and here the media can help vitally in the effort to make football violence unfashionable. The game and the police can preach and warn all they want, but no one listens, and tragically, no one cares. Yet if they worked together and involved both the media and, most importantly, the fans, we may actually get somewhere. It simply needs someone to grasp the initiative and make a start. It may be a sad reflection on this country that the long-term solution to football violence could well come from a tabloid newspaper, but it is almost certainly a fact, and the post-Euro 96 euphoria surrounding football constitutes a valuable opportunity to start things moving.

Chapter 20
People Power

One of the major frustrations of being a football fan is that no one ever listens to what you have to say. Despite the fact that over the years you will have spent thousands of pounds to pass through the home turnstiles or travel the length of the country to put money in some other club's bank account, those who run either your club or football imagine you have nothing of value to say. If you offer an opinion on the style of play or a particular player, you are told that you don't really understand the game and if you put forward anything to do with the club, then you don't understand the business side of things. This incredibly patronising condemnation has been allowed to continue at almost every club in this country because the people on self-important ego trips – the board, if you like – need to know that they are more important to the club than you are. That is why they are there, after all. The fact that we pay our hard-earned money at the gate means very little despite what the clubs say because they know that this income is, to a great extent, guaranteed. They are astute enough to realise that we, as football fans, are obsessives and need our fix on matchdays and therefore, come rain or shine, we will be there. The board know that if they sell our favourite player, we won't mind too much and will soon forget him, or if, as in the case of Watford, they sign a player from your local rivals, we won't mind too much and we'll soon accept him as one of ours.

And so it goes on. They want to sell our ground? Great. It's only historical, but it is the perfect place for a supermarket. What about ground sharing, that'll save a lot of hassle, won't it? And it's only fifty miles up the road, not that far by car. And what about a new strip? We've had the old one two years now, or even two months if you're a United fan, so we'd better change that; but we won't stick to those boring old traditional colours, let's let the chairman's grand-daughter design something, or we may just let the kit suppliers pay someone a fortune to design one. The fans won't mind, they'll buy it anyway. Of course, we do mind, a lot, but the tragedy is that we allow them to get away with it because there is nothing we can do. Ask the supporters of Aldershot, Gillingham, Orient and Exeter, to name only a few.

Our lack of influence at both our clubs and the FA can easily be proven. What club in this country, for instance, has a supporters' representative on its board? Exactly. The clubs themselves will argue that the supporters' club provides a forum for the fans to have a say, but in reality, it doesn't. The average bloke uses the supporters' club as a convenient drinking hole on matchdays – no more, no less – and any contact with the board is a token gesture only. The growth of the independent supporters' club movement is proof of that, and these organisations do tend to have a higher profile at clubs, but in truth, usually because they are far more vocal than really influential. The fact is, whatever gesture the board of any club makes towards the fans it is usually of the token variety; it is rare that a board will listen to criticism or do anything of value.

So what else represents us? The Football Supporters' Association! Here's a fine body of men, ready and willing to appear on television at a moment's notice to talk bollocks for a couple of minutes – the perfect advert for the trendy fan or the football anorak. This is the organisation that claims to represent the concerns of all supporters to the FA, and yet who did almost nothing when Chelsea fans were battered senseless by the police in Bruges, or Manchester United fans were subjected to the most horrific abuse in Galatasaray. This is the organisation that set up the supporter embassies at European Championships and World Cup campaigns with the aim of helping supporters with any problems and guidance, yet didn't want to know when fans were complaining of attacks by police and home supporters at Italia 90. This is the organisation that makes the outrageous claim that it defeated the ID card scheme for football fans, when this scheme was dead in the water even when proposed, for any number of reasons. The primary one was that the clubs didn't want it because it stopped the casual supporter from attending matches. While criticism of the FSA is in most cases deserved, it is still unfortunate that the only viable route for anyone with a grievance seems to be in demise.

For the day-to-day running of your club, you have no alternative other than to leave it up to the board, who will happily do what they like without any consideration for your wishes whatsoever. The growth of the fanzine movement is symbolic of this because these cheap, easily produced and readily available magazines finally provided a platform where fans could really have their say. Criticism of the chairman, the manager or the players were and are positively encouraged, but the fact that they were outside the control of the clubs themselves led to the complaint from most chairmen that 'they are taking money away from the clubs'.

The FA are just as guilty as any club because they cannot see past the corporate money thrown at them by the bucketload and let those who throw it run roughshod over our game and dictate to them what they want, and force us to accept it. They refuse to listen to us, and then complain because no one goes to Wembley to watch England or buys tickets for semifinals. While we moan and gripe for all we are worth, we, as supporters, have to face the fact that we are dictated to by Lancaster Gate and our own board.

In the case of the England team, the problems are somewhat

easier to deal with because we have the ultimate weapon: we don't go, and many don't even care. Unlike our club sides where, no matter what is happening, we have to be there just in case this is *the* game, if you don't like the manager or the tactics England are employing, stay at home. We can do that, and we don't have to have the very latest fashion statement/ excuse for a shirt that Umbro have put together because we can register our disapproval by not buying it, which is not a strain for most of us. In truth, many fans see the England set-up as the epitome of all that is wrong with the game in this country. The ultimate proof of this was in the failure to appoint Brian Clough as England manager, despite the fact that almost every football fan in this country was willing him to get the job. They didn't listen to us because they wanted exactly what Clough wasn't – a yes man – and so the people's choice, the right man for the job, was overlooked, in a decision that was tragic for the international side.

The formation of the Premier League has transformed football in this country, and it has to be said that the standard at the top has changed out of all recognition from twenty years ago. That does deserve huge amounts of credit. Even the Sky deal was a great thing for the armchair fan, or at least those with Sky, and brought millions of pounds into the top flight. That's all fine, but once again there was little consultation with the real supporters who saw an instant end to the tradition of Saturday football. Still, who minds travelling to the other end of the country on a weekday, just because Sky want the game on, even though you may possibly miss a day's work? Not us. Seriously, the only people who were asked about the Sky deal were the boards of the clubs, who saw nothing but pound signs, the television schedulers and the sponsors. It seems that the only real power the FA have in the scheduling of games is on the last day of the season, because even they realise the dangers of staggering kick-off times at such a crucial time; but let's be honest, if they thought they could, they would.

One of the more disturbing aspects of the Premier League is that it is in the process of destroying the remainder of the

Football League as every season passes. The gap between the first division and the top flight is huge and growing all the time – ask any Bolton, Palace or Swindon fan – and any club winning promotion is looking at a massive expenditure even to think about maintaining that status for more than a season. However, that struggle is being transposed down to the second and third divisions, which now face the real possibility of part-time regional football. One has only to look at the list of clubs facing severe financial problems, or even ruin, to realise that what is a disturbing worry for supporters may well be warmly welcomed by the odd chairman.

However, there are occasions when supporters are taken too much for granted and finally fight back. When that happens, supporters make the news primarily because such events are so rare, but also because the people of this country like to see the odd group rebelling against authority. At most clubs, these rebellions take the form of abuse and protests directed at managers or the chairman for their total ineffectuality and, in most cases, the complaints go largely unheeded. This then forces those who protest to become more vocal or, sadly, violent on occasion.

A classic case in point is Norwich and, as a football fan, one can only feel sympathy for what is going on in East Anglia. Despite the success enjoyed by the club in the Mike Walker era, they have been stuck with a chairman who obviously advocated a sell, sell, sell policy with regard to their best players. This strategy can be understood to a certain degree (look at Wimbledon to see that it does work), but at Norwich the problem is that the money raised has not been reinvested in the team and, as they now languish in the First Division, supporters are getting a bit miffed. Since Walker's departure, there have been concerted campaigns to force Robert Chase out; but he refused to bow to pressure from the fans who keep the club afloat with their entrance money, and he refused to resign. Then, out of the blue, at the end of another season of First Division football, Chase called a press conference and announced that he had sold his shares in the club and would be leaving . . . just like that. The ultimate and final action of a stubborn man. The tragedy for the Norwich fans was that this unrest obviously had a major effect on the players during the 1995/96 season, and one can only hope that a new broom will see Norwich return to the top flight in the near future.

Similarly, the on-pitch disturbances at Brighton at the end of the 1995/96 season showed just what can happen if fans are not consulted or considered when major decisions are made at their club. Quite how the club found itself in the region of £8,000,000 in debt is unclear, but the fact is that it did. With seemingly no other option available, the board decided to sell the Goldstone ground and ground share with Portsmouth to save the club. The main problem with this course of action was that the board didn't bother to tell anyone. The FA were far from happy and refused to sanction the ground-sharing plan because no submissions had been made for a new ground – the local council were not being very helpful. The Portsmouth fans were unhappy because they would be saddled with supporters of one of their fiercest rivals. And funnily enough, the Brighton fans weren't too thrilled, either. Not only did it seem that they had lost their ground, and therefore their historical home, but they were faced with a trip along the coast for every home game, where they would also have to run the gauntlet of local rivals. Protests against the board, the local council and anybody else who could be blamed were organised, but no one listened. So on Saturday, 27 April 1996, with Brighton seemingly playing their last ever game at the Goldstone ground after ninety-four years, and having already been relegated to the Third Division, the match against York City was disrupted when the crowd spilled onto the pitch. After only sixteen minutes of play the game was eventually abandoned, with the goals in tatters. With the final day of the lease due on the Tuesday, and despite a last-ditch plan to save the club by a consortium involving Liam Brady, the supporters were faced with the very real possibility of waking up and finding their club extinct, and there was nothing they could do about it. Luckily, the new owners had offered the board the opportunity of leasing the ground for another year, but up to the last minute this had been refused, primarily because of the £480,000 fee. In the end, the board had no choice but to agree if they were to save the club.

At Watford in the mid-nineties, the chairman was adamant that no money would be released for the then manager Glenn Roeder to spend despite yet another, but this time seemingly terminal, relegation battle. Weeks of demonstrations by the fans culminated in a pitch invasion and an attempted takeover of the directors' box following a game against Grimsby and this finally forced the chairman to stand down and release funds. So Roeder bought and we escaped relegation. The violence was the direct result of the fans' wishes going unheard, together with a stubborn chairman, and if either one had talked or listened to the other this would have been averted. These type of demonstrations are, however, generally spontaneous. It's when they become organised that they can become far more dangerous. The peril of a group of fans actually planning to use violence or intimidation to get their point across is becoming more and more real. We are not talking about frustration and last resorts: we are talking about first resorts – straight to the quick, as it were. There are, sadly, a number of examples of this, but three of the more infamous include the campaign against Ian Branfoot at Southampton, and the attacks on Jimmy Mullen at Burnley and John Lambie at Falkirk. A section of the Southampton support subjected Ian Branfoot to a systematic campaign of hate mail and intimidation, during a period when the team was experiencing problems. Probably the final straw came when the headline 'Hope You Die Soon' appeared on one of the Southampton fanzines. Branfoot's refusal to bow to this type of intimidation was admirable but ultimately doomed, as he eventually had to stand down to protect his family from further distress. Similarly, in February 1996 Jimmy Mullen and his wife were in a takeaway when some supporters came in following the defeat by Crewe. After a heated discussion, one fan attempted to set Mrs Mullen's dress alight. Mullen resigned the next day. And in that same month John Lambie was driving along with his wife, following a midweek defeat, when some supporters attempted to run him off the road, with obvious consequences. One has to ask what it is that drives these people to this end. Is it simply the lack of a platform, the fact that no one listens to them? Or that they feel that something so important to them, their club, is in real danger, and they will do anything to save it? Whatever it is, these acts are despicable and those that not only take part in them but advocate such direct action bring shame on every football supporter in Britain.

Very occasionally, however, when something terrible or threatening is happening to their club, someone manages to harness the feelings of the supporters in a positive way and attempts to force change by positive and constructive means. The first real example of this phenomenon was back in the Robert Maxwell era, when the astute businessman we know and love had the quite clever idea of merging Oxford United and Reading to form the Thames Valley Royals. On paper, this did make quite a bit of sense. The proposed club would have had a massive catchment area and a brand-new ground; but there was one problem, which Mr Maxwell did not really consider and which he had no control over: the fans. Strange as it may seem, the supporters of both clubs did not take too kindly to the plan that they should merge with their local, and very bitter, rivals, and after a concerted campaign of complaints in the media and protest from all sides, including the new chairman of Reading, Mr Maxwell finally took the hint, and bought Derby County instead.

There are many other well-documented cases of supporter-led movements against decisions supposedly made on their behalf, but the ultimate example of fan power simply has to be the emergence of the Valley Party in Southeast London. Having seen their beloved Charlton forced to leave their spiritual home in 1985 after the Greater London Council condemned their East Stand, a group of the club's supporters began a concerted campaign to take their club home. As the protest movement continued, Greenwich council opposed a plan to renovate the stadium and, in 1990, the Valley Party was created to gather publicity and momentum for the protest movement. Its one policy concerned Charlton Athletic and the Valley, and when it stood at the local elections that year, polling over 14,000 votes, the local council finally saw the light. In 1991, Charlton returned home. This one example proves that it is possible to force change if supporters get themselves organised, and the best way to do this is to use political pressure: votes are what matters at the end of the day and it has to be the way forward. It may seem trite to say it, but at regional level, to a great many people, football is more important than local government, and if Brighton fans had been able to get themselves really organised and followed Charlton's lead, the problems they experienced may well have been avoided.

This opens up another interesting debate. If someone knocked at your door and said he was standing in a local election to force the council to do something about the local club, would you vote for them? At a time when many local elections experience turnouts of less than 30 percent due, in no small part, to apathy, anyone who campaigned for football would generate a huge amount of interest and would be in with a realistic shout of getting elected. In a town or city with a big club, anyone with the time, finance and bottle to do this would cause tidal waves of unease among those already in power. And, if nothing else, it would certainly be worth seeing! We are not advocating the formation of the National Football Supporters' Party – not yet anyway. But it is a great idea: remember, the World Cup semi-final between England and Germany was watched by approximately 25 million people, 12 million more than voted for the Tories at the 1992 general election.

In the meantime, what needs to be done? If the clubs actually bit the bullet and employed someone to liaise with the fans, that would be a major step forward. Similarly, if the FA had a supporters' representative available then they would gain a huge amount of insight as a result, not to mention credibility. These aren't radical ideas, they're common sense, and they have been put forward by more than one MP in the past. Not all those in government agreed with Colin Moynihan's labelling of English fans, in the run-up to Italia 90, as nothing less than the scum of the earth. The Labour MP Keith Vaz called for greater dialogue between supporters and the police, and Tom Pendry, another Labour MP, called for the Football Supporters' Association and the National Association of Football Supporters Clubs to be represented on Football Trust (although with no success). It isn't just our illustrious government members who propose these staggering concepts, either. In 1993, the chief executive of the Premier League, Rick Parry himself, called for greater cooperation with supporters – by which he really meant only those of the Premier League – and actually said, and I quote, 'Until we've asked the fans, we shouldn't really be debating it,' and, 'Every business carries out consumer research and if it ignores what the customer is saying then it tends not to succeed.' Despite pilot schemes being set up at a number of clubs, including Norwich, Coventry, Chelsea and Arsenal, it is doubtful that anything of value ever came of these meetings.

It is easy to be critical of clubs and the FA; but let's be honest, there isn't a member of Joe Public on the board of Tesco's or Marks and Spencer, and neither is there any real chance of the average bloke ever being invited to take his seat in Westminster, so do we really have any right to complain in this manner? Those who work at the FA may be fans of the game but have they ever been subjected to the treatment dealt out at almost every game to visiting supporters? Have they ever been herded along a road by some overzealous policemen? Highly unlikely; so how can they understand the frustration and annoyance the average supporter feels towards the FA? Similarly, how much consideration does Ken Bates give to what the average family man/fan thinks about the way he runs Chelsea? Look at the Matthew Harding saga. Ken Bates is able to adopt such an approach for the same old reason: supporters have not only accepted the status quo, but the chairman knows that their entrance money is as good as cash in the bank. The same can be said of any club in the country because all boards know what their average gate will be and to a certain extent, that number is as good as a fixed asset. As a result, they know that their supporters will turn up, come rain or shine, so why should they bother to ask their opinions on anything? If they don't like it, they don't have to come, do they? Well, choice is important, and if we don't like Tesco's beans, we can go to Sainsbury's. But football isn't Tesco's: we have to go no matter what, because it is ingrained in us; it is our obsession; we cannot stay away. And the game knows that and takes advantage of it, and therefore us.

CONCLUSION

You are never going to solve the problem of violence at football matches; never. The fact is that there will always be an element of confrontation among the supporters, just as there will inevitably be the odd problem on the pitch, among the players. That element of confrontation exists because for some, their country or their club means so much that they will use violence against anyone or anything that attacks it. These people would never get involved in violence away from football, but an attack on what they see as 'theirs' will provoke a reaction. There are also those that love to fight, those that love to prove themselves to the people around them, and football provides them with that opportunity.

That may be difficult to grasp for anyone who has not been involved in football violence, but fighting at games is a tremendous buzz and is still seen as a trendy thing to be involved in. The people willing to do it are in a minority, and they will always remain so, yet they have influence over the rest of us because we have to watch the game in a certain way as a consequence of their (and yes, our) actions. But why, if they are the minority, isn't more being done to erode their influence further? In fact, to take that question further, just what is being done? Go to any ground and buy a programme, and you will see the 'Kick Racism Out of Football' slogan

271

inside; but where are the 'Kick Violence Out of Football' slogans? Pick up any football magazine and you will see plenty of adverts for everything from new trainers to Radio Five Live, but nothing about anti-hooligan initiatives being implemented by either the FA or the clubs themselves.

To those who don't fully understand the problem, the hooligan issue seems to be a police matter, but actually it isn't. We are no fans of the old bill for any number of reasons which you may have already gathered. Their primary function around football is to uphold the law of the land by reacting to potential problems, and to deter. If things do kick off, or are likely to, then it is indeed down to them to sort things out and deal with anyone they manage to detain in the correct and proper manner. But the search for a long-term solution is not their responsibility, and there are far more pressing problems within our society than this one. No, the responsibility for this issue lies firmly with two groups, the FA and the fans.

Having read this book up to this point, you may well have formed the opinion that the two of us are pro-violence. Bearing in mind that we have a history of involvement and that many of the accounts of trouble contained within these pages are graphic, it is an easy opinion to form. But it is wrong. Our books may be about football violence, but they have been written to tell it like it is, or was to us in any case, in the hope that we can reopen and contribute to a debate that has largely been conducted in entirely the wrong manner. But the blame for this lies totally with those who take part because if they didn't fight at football, there would be no football violence. We freely admit that the police were all over us during Euro 96 because of what we, and people like us, did in the past and others are still doing today. We readily admit that what we did in the past was wrong, and totally futile; what possible purpose does it serve to travel somewhere, cause trouble and then go home? It *is* pointless; it *is* ridiculous; but unfortunately, hundreds of football fans have done it and are still doing it. Similarly, why travel abroad with England to another country which you may never visit again, and then get caught up in trouble? But it happens, and we have tried to explain why and how it happens using our own and other people's experience. Now we need to look at ways in which it can be stopped or, at the very least, reduced. But believe us when we say that it is not that simple: there are two sides to every story, and in this case, the other side is very much the FA.

There is no doubt that we will get slaughtered for this, but we believe the FA are quite content that the hooligan issue is still around. That isn't to say that they weren't relieved that Euro 96 went as well as it did, because they obviously are, but it is our belief that what trouble there was did the FA no harm at all. You see, every time a major off, such as the two during Euro 96, occurs, another nail is driven into the male-dominated terrace culture we grew up with, and they are thankful for that. They know that the hooligans are busy destroying their own arena and in fact have already done so in the Premier League because their spiritual battleground, the end, has all but vanished forever now. They know that in truth, even though it is a concern to most of us, the hooligan problem is actually fairly self-contained among those who fight each other, but the fact that hooligans intimidate others provides them with the excuse to continually change their fan base and attract more family support. Can you think of a single constructive thing that the FA are doing to actually deal with the hooligan issue? They have abdicated responsibility and put it in the hands of the police, who are purely reactive, not proactive. The simple fact is that this problem affects all football, from the national side to the midweek five-a-side local leagues, so the FA have a duty to deal with it. Furthermore, when England travel, the FA should uphold that duty: it is up to them to take responsibility for the team and its supporters, who are, after all, representing both them and the country.

It is, however, important to remember that those still involved in the violence will never talk. They love what they do, and would never trust anyone outside their own group. But there are those that have left the fighting behind, who know what it is all about and who know how the whole thing works. That is where hope lies. If the FA really are serious, then they will have to swallow their pride eventually and sit down and talk to these people – the very ones they despise so much – if we are ever to reach a long-term solution that will benefit the game. It's not a unique concept. This type of initiative almost worked in Italy when the Ultras called a truce after the death of a supporter. There has never been a better opportunity for the FA to tackle this problem head on than the one given to them by the success of Euro 96.

We will never know whether the FA were either very clever or just very lucky, but it is clear that the fan base they have been so desperately looking for came out of the woodwork for the tournament. If that is what they want, then it is up to them to nurture it and ensure that those fans, who were so colourful at Wembley, return. However, they have to realise that they will not get the backing of everyone. We have stated throughout this book that the way in which the Dutch follow their national side is not the way we would like to follow ours. We believe the English are different, and we like that. Personally, we don't like the face-painting, the dressing up, the Mexican bloody wave and all that bollocks, but if that is what the FA (and it must be said, the majority of those that attended the Wembley matches) want, and it leads to ending the violence, as it did at Wembley, then they must have it. Those England supporters proved to the world that they can, and indeed want to, behave.

As we have attempted to show, the problems among fans at national level rarely occur when England are playing at Wembley, but almost always abroad. So, as it is impossible to stop people travelling, the FA must encourage the people they pulled into Wembley to follow the national side abroad. That doesn't mean that they should rip them off; it means that they should make it easier and more affordable for these people to travel on the official tours so that they can develop that kind of support under the watchful eye of the England Travel Club. Furthermore, if the FA want this type of support then they must be prepared to stand by the fans when they are treated poorly. We have already pointed out many of the problems that the home support and the authorities can give England fans when travelling abroad, and there will always be someone willing to take on the English; and further – when you know that there is no one else on your side you have to defend yourself. So the FA must be seen to defend their rights and bring pressure upon the government when things get out of control.

Another problem the FA faces, which we have mentioned, is the fact that it is still considered trendy to be involved with a mob at football. Just how do you deal with that? How can you harness that perceived loyalty in a positive rather than a negative way? It is a well-known management ploy (certainly within the Forces) that if you have a disruptive element, you give it responsibility and believe me, it works. Maybe the hooligans should police the hooligans; this has worked at various League clubs, so why not the national side? Surely the best type of steward would be someone who knew what to look for?

It is all well and good encouraging the new breed into following the side, but what about those that will cause trouble no matter what? They will not simply walk away just because a few families travel. Well, we firmly believe that the best deterrent is for any fan that plays up, be they English, German, Dutch, whatever, to be dealt with, and seen to be dealt with, in the country where the incident took place – not sent back home. The thought of going to Pentonville is one thing, but five months in a foreign jail is something else entirely.

The media also have a role to play in all of this. The jingoistic rantings seen during Euro 96 should never be seen again, and they should concentrate on the field of play which is, after all, what they're there for. We wouldn't want them to ignore problems abroad, but we do want them to report incidents fairly and truthfully. For some journalists, this may be a problem. After all, some of them did a great job of covering up everything which occurred during the 1995/96 English domestic season, but they could not resist publishing plenty of complete bollocks in the build-up to Euro 96. However, while the FA, the media and the police have their bits to do, the key role remains with the fans. If they continue to play up abroad, nothing will ever improve. The targeting of individuals by the police has not worked, as was proven in Dublin, but the responsibility lies with the rest, who have to let them know that their behaviour is unacceptable. The hijacking of England games by political groups is just not on any more. Football should and must be kept separate from politics, something that would be assisted no end if the EU banned the display of political banners inside all grounds.

There is no doubt that Euro 96 saw the new face of football fandom in England, and one which most people came to like. Certainly it did wonders for the performance of the national side and, to a certain extent, the country; but most importantly it did the English game an awful lot of good. After all, football is the people's game: it belongs, ultimately, not to some giant corporate empire, not even to the United Colours of Commercialism, but to the people who play it and those of us who watch it. It is also a simple game in every respect – just twenty-two people aiming to get a ball into the opposition goal, no more, no less. Every detail is recorded and scrutinised while the players and the managers pore over the statistics to discover anything that will improve things, but the aim is always to learn. Similarly, the performance of the fans, good or bad, comes under a different type of scrutiny but again, everything is studied and recorded. The difference is that nothing is ever learnt. If it was, we wouldn't be writing this book, would we? The 1998 World Cup will hopefully see the England side cross that small strip of water to France, and it is clear that the potential for violence is huge, possibly bigger than Euro 96, because England will be playing away. Everyone should be thinking about that and we should all be working to ensure that when people talk of the Dutch, Danish and Irish fans, they talk about the English fans in the same light. We've possibly made the first step; let's make sure that we continue moving in the right direction.

Conclusion

Of course, the tragedy of all this is that what we say is nothing new, nor is the way we say it. You only have to walk into any pub on a matchday to hear much of what is contained within these pages. The problem is that no one is listening. We have said already that you will never stop fighting at football, but what you can do is work to reduce it, make it unfashionable and unacceptable, and that will only happen when all concerned acknowledge the problem as theirs and then start to discuss it. Everyone has a role to play within football in this country. The opportunity has to be given for the fans, finally, to play all of theirs.

This book would not have been
possible without the help of football supporters
from all over the country.

If you have any views on the contents of this
book or would like to help us with our football-
related research please do not hesitate to
contact us at the address below.
We will add your name to our database
and send you regular questionnaires on
the issues that affect *you*, the
football supporter.

This is an opportunity to have your say.

All correspondence will be treated with the
utmost confidentiality.

Please write to:
Fandom
P.O. Box 766, Hemel Hempstead, Herts,
HP1 2TU